than the bus journey preceding it.

In all weathers the colourfully patterned traditional blanket is the chief item of clothing for man and woman alike, each person having a special blanket reserved for gala occasions. According to tradition, only men wear the famous conical rain hat.

AFRICAN HERITAGE

AFRICAN HERITAGE

Barbara Tyrrell and Peter Jurgens

M

Dedication

To Mr and Mrs G. van Zyl, for 'Paper Cathedral' where this text
was written, and to the memory of Pete, husband of Barbara and
father of Peter.

© Barbara Tyrrell and Peter Jurgens 1983

ISBN 0 86954 116 1

First published in 1983 by
MACMILLAN SOUTH AFRICA (PUBLISHERS) (PTY) LTD
Braamfontein Centre, Jorissen Street, Johannesburg
Associated companies throughout the world

House editor: Eleanor-Mary Cadell

Text set in 11/13 Paladium Compugraphic
Typeset in Hong Kong by Graphicraft Typesetters
Printed and bound in Hong Kong

CONTENTS

ACKNOWLEDGEMENTS

THE authors wish to acknowledge their debt to the time and generosity of all those who helped to make this book a reality. Chantal Bertrand, Jean Anderssen, Bonukele Mbangwe, Rose Handler, Professor M. West, Professor W.D. Hammond-Tooke, and Ted Hart are due for special thanks.

The authors and publishers wish to thank the following who have kindly given permission for the use of copyright material:
African Studies Centre, University of Cambridge, for the extract from *Rainmaking Rites of Tswana Tribes*, by I. Schapera; H.S. Alverson for the extracts from the essay 'Africans in South African Industry'; A.K. Boshier for the extract from *Parapsychology in South Africa*, ed. by J.C. Poynton and published by the South African Society for Psychical Research; the *Cape Times*; F. Cass & Co. Ltd for the extract from *The Swazi*, by B.A. Marwick; *Drum* magazine; C. Hurst for the extract from *Zulu Thought-patterns and Symbolism*, by I.A. Berglund; International African Institute for the extract from *The Realm of a Rain Queen*, by E.J. and J.D. Krige; A. Kiev for the extract from his book *Transcultural Psychiatry*; Mission Press, Lovedale, for the extracts from *The Ama-Xosa*, by J.H. Soga; Oxford University Press for the extracts from *The BaVenda*, by H.A. Stayt; Penguin Books Ltd for the extract from *Married Life in an African Tribe*, by I. Schapera; David Philip for the extracts by A. Mafeje in *Religion and Social Change in South Africa*, ed. by M. Whisson; Routledge & Kegan Paul for the extract by W.D. Hammond-Tooke from *The Bantu-speaking Peoples of Southern Africa*, ed. by W.D. Hammond-Tooke; and from *Sex, Custom and Psychopathology*, by B.J.F. Laubscher; Margaret Shaw; Shuter & Shooter for the extracts from *The Zulu People*, by A.T. Bryant; C. Struik Publishers for the extract from *The Annals of Natal* 1495-1845, by J. Bird; University of Natal Press for the extracts from *Zulu Transformations*, by A. Vilakazi; University of the Witwatersrand Press for the extract from 'The praises of the divining bones among the BaSotho' by F. Laydevant in *Bantu Studies*, 7; Van Schaik for the extract from *The Pedi*, by H.O. Mönnig; Professor N. van der Merwe for the extracts from his essay 'The Iron Age: a prehistory of Bantu-speaking South Africans'.

LIST OF COLOUR ILLUSTRATIONS

PREFACE

THE 150 million Negro peoples living in sub-Saharan Africa speak some 300 related languages. In 1861 a researcher, Bleek, dubbed this family of languages the 'Bantu' group after the ubiquitous word-root for person, *ntu*, and the plural prefix *ba*. It is thus, as a linguistic term, that the word 'Bantu' is used in this text.

The black traditional communities of contemporary Southern Africa comprise Bantu-speaking Negroes. Two centuries ago, before the European invasion, these peoples shared Southern Africa with other subsistence-level communities, the Khoikhoi (Hottentot) and San (Bushmen), both now virtually extinct. Today, the Bantu-speaking Negroes of Southern Africa are fast abandoning their traditional ways of life under the impact of Western life-styles and ideas.

Nowhere can the student find a wholly traditional and untouched African life-style and many urban blacks may be described as almost completely Westernised. Thus, in any description of the Bantu-speaking peoples of Southern Africa, one is forced to delimit the field.

This book presents a picture, through Western eyes, of the more traditional ways of living and thinking. But this delimitation does not avoid the need for making repeated mention of the ubiquitous changes in order to qualify the picture. The reason for this lies not only in the far-reaching impact of Western culture on different groups and individuals, but in the differing susceptibilities to change of different components of traditional African culture. The mere fact that political domination and economic necessity have forced the township or farm-dweller to adopt a pseudo-Western facade does not imply that he has rejected his traditional African beliefs. Why should he? These beliefs are no more incongruous than those sanctioned by Western society. No matter how extraordinary their coexistence with Western life-styles may seem to the Westerner, it is no more surprising than the continued existence of traditional Western forms of worship in this day and age.

The reader will note my preoccupation with the magico-religious side of traditional life. I make no apology, for two reasons. First, these beliefs are among the most enduring aspects of African culture. Second, the simple fact is that they interest me and represent to me an alternative reality to that of my own Western culture. It seems to me that the loosely defined magical materiality of Africa might contain the seeds of a world-view that could deliver Western man from the dilemma of choosing between the irreconcilable divine and material worlds, which have been competing for his soul since the time of Newton. It is essential to the well-being of Southern Africa and the world that the Westerner, complacent and perhaps patronising in his self-image as the 'giver', should clearly see that this image holds true only within a fairly narrow definition of nature and the relevance of life: he too can, and needs to, benefit in the role of 'receiver'.

It is perhaps a truism to state that it is becoming more and more apparent that the different races inhabiting this subcontinent must begin to share it rather than to compete for its riches. This will become possible only when, in their mutual dealings, these races can transcend the all-too-frequent utilitarian caricatures they have of each other. This book is written in the hope that it will make the culture of the black man real enough to a few white individuals to suggest to them his evaluation in terms that are not bound to economic considerations. My dream is that, hidden in the overt features of this African culture, Westerners will pick up the threads of another reality with which to enrich their world and will, within this larger world, find a caring contact with Africa and her people before it is too late.

ETHNIC GROUPS

MORE than nine-tenths of the Bantu-speaking peoples of Southern Africa are accounted for by two loose groupings: the Nguni, found mainly on the east coast; and the Sotho/Tswana peoples, whose home is the plains of the Southern African plateau. The balance of Bantu-speaking Southern Africans are accounted for by three groups, varying in numerical strength from minor — Tsonga and Venda — to insignificant but nonetheless interesting — the Lemba.

These groups are conveniently broken down into subgroups composed of related traditional political units, loosely termed tribes, numbering from a few individuals sharing a king to hundreds of thousands. The defining criterion of a tribe, as opposed to the clan or kinship group, is that the unifying principle is political rather than based on blood ties. This is the only sense in which the term 'tribe' is used in this book: no association is intended with the adjective, 'tribal'.

NGUNI

The Nguni are basically pastoralists, whose traditional lightweight grass huts (now largely replaced by more permanent wattle-and-daub dwellings in rural areas) tell of a wandering existence. Their small homesteads comprise clusters of huts, housing from a single family to twenty or more related souls. A distinctive characteristic of this group is their very strong sense of clan ties and their practice of exogamy — a man may not marry a woman of his own *isibongo* (clan-name), or a close relative on his mother's side.

The Nguni, who account for some sixty per cent of the Bantu-speaking people of Southern Africa, can be divided into two subgroups, the coastal tribes and the Transvaal Ndebele, who live in the interior among the Sotho/Tswana peoples.

Nguni of the Interior: the Transvaal Ndebele

The Sotho have long referred to their Nguni neighbours as Ndebele and the Nguni living among these Sotho have adopted this name for themselves. The Ndebele people (comprising some two and a half per cent of Bantu-speakers) are composed of two separate groups which apparently do not share a common origin: one group resides in the more northerly areas, and the other in the south-central Transvaal.

Northern Section

Those to the north, the Northern or 'Black' Ndebele, have all but discarded their Nguni identity in favour of Sotho language and culture. All that remains of this identity is a tradition, unsubstantiated by history, of origins in Nguni territory. Today small tribes of these people are to be found spread across the northern Transvaal from the Botswana border in the west to the Zebediela district in the lowveld of the east.

Southern Section

Living on the Transvaal highveld and separated from the Northern Ndebele by the Springbok Flats, are the Southern Ndebele who, with their abundant beadwork and gaily painted houses, have made the name Ndebele famous in South Africa.

These people trace their origin to one Musi or Msi who lived, according to contradictory legends, either in Natal or near modern-day Pretoria. Musi, so the story goes, was father to five sons, each of whom founded a tribe. One of these tribes are the Makopane, but the most numerous and well known are the Manala, who live outside Pretoria, and the Ndzundza who, after being totally defeated and dispersed in the days of the Transvaal Republic, gathered together in small groups in the Middelburg, Springs and Rayton districts.

Coastal Nguni

The numerous coastal Nguni are best characterised as a kaleidoscopic collection of some hundreds of important and minor tribes scattered along the eastern coastal belt, whose cultures and languages merge to form a continuum. For the purposes of description, three broad divisions can be made: the Southern Nguni, the Zulu-speaking tribes, and the Swazi.

Southern Nguni

These people speak closely related dialects and are collectively referred to as Xhosa. They account for more than thirty per cent of Bantu-speaking South Africans. The tribes constituting this group live in southern Natal, Transkei and the eastern Cape.

The largest of these tribes are the Xhosa, resident mainly in Transkei and Ciskei, and composed of several factions, the greatest being the Ngqika and the Gcaleka. To the north-east of these tribes live the Mpondo, Mpondomise and Thembu, and to their east, the Bomvana. Two latecomers in the picture are the Bhaca, resident in north-eastern Transkei and southern Natal, and the Mfengu, who live among the Xhosa.

Zulu-speaking Nguni

The Nguni of Natal and Zululand (northern and north-east Natal) speak dialects collectively referred to as 'Zulu' and are marginally less numerous than the Xhosa-speakers. In pre-nineteenth-century Natal and Zululand, each of the hundreds of small tribes living in this area was autonomous. After the Zulu conquests, the status of these tribes varied from still autonomous to those who identified themselves as basically 'Zulu' though aware of a more immediate ethnic identity. In Natal one encounters individuals who, while dressing differently from the Zulu of Zululand and paying homage to a local

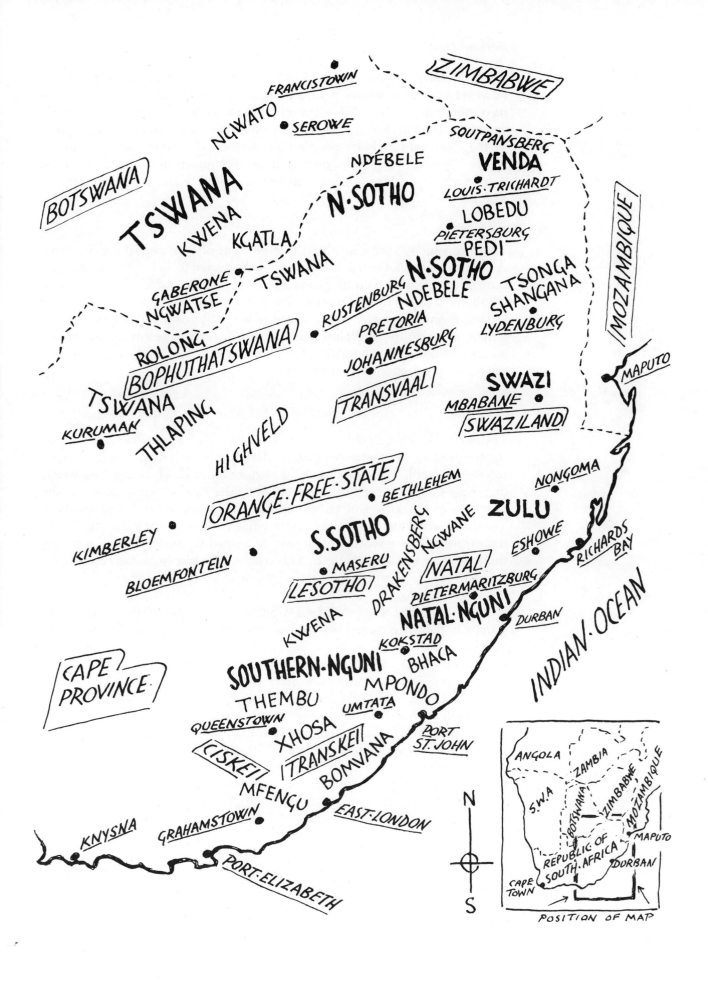

chief, identify themselves as Zulu. An equally probable response is, however, a proud assertion of affiliation to some small tribe reputed to have stood up to — evaded — the might of the Zulu. The term 'Natal Nguni' generally refers to those tribes whose identity has not been swamped by that of the Zulu, and includes people such as the Cele, Nhlangwini, Dlamini, Khuze, Ngwane, Hlubi, and dozens more, too numerous to mention. Those people whose old identity has been lost to that of 'Zulu' are to be found in Zululand.

Swazi
The Swazi today comprise about five per cent of Bantu-speaking Southern Africans and speak the *tekela* dialect, closely related to Zulu. About sixty per cent of people identified as Swazi live in Swaziland, while the rest live in adjoining areas of the Transvaal. The present-day Swazi nation boasts the longest reigning monarch in the world, King Sobhuza II. The nucleus of the nation is a group of Nguni who settled in their present home in the nineteenth century, subjugating the local Sotho and skilfully incorporating them into the modern Swazi nation.

SOTHO/TSWANA

The hallmark of the Sotho/Tswana , who account for just over one third of Bantu-speaking Southern Africans, is totemism. Each clan has its specific totem, be it animal or, more rarely, a plant or mineral. There are the Kwena, or people of the crocodile, for example, or the Kgatla, whose totem is the monkey, or the group of tribes now settled in the central and northern Transvaal who have the pig as their totem. In days past each clan venerated its totem and those whose totem was an animal would not think of killing this species or of eating its flesh. This religious reverence of each clan for its totem has been considerably watered down and today, for many, the totem has little meaning.

A distinguishing feature of the Tswana and to a lesser extent of the Sotho groups is their preference for large settlements. Among the Tswana these may embrace 20 000 or more people. Unlike the Nguni the Sotho are traditionally endogamous: they have no taboo on marriage with a clan member and, in fact, prefer such unions.

The Sotho/Tswana inhabit the interior of Southern Africa — the Transvaal, the northern Cape, eastern Botswana, and Lesotho. They can be conveniently divided into three broad subgroups: the South Sotho, living in Lesotho and surrounding areas; the Tswana, apparently closely related to the first subgroup and living mainly in Botswana, Bophuthatswana, the northern Cape and western Transvaal; and the North Sotho of the central, eastern and northern Transvaal, a scattering of tribes ethnically diverse in comparison with the South Sotho or Tswana.

South Sotho
The South Sotho, who account for just over one sixth of Southern Africa's Bantu-speakers, are defined by their ethnic and linguistic homogeneity and their geographic location. Their main stronghold is Lesotho, although many people live on the adjacent European-owned areas of the South African high-

veld. The wars of the nineteenth century caused considerable disruption among the old tribal groups. However, many fairly strong ethnic subgroups survive today in the form of various Fokeng groups in northern Lesotho, the hardy Tlôkwa of mountainous eastern Lesotho, the Kgwakgwa of Butha Buthe, and many more. Today, these peoples' identity as baSotho (members of the modern nation) is more important than their more immediate tribal affiliations.

Tswana (Western Sotho)

The Tswana people, comprising one tenth of Southern Africa's Bantu-speakers, appear to share common ancestry with the South Sotho. They live in eastern Botswana, the northern Cape, and the west-central Transvaal. Those people living towards the west identify themselves as Tswana, while those in the east are equally happy to call themselves Sotho.

In Botswana one encounters several large tribes, such as the Ngwaketse and Ngwato. Along the Cape-Botswana border live the Rolong, whose totem is iron, and to their south the Tlhaping, whose fish-totem gave the little town of Vryburg its coat-of-arms. In the Transvaal, one encounters various tribes including the Huruthse in the western Transvaal near Rustenburg, and the Mosetla-Kgatla near Pretoria. Further towards the north-west are the Hananwa.

North Sotho

Of all the ethnic subgroups mentioned in this book, these people, nearly as numerous as the Tswana, are culturally the most diverse. While these inhabitants of the central, northern and eastern Transvaal speak related dialects, testimony to some relationship, their cultural and linguistic links are sufficiently tenuous to suggest caution in imposing this category.

Among the most noteworthy peoples in this group are the Pedi. They are most accurately described as a loose confederation of small central Transvaal tribes, paying homage to their Pedi conquerors of three centuries ago. These tribes identify themselves today both with the Pedi and with their more ancient and more immediate tribal names.

The other more noteworthy tribe among the North Sotho are the Lobedu, who live just beneath the Drakensberg escarpment in the north-eastern Transvaal. These people, who are related to the Venda, are today basically Sotho in culture and language. They owe much of their power and security to the line of Modjadji rain-queen rulers, whose formidable rain magic has always ensured a steady stream of tribute and has protected the Lobedu from military attack.

Further east are a group of tribes contemptuously termed 'Roka' by their neighbours: the Narene near Tzaneen and, still further east, the Koni group, which includes the interesting Kgaga tribe and the ancient Phalaborwa people.

With the exception of the Lobedu, these North Sotho tribes mentioned so far seem reasonably homogeneous. But in the far east of this area are a collection of tribes, the East Sotho, who have only a nominal membership in this category and, on the plateau to the north of the Olifants River, whose local tribal cultures and traditions show more affinity with the tribes of modern Zimbabwe.

VENDA

The Venda are a group of tribes living in and around the Soutpansberg mountains of the northern Transvaal. Despite their relatively small numbers (they comprise only two per cent of Bantu-speakers in Southern Africa), they are regarded as an important people. Culturally and linguistically, the Venda are distinct from their Sotho neighbours. However, contact with Sotho culture and language has influenced the Venda in the west and south to a considerable extent. The true heartland, where the distinctiveness of Venda culture is really apparent, is in the north-east, home of the two most important tribes, the Tshivhase and Mphaphuli.

A characteristic Venda village, perched high on a mountain ridge as a natural defence against enemy attack. Today more and more villages are being sited in the more accessible lowland areas.

Lemba

A numerically insignificant but nonetheless fascinating people are the Lemba, whose arrogant aloofness from their Venda and Sotho hosts has always elicited comment. Termed the 'Black Jews' for their custom of kosher killing, these proud people are highly respected as wandering iron-smelters and potters. All evidence, notably their features and names, supports their tradition of a descent from Arab traders who 'went native' after the sack of their home city while they were trading in East Africa.

TSONGA

These people, though one and a half times as numerous as the Venda, are not as significant in the context of this book because most are nineteenth-century settlers whose cultural nucleus is in Mozambique and not a subject of this text. Wandering in as refugees, these rather despised people were unsuccessful in establishing any real, strong political institutions and still live in isolated pockets, mainly in the eastern Transvaal, but spreading west to beyond Pretoria.

Venda women stamping grain according to the traditional method.

ORIGINS AND HISTORY

ORIGINS

WHERE do the Bantu-speakers come from? Researchers have placed most reliance on two avenues of research in seeking an answer to this question: archaeology and glottochronology, the statistical study of the evolution and diversification of language with time. These methods have spawned a plethora of theories and subtheories and the story I present here is based on currently respectable theories. The reader who wishes to penetrate beyond this level of examination is referred to the bibliography.

Linguists point to the Niger-Cameroons area as the most likely point of emergence of the first, so-called proto-Bantu languages some 2 500 years ago. This finding appears to corroborate discoveries by archaeologists that iron was smelted in this area for the first time about 500 B.C. Theorists describe a community of proto-Bantu-speaking Negroes living on the savannahs fringing the great Congo rain forests. When these people learned the art of smelting iron, possibly from Berber tribesmen who traded across the Sahara with the rich Nile civilisation, the tempo of life changed considerably. The change was probably accelerated by the introduction of several species of millet.

With iron hoes and cereal crops, local agriculture changed from the tentative scratchings that archaeologists have dubbed vegeculture to something more akin to modern agriculture. With this improvement came a population explosion which in turn brought war fought with iron assegais, and the first movement of the early proto-Bantu-speaking Negroes towards the south.

Linguistic evidence suggests that a community of these migrants may have lived and multiplied in the vicinity of Zaïre's Shaba province before spreading east and south to bring the Bantu family of languages to the southern subcontinent.[1] Certainly, early historical records indicate that trade existed between sturdy black men and the Arabs who sailed to the East African coast in the early years of the Christian era.

The Early Iron Age
Archaeologists divide the Iron Age in sub-Saharan Africa into two periods, the Early and Later Iron Ages. The Early Iron Age tells the story of the fairly rapid spread of iron-smelting peoples in equatorial Africa during the second

century A.D. and their movement southwards in two streams. It was the more easterly of the two which brought the Early Iron Age to South Africa around A.D. 300.

It is common knowledge that Stone Age man, in the form of San (Bushmen) and Khoikhoi (Hottentots), inhabited Southern Africa long before the advent of the European. However, the popular history of Bantu-speaking Southern Africans (the most likely candidates for Early Iron Age man) has dated their arrival in Southern Africa as contemporaneous with that of the European, in the mid-seventeenth century.

This false view of history, which has suited some politicians, has been sharply criticised by one of South Africa's most eminent Iron Age archaeologists, Professor Nick van der Merwe:

> The history of South Africa, as taught in its school system, views the past as if through the wrong end of a telescope. The discovery and settlement of the country is seen as being little more than three hundred years in duration and is described primarily from the point of view of European immigrants; the rest is compressed into insignificance. The result is a series of historical myths, perpetuated from one generation to the next, which is accepted without much questioning as 'the truth' by the vast majority of white South Africans.[2]

Bantu-speakers in Southern Africa

Though this myth, as Professor van der Merwe has called it, has now been flourishing for decades despite evidence to the contrary, the last ten years have seen the discovery of more and more Iron Age settlements dated by radiocarbon methods to well over 1 000 years before the arrival of the first European settlers in the Cape in 1652. It is for this reason that I have felt it essential to give an account here, however briefly, of the early history of Southern Africa 'from the right end of the telescope'.

We know that by A.D. 300 the Early Iron Age people had settled in South Africa, probably reaching the vicinity of modern East London on the coast and the southern Orange Free State inland by A.D. 500 or 700 at the latest. What has also become apparent, and a revelation to the locally educated South African, is that these people (like the later Bantu-speaking settlers encountered by the Europeans) moved no further south because weather conditions there did not suit them: the Karoo, inland, was too dry, and on the coast the Cape's winter rainfall region was unsuitable for African methods of agriculture. The 'southward-moving stream of Bantu who encountered the northward-moving European in the vicinity of the Great Fish River' is a myth.[3]

We know that these Early Iron Age people were Negro. What the archaeologists cannot tell us is what language these early settlers spoke. Again using the words of van der Merwe: 'We can only prove they were Negro people with an Iron Age culture, and we can surmise with confidence that they spoke Bantu languages.'[4] In fact, it would be extremely surprising to find that these early Negroes did not speak Bantu languages.

However, it is unlikely that these Early Iron Age Negroes will remain anything more than an enigmatic presence for some years to come. The story of the present-day Bantu-speaking inhabitants of Southern Africa is that of the Later Iron Age.

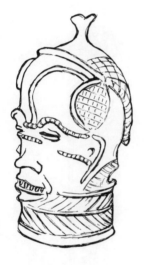

One of the so-called 'Lydenburg' masks, discovered on a farm near the Transvaal town of that name and dated to A.D. 500. Early Iron Age pottery found in association with the masks has been associated with contemporaneous Natal styles, suggesting a very early and widespread settlement of Southern Africa by people who were probably the ancestors of the Bantu-speaking inhabitants of present-day Southern Africa. [S.A. Museum, Cape Town.]

Later Iron Age

Throughout sub-Saharan Africa, according to archaeologists, there occurred in the tenth century a dramatic change in the styles of pottery being made — a change which could have come about only through the emergence of a new and energetic group of people, the carriers of the Later Iron Age. The origin of these people is obscure. Ruin excavation shows a continuity between Early and Later Iron Age styles only in the vicinity of the Angola-Zambian border. This might indicate that it was here that the new, virile, Later Iron Age people emerged from Early Iron Age society. Corroborative evidence comes, perhaps, in the form of language analyses which point to the adjacent Shaba province of southern Zaïre as the point of dispersal of modern Bantu languages.

HISTORY OF THE SETTLEMENT OF SOUTHERN AFRICA

Whatever their origin, the carriers of the Later Iron Age culture were Bantu-speaking Negroes, who appeared in Southern Africa between A.D. 1000 and 1100 to become the ancestors of most of the present-day inhabitants of the region.

It is currently believed that the new settlers did not come as a great conquering force but rather diffused into the area in smallish groups, overcoming their predecessors by weight of numbers over a long period of time rather than in a military campaign. These predecessors were of course their Early Iron Age counterparts, who were apparently not very numerous, and the Khoisan (Khoikhoi and San) people with whom they co-existed.

Settlement of the Interior

The Western Migrations

Of all the modern-day Bantu-speaking peoples of Southern Africa, those whose history and current life-style link them most clearly to the tenth-century Iron Age settlers are the various members of the Sotho group and, of these, the South Sotho and Tswana (Western Sotho) subgroups are the most notable. It was the Tswana and South Sotho who built the thousands of stone huts whose ruins today dot the South African highveld. They were the inhabitants of the great towns built of stone reported by the explorers of the early nineteenth century. For instance, the missionary Campbell[5] who visited the town of Kaditshwene in 1820 estimated its population at 16 000. Recent aerial surveys[6] have revealed at least twenty urban settlements of a similar size and density and hundreds of others of a more dispersed nature. When, in 1801, the trader Borcherds[7] tried to sell these people knives they were not interested: their own, ornately decorated, were superior.

While the oral histories of the South Sotho and Tswana give a fairly reliable story of their settlement of Southern Africa, the origin of these peoples is vague. One tradition tells of a long journey from a place where 'the sun shone on the other shoulder' — apparently somewhere in the northern hemisphere. Another legend tells of an origin in a land of lakes and mountains, which suggests that the Sotho come from the Lakes Region of Africa. It is likely that, in both Early and Later Iron Age times, the Great Rift Valley and associated lakes and highlands were used as a migration route by

This nineteenth-century, Tswana carved ivory sheath knife is typical of the pre-European tradition. Such knives are individually carved and therefore not only very meaningful to their owners but forged of better quality steel than those brought by early traders, who found that they could not sell their mass-produced equivalents. [S.A. Museum, Cape Town.]

Bantu-speaking pastoralists, as the highlands were free of tsetse fly and the deadly nagana disease it transmitted to their cattle. A further tenuous link with more northern regions is the arcane teaching in the girls' initiation lodges of some South Sotho tribes that their people are the 'fathers of the Swahili', the Swahili being an East African tribe.

Whatever their distant origins, now all but lost to the ethnic memory, the ancestors of the South Sotho and Tswana were one of the most important groups of people to settle on the South African highveld. For centuries they bickered and spread across the central plains, and today their descendants are scattered over the southern, central and western parts of the Transvaal, the northern Cape, eastern Botswana, the Free State, Lesotho and the various homelands. The precis that follows cannot do justice to the rich and fascinating oral histories[8] which reach back to the time when the first settlers crossed the Limpopo some thirty generations — nearly a thousand years — ago.

Among the first colonists were the Kgalakgadi, followed by the Rolong and Thlaping and various splinter groups. Later, at some time during the fourteenth and fifteenth centuries, a settlement near the confluence of the Crocodile and Marico rivers in the western Transvaal became an important centre of population dispersal, and the Huruthse people living there saw descendants heading for all points of the compass. Most important were the Kwena who, in their turn, fragmented to produce many and varied tribes, including the Ngwato and Ngwaketse. Related, it is surmised, to the Huruthse, are another tribe, the Kgatla, who probably lived in this area at much the same time and who, in their turn, spawned several tribes, including the Tlôkwa and Phuting of Lesotho. The Pedi, another Kgatla offshoot, wandered into the central Transvaal in the mid-seventeenth century to subjugate the local peoples and create the only substantial Sotho empire.

The Northern and Eastern Migrations
The story of the settlement of the central, northern and eastern areas of the Transvaal by their present-day occupants is confused and the origins of the different groups diverse. For this reason I will not deal with their histories in detail.

Two broad groups of people settled in this area: the Venda in the Soutpansberg and the North Sotho in most other areas. The Sotho,[9] for the most part, appear to have been in the area for a considerable time: the Phalaborwa, who give the modern mining centre its name, were mining copper on that site for nearly a thousand years before their European counterparts. These same people were possibly the prehistoric copper miners of Messina in the far northern Transvaal.

The Venda entered the area much later than most Sotho, displacing those people they found in the Soutpansberg to make this mountain range their home and a fortress which has secured them against most attackers. The Lobedu people, now culturally more Sotho than Venda, are a Venda offshoot who migrated further south. Venda tradition tells of a journey from the vicinity of a great, silent pool of water, probably Lake Malawi, followed by a sojourn among the Karanga nobility of Zimbabwe, to whom they are related. The other peoples of the northern Transvaal who are related to the Zimbabwe tribes probably entered the area considerably earlier, and the rich archaeological site of Mapungubwe near the Limpopo river points to a very early period of occupation.

Settlement of the Coastal Areas

The plateau on which the Sotho peoples settled is part of a huge basin which used to be the bed of an ancient sea. Surrounding this basin is a range of mountains, stretching in a vast loop down the western periphery of the southern subcontinent and then on and up the eastern seaboard. In the east this range of mountains reaches its most impressive proportions in the form of the magnificent Drakensberg escarpment, which looms above Natal and tails off to the south in Transkei. It is here, in the rich, well-watered belt between this escarpment and the sea, that the early, unknown ancestors of today's Nguni built their sturdy grass huts.

Unlike the Sotho, the Venda, and the tribes to the north, whose histories can be traced to some kind of foundation, the Nguni have been called the 'invisible' people of South African history. Trying to glimpse the distant past of the Nguni is like peering into the mists of the Drakensberg mountains which border their lands. The more recent happenings are clear, bloody, and larger than life, but as events recede in the mists of time they become formless and confused, beyond the probing of even the most diligent and perspicacious student.

Archaeological evidence suggests the advent of the Later Iron Age in Nguni territory around A.D. 1000, which probably establishes that date for the settlement of Zululand, Natal and Transkei by at least some of their present-day inhabitants.[10]

We have seen, too, that the Early Iron Age, eclipsed by this culture, reaches back to A.D. 700 at the very least in this area. Furthermore, it has been suggested that this area was possibly a point of evolution from the Early Iron Age of at least one component of the Later Iron Age culture which is hypothesised as having spread from Natal to Zimbabwe. This hypothesis might be corroborated by traditional histories which tell of the Lala people, reputedly very ancient and renowned metal-workers, who were encountered by the ancestors of the modern Nguni when they settled in Natal — a people who can be tentatively associated with Zimbabwe.

An early student of Nguni oral histories, the Reverend A.T. Bryant, believed these modern Nguni ancestors entered Natal in several streams, the parent stock having split up somewhere in the interior. One group, the Mbo-Nguni, entered Natal after travelling down the Lebombo Mountains on the modern Swaziland–Mozambique border. Along with several clans and tribes in Zululand, Natal and Transkei, the Swazi are descended from these people.[11]

The Mpondo and Mpondomise of Transkei are, perhaps, related to the Swazi. These two tribes, like other Southern Nguni, are established by a combination of traditional histories and accounts of early shipwreck victims, as having been settled in present-day Nguni territory since, at the latest, A.D. 1300.[12]

Bryant who, along with the Reverend J.H. Soga,[13] made a study of early Nguni history, hypothesised an early wave of Nguni immigrants whom he called the 'ntungwa'. Among these 'ntungwa' Nguni was the small Zulu clan which contained the seeds of the terrible Zulu war machine.

THE GREAT BANTU REVOLUTION

To summarise briefly: various sources have been combined to tell the story of the direct ancestors of the modern Bantu-speaking peoples of Southern Africa; people who wandered into the region nearly a thousand years ago to settle the interior plateau and coastal regions. This settlement was followed by a period of relative peace and stability lasting some eight centuries. As a clearsighted if romantic missionary, Bryant had the vision to see past the dearth of material and artistic culture into the spirit of this age. He called the society he saw in Nguni territory 'an African Arcady'. In this era of South African history even the serious business of warfare was hardly distinguished from sport. Battles were fought on pre-arranged days between armies numbered in dozens. Casualties were light and, as often as not, the end of the battle would find an erstwhile warrior paying a visit to a sweetheart in the enemy clan.

But this happy-go-lucky state of affairs had to vanish. In the late eighteenth century a process of empire building began in Zululand, a process exploited by Africa's Napoleon, Shaka, king of the Zulu. He used his clan to create a nation and he used the armies of that nation like a blood-filled pen to write, with a wanton genius, the nineteenth-century history of Southern Africa.[14]

Up to this time the history of Southern Africa's Bantu-speakers is vague and blurred, but, from this point on, the story of Southern Africa becomes larger than life.

The hills of modern Natal and Zululand were, in the late eighteenth century, inhabited by literally hundreds of tiny and not-so-tiny clans. One of the larger and more important of these clans, the Mthethwa, entered Zululand during this period after a sojourn among the Tsonga in what is today called Mozambique.

Early in the nineteenth century, they were ruled by a very resourceful man named Dingiswayo. Not content with the happy, bickering, humdrum way of life led by his clan and those around him, he set out to conquer his neighbours and to absorb them into a bigger kingdom. He little realised that his tiny efforts at improving the politics of his people were the first stirrings of the Nguni giant, which was to produce the most efficient and deadly fighting force ever seen in this part of Africa.

Dingiswayo's most important contribution to history was in fact the organisation of his fighting force. He schooled initiates thoroughly in the arts of war. When he conquered another clan, their young men, too, were trained under the banner of the Mthethwa royal house in age-regiments, to form units which cut across all clan differences, thereby precluding a revolt by any single clan or group under his power.

Shaka

One of the young warriors in Dingiswayo's fighting force was destined to reach the very pinnacle of power and infamy. He was a princeling of one of the tiny clans in Zululand. This clan bore the name of their founder — Zulu, meaning 'heaven'.

Tribal history tells us that Sezangakona, a late eighteenth-century chief, descendant of Zulu, was a great success with the ladies and, like many a young man before him, enriched his life with the usual flirtations and paramours. And, like many who preceded him and many who have followed, Sezangakona made a mistake: from a homestead of the neighbouring eLangeni clan, a message was sent to the Zulu chief to the effect that subsequent to his attentions one of their royal daughters was pregnant. Immediately a messenger was sent back to the eLangeni homestead: the lady in question, Nandi, was not pregnant but was in fact suffering from an infestation by an intestinal beetle, or *iShaka*. Thus it was that, when the child was born, there seemed to be no better name for Nandi's son than Shaka. Sezangakona was forced to accept, grudgingly, mother and son as part of his household, where they stayed some years, during which time Nandi also bore a daughter. However mother and children were unhappy, despised and saddled with an apparently well-earned reputation for being badtempered and fractious. The situation came to a head when the young Shaka allowed a dog to kill one of his father's favourite fat-tailed sheep, and Nandi and her two children were given their marching orders.

They returned to her eLangeni people, where, tradition relates, her son was incessantly bullied and mocked and as unhappy as he had been at his father's home.

Shaka developed what can only be called a king-sized chip on his shoulder. He resented his father, and refused to accept from him the *umuTsha* (loin cover) customarily presented by a father to his son to cover his nakedness. After her stay with her family, Nandi sojourned discontentedly in several homesteads until she finally settled among the Mthethwa in a district headed by one Ngomane. Here, at last, the little family found kindness — never forgotten by the young Shaka who, when a mighty monarch, made Ngomane the most powerful man in his kingdom after himself.

PAGE 25   Respect is always shown to traditional beer by receiving and drinking it in the squatting position: it is an insult and breach of good manners towards the host, his family and his ancestors, to accept and drink beer when standing. The cattle kraal is the traditional venue for men to gather for drinking and discussion.

This Zulu man, in his traditional animal skins and feathers, wears bead bands which indicate marriage or betrothal. On his collar of skins is pinned an inflated gall bladder from a sacrificial goat. The black pompom and tuft of black feathers on his head are made from the tail feathers of the widow bird. The blue crane feathers and leopard skin are prerogatives of rank. His shield is of the small type used for dancing and on ceremonial occasions.

PAGES 26-7   Modern Sotho huts on the borders of the Orange Free State show a new look in mural design. In many areas, bright commercial paints are replacing the ochres and whites and blacks of the traditional patterning.

Most common are the flat-topped, back-sloping houses with their colourful frontage. Shallow-relief modelling gives form to the colour divisions, and low walls may also divide the family 'yard'. The house on the left is of this style, while the owner of the hut on the right has retained the use of the traditional reed enclosure for the 'yard', to which a front wall has been added and brightly decorated. In the left foreground is a pile of cowdung patties, ready for use as fuel for cooking fires because of the scarcity of firewood on the highveld — a loss to the fields of valuable manure. (Assisted by photographs by Aubrey Elliot)

While Shaka was resident among the Mthethwa, Dingiswayo became their chief and Shaka soon joined the army. Brave and resourceful, Shaka became Dingiswayo's favourite. His principal claim to attention was a manner of attack which dumbfounded his enemies: instead of standing at a distance and hurling his assegai like any other respectable warrior, he would rush in and make quite certain of the kill by using the assegai as a stabbing weapon. When Sezangakona died and was succeeded by a half-brother to Shaka, Dingiswayo gave his favourite his blessing and a troop of warriors with which to usurp leadership of the Zulu clan.

Once in power, Shaka wasted no time. First he purged his home of all those who had been unkind to him or his mother. Then he paid his first visiting call — on the eLangeni people who had treated him so cruelly. Every person who had ever done the young boy any wrong was impaled on a stake and a fire kindled under him. These goings-on doubtlessly brought great satisfaction to Shaka's bitter heart, but were only portents of far worse atrocities to come.

The first revolutionary fighting technique of Shaka's rule had long been in his mind, and one day he divided his small army into two groups, both of which were provided with reeds instead of assegais. These two armies were then ordered to oppose one another, the one side throwing the reeds and the other using them as stabbing weapons. The results were spectacular, and from that day on, Shaka's armies were equipped with the stabbing spears for which they became famous, and a soldier returned from battle with his weapon or not at all.

Like Dingiswayo, Shaka understood the soundness of the age-regiment system, which provided an army with no loyalties other than to himself. He carried the concept further, however, by appointing indunas or headmen in charge of his armies, who were loyal to him alone and owed their position — and indeed their lives — solely to him.

But the heights of power were yet to come — with the disintegration of the Mthethwa empire of which the Zulu were a part. The agent of this destruction was Zwide, the ambitious chief of the Ndwandwe people. The Ndwandwe and Mthethwa clans clashed and, possibly as a result of extensive magical preparations on the part of Zwide, his people were doubly victorious: not only did they defeat the Mthethwa army in battle but they managed to capture and later put to death their monarch, Dingiswayo.

Shaka (whose soldiers had been conspicuously absent from the ranks of Dingiswayo's army) took advantage of the situation and set about

A small Zulu dancing shield. When the Zulu were a warring nation, each regiment was recognisable by the characteristic hide markings on their fighting shields.

PAGE 28   White is the colour of gala dress for Xhosa, Mfengu and Mpondo. The Mfengu blanket may be recognised by the particular use of beads, braid, buttons and tippets of fur. The black headcloth is edged with blue beads and heavily encrusted with pearl buttons, many of which date back to the days of early white settlers. Most Southern Nguni coveted these buttons and obtained them by fair means or foul, sometimes catching white children herding cattle simply to remove their buttons. Mfengu beadwork is characterised by the plentiful use of animal motifs.

A nursing mother and child have whitened faces, the mother's facial decoration often a work of art. In the background a man and woman set off on a journey, the man in front with his fighting sticks ready for any contingency, while his wife follows with all the luggage on her head.

reorganising the Mthethwa army. This soon attracted the attentions of Zwide's militia and, unequipped to face this force in battle, Shaka lured them ever southward, using a scorched-earth policy, until hunger forced them to turn back, weary and weakened. Then Shaka's army dogged their heels, using guerrilla tactics and waiting for an opening that would spell defeat for Zwide's Ndwandwe.

This opening presented itself at the Mhlatuze River where the Zulu attacked the much larger Ndwandwe force. The water ran red with blood as the battle raged to and fro in midstream, but the Zulu army could not get the upper hand. When the battle hung in the balance, Shaka showed his genius: he ordered one of his regiments upstream to cross the river and attack the enemy on their flank. Fighting on two fronts, the Ndwandwe resistance crumbled and a massacre followed.

From the time of this victory in 1819 until his death in 1828, Shaka's armies roamed almost at will, trampling the yellow winter grass to kick up a cloud of dust which hung over the once sunny land. Confronted by these armies, smaller tribes had little choice: resistance, followed by defeat and bloody subjugation — or flight. Most of the peoples of Zululand faced Shaka's wrath and were welded into the growing Zulu empire. Today, much of their identity lost, these various tribelets have only their clan names to remind themselves of their one-time independence.

The Mfecane

Many clans, however, chose flight in preference to servitude or the annual winter raids by the Zulu armies. Like the ripples on a pond, these displaced peoples poured out across Natal — and Africa — disturbing the pattern of ages. The impact of the mass flight and the chain reaction it caused was so great that, before Shaka's armies ever penetrated south of Zululand, Natal had been transformed into a mass of desperate, battling bands, each a victim and at the same time and agent of the destructive force unleashed in Zululand. In Nguni territory this orgy of violence became known as the *Mfecane* or 'crushing'.

The Bhaca

In southern Natal, two bands of homeless desperadoes emerged, to begin a ten-year running battle. The eventual victors were led by one Ncapayi, described by a certain Captain Gardner as 'one of the most desperate Characters in this part of Africa'. The descendants of his followers are the Bhaca, a proud but somewhat despised people.

The Mfengu

The remaining refugees in Southern Nguni territory were a sorry lot, named the Mfengu after their continual begging for food (*ukufenguza* — to beg for food). These homeless beggars saw their salvation in the white man and ingratiated themselves with the early missionaries who, impressed by such excesses of devotion, obtained permission from the authorities to move a large number of Xhosa off their land to make way for the Mfengu. The Xhosa in question understandably refused to move, with the result that the Mfengu, when they settled, found themselves surrounded by extremely hostile people. Lacking a homeland and dependent on the Europeans, the Mfengu

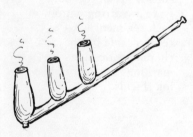

Not for the faint of heart! An unusual early Xhosa pipe which, but for the two extra bowls and the European derived peg beneath the end bowl, resembles those in use today. [From Shaw, 1938, Plate 92.]

were quick to adopt Western ways of living and thinking, producing a disproportionate number of Southern Africa's black intellectuals and academics.

The Ngoni

While indiscriminate scrimmaging was spreading to the south, the Nguni revolution was exploding northwards. The defeat of the Ndwandwe by Shaka sent three leaders, each with a tiny following, into Mozambique. After hacking their way through the surprised and peaceable Tsonga peoples living there, two of these bands plunged further northwards, striking the death-knell of the ancient Changmire empire of Zimbabwe and then battling still further north, their numbers swollen constantly with conquered people. These people, who became known as the Ngoni, carried the violence as far as the southern shores of Lake Victoria. Today there are still small groups of their descendants scattered about East Africa.

The Shangana

The third band, under the leadership of Soshangane, remained among the Tsonga of Mozambique when the other two fought their way northwards. Soshangane carved out an empire for himself which became known as Gaza after his royal lineage. The Gaza empire was the last surviving black empire in Southern Africa, falling to the Portuguese only in 1895.

The Tsonga, ruled by the royal house of Gaza, became known as the maShangana or 'Shangaans' after the founder of the empire. With the collapse of the empire, many Shangana fled west into the Transvaal where today they inhabit mainly the southern lowveld areas. Always despised and unwelcome, small groups have wandered as far west as Pretoria.

The Swazi

At the beginning of the nineteenth century Sobhuza I, leader of the Ngwane people (descendants of the Mbo-Nguni), was an ambitious and moderately successful king. By conquering the surrounding tribes along the Pongola River and to the north, he ruled an area half the size of modern Swaziland. He made the mistake however of laying claim to some of the Ndwandwe land along the Pongola. This soon led to his defeat at the hands of Zwide, and flight to central Swaziland. Here, undeterred and using Zulu fighting methods, Sobhuza built a kingdom from the surrounding Sotho and Nguni tribes. He wisely treated the conquered peoples well, allowing them to retain their own royalty; yet such was his genius that at the same time subject communities developed a sense of belonging and pride in the larger nation, and their young men were given the honour of joining the national army.

Shaka never attacked the Swazi. His armies used their country as a thoroughfare to the north but it was spared the agony of so many other nations, probably owing to the Swazi monarch's ability to make himself unobtrusive and to judicious marriages of Swazi maidens to Zulu royalty. Even when Shaka's Swazi princesses were put to death on becoming pregnant, Sobhuza kept his counsel.

However, in 1836, some years after Shaka's brother Dingane had become king of the Zulu, his armies attacked the Swazi. Sobhuza's armies melted into the hills and caves of their country to elude their pursuers. After

Mswazi had succeeded his father as chief, the Zulu attacked again — this time aided by European hunters and adventurers — and were victorious. However, they did not press their victory, and merely confiscated some cattle.

Mswazi died in 1868, leaving the nation his name. During his reign and those of his successors, European pressures mounted until, from the time he took office in 1875 until his death in 1889, king Mbadeni signed his whole kingdom away several times over to a renegade and colourful crowd of concession-hunters, involving his people in a fiasco of epic proportions. The Swazi nation and its royalty are fortunate to have survived intact.

The Difaqane: Revolution in Sotho Territory

Although neither the Hlubi nor the Ngwane are today tribes of any consequence, I will tell their story in some detail, not only because of their part in carrying the revolution to the Sotho (where it became known as the *Difaqane* or 'hammering'), but as an example of the life of small tribes during this harsh and turbulent period.

The early part of the nineteenth century found the Ngwane people a fairly powerful clan, living in northern Natal and ruled by Matiwane. Immediately to the south-east of the Ngwane lived the Hlubi, one of the most powerful tribes in Nguni territory.

The Hlubi were the first victims of Matiwane's Ngwane people. Unsettled by successive attacks by Dingiswayo to the east, and bitter over being cheated by the Hlubi in a cattle deal, the Ngwane decided to seek peace in a new home further west, beneath the Drakensberg escarpment. Before they left, they set upon the Hlubi, defeating them in a surprise attack, sowing death and destruction everywhere and capturing virtually all their cattle. After the attack, the Hlubi split into two sections. One fled to the south, to become part of the faceless, starving mob later known as the Mfengu. The larger part, however, chose a warrior existence. In 1822 they rallied under the young and zestful Mpangazitha and scaled the Drakensberg, intent on a career of destruction among the peaceful Sotho people.

The first Sotho tribe encountered by this section of the Hlubi were the Makotleng Tlôkwa, one of the Kgatla group. Led by MmaNthatisi, until her son Sekonyela's majority, they faced Mpangazitha's Hlubi in battle, but were totally defeated, losing their cattle to the enemy. Forced into a life of plunder, MmaNthatisi moved down the Caledon river, attacking the peace-able Fokeng, Kwena and other peoples whom she encountered on the way, taking their cattle and repeatedly fighting off Mpangazitha, who followed her path of destruction.

On one occasion, after an attack on the Hlubi by MmaNthatisi's Tlôkwa, a counter-attack was launched a few days later while MmaNthatisi's warriors were away from camp. Here MmaNthatisi showed her notorious resourcefulness. She formed all the women and children into such a long and formidable-looking line behind the shields of the absent army that the would-be attackers turned away, completely demoralised, and were caught unawares by the returning Tlôkwa army. After this, MmaNthatisi's people roamed up and down the Caledon, living by death and plunder, dislodging many Taung, Phuting, Kwena and Fokeng tribes and generally becoming so infamous that all the warring bands that wandered across the plains of the interior were 'Mantatees' (after MmaNthatisi) to the early white settlers and traders.

After their plunder of the Hlubi, Matiwane and his Ngwane had little opportunity of enjoying their new home beneath the Drakensberg escarpment. In the winter of 1821 a Zulu army appeared on the horizon, forcing Matiwane to lead his Ngwane westwards, up the escarpment and into the land of the Sotho where, plundering and pillaging, he achieved abysmal notoriety among the local inhabitants.

These two groups of master pillagers — the Tlôkwa and the Hlubi — were soon joined by a third group, the Ndebele.

Mzilikazi

The unfortunate Sotho, however, had additional problems. Around 1820 there appeared on the central plateau one Mzilikazi, a rebel Zulu general fleeing Shaka's vengeance. Accompanied by a handful of warriors, his natural resourcefulness and Zulu fighting techiques enabled Mzilikazi to create a warlike nation, the Ndebele (later called the Rhodesian Ndebele or Matabele by Europeans) whose armies were, for nearly twenty years, the most destructive force in Sotho territory. They wandered at will over the central plateau, conquering the most powerful Tswana tribes and sending even the mighty Pedi scurrying off to hide in the Soutpansberg. Mzilikazi's defeat at the hands of invading Voortrekkers sent him and his people fleeing northwards to establish themselves in Zimbabwe (where they were finally defeated by European settlers some sixty years later).

A dark fate also awaited the Hlubi and Ngwane. The Hlubi were crushed by Matiwane's Ngwane in an epic five-day battle on the west bank of the Caledon. Some joined the ranks of their former adversaries, while others set out on a remarkable warring career during which they saw service in Mzilikazi's army on the highveld and, later, defeat at the hands of Ncapayi's Bhaca in far-off Transkei. This battle-weary band, like many others, eventually found peace under Moshweshwe, the Basotho chief. Today their descendants live in the Herschel district of the Cape Province.

The fate awaiting Matiwane was no less bloody than that of his defeated adversaries, the Hlubi. The victory over Mpangazitha and the Hlubi opened up extensive new territory to him, but the beginning of the end for Matiwane came in 1827 with the appearance of the very people that had sent him scurrying from Natal — a marauding Zulu army.

Desirous as ever of keeping a large gap between himself and the Zulu, Matiwane fled. His flight took him to the banks of the Mthatha river in Transkei where he had the misfortune to be confronted and defeated by a colonial army, mustered not against him but for battle with the Zulu.

The majority of the defeated Ngwane merged with the Mfengu horde, but Matiwane and a small following set off to seek a pardon from Dingane, who allowed them to settle in their ancestral home. However, the presence of so famous a warrior unnerved Dingane and one day a messenger arrived to summon Matiwane into the presence of the Zulu king. Fearing the worst, he told his son and heir, Zikali, to remain at home. At the Zulu capital, Matiwane's men had their necks broken. Their leader, caught at last in the web of violence, had his eyes gouged out and pegs hammered through his nostrils into his brain.

Matiwane's son, Zikali, settled with his Swazi queen on the old Ngwane lands below the Drakensberg. Here many of the battered and scattered Ngwane remnants gathered and their descendants live to this day in the Cathedral Peak area.

Moshweshwe and the Basotho Nation

While Mpangazitha, Matiwane, MmaNthatisi and their likes were tough and resourceful, in the light of history they can be seen to have been helpless participants in an explosion of violence over which they had no real control.

Moshweshwe towered above this horde as a man of stature. The way in which he received his name illustrates his qualities. Close to his home lived one Ramonaheng, a particularly wealthy and important man. To steal the cattle of this individual daunted the heart of even the coolest young man in search of adventure. Yet young Lepoqo — as he was then called — in the manner of Drake of Elizabethan England who 'singed the beard of the King of Spain', was said to have 'shorn the beard of Ramonaheng' and was named accordingly after the sound a razor makes when it cuts through a beard — Moshweshwe.

A courageous man and a wily statesman, Moshweshwe had a sound understanding of human nature. Tradition tells us that he learned the principles of forgiveness, compassion and justice from one Mohlomi, a famous sage whose advice tempered the hot-blooded prince's attitudes. On one occasion, in reply to Moshweshwe's query as to which medicine would turn one into a great chief, the sage replied, 'Power is not acquired by medicine; the heart is the medicine'.

The Basotho nation, now known as the South Sotho, was as much a product of the geological peculiarity of its homeland as of its founder's genius. This peculiarity was the numerous flat-topped mountains in eastern Lesotho. With the war-clouds gathering, Moshweshwe and his followers retired to their first mountain home, Butha Buthe, between the headwaters of the Orange and Caledon rivers. This home he defended against all comers until MmaNthatisi's son, Sekonyela, besieged him there for two months, leaving only after consuming all his crops.

After the privations of this siege, Moshweshwe repaired to a remarkable mountain fortress found by his spies — Thaba Bosiu, 'Mountain of Night'. This was to become a centre of attraction for desperate and war-weary people throughout the duration of the *Difaqane* and later, when refugees poured back from the Cape. Moshweshwe's attitude towards this human rabble was illustrated by his treatment of the cannibals in the vicinity. On the long march from Butha Buthe, Moshweshwe's father, among others, had been eaten by these people. Yet Moshweshwe wanted to rehabilitate and include them in his kingdom, a scheme to which his subjects objected strongly. Their leader talked them round, however, pointing out that as the living tombs of their victims the cannibals should be protected. When allowed to live on Moshweshwe's lands and to drink the milk of his cattle, these former cannibals became some of his most loyal and devoted followers.

Moshweshwe exercised tolerance towards those weaker than himself, and tact and diplomacy towards those stronger than himself. To Shaka he sent an annual tribute of cattle and crane feathers for the great monarch's armies. When this tribute failed to materialise one year, the Zulu king, quick to take offence, sent messengers to Moshweshwe to demand the tribute. The Sotho statesman begged forgiveness: owing to the depredations of Matiwane's Ngwane he had been unable to send anything. This answer soon brought the Zulu army to Sotho lands, a presence which sent Matiwane scuttling southwards and freed Moshweshwe from a major menace.

Moshweshwe, like many leaders of the period, sensed and feared the power behind the apparently puny little bands of Europeans in the area and realised the need for loyal ambassadors to the European colonisers. In missionaries he saw potential ambassadors, and three pioneer members of the Paris Evangelical Mission Society found in Moshweshwe a protector. Over the years Lesotho welcomed a large number of helpful and useful missionaries — insurance against future problems with the Europeans.

Destruction in the West

It took perhaps a year for the chaos along the Caledon to spread northwards and westwards across the Vaal River. The first major victims were the Huruthse whose capital Kaditshwene — home to 16 000 people — was sacked. The starving, plundering band that developed became known as Mantatees, and their arrival, after a plundering career, at the Thlaping capital of Kuruman was preceded for weeks by rumours of a horde who sent hornets into battle ahead of them and found nourishment at the breasts of their leader, a one-eyed giantess. The missionary Robert Moffat, who was based in Kuruman, summoned a Griqua army who used firearms to defeat, without any loss to themselves, what was in fact a pathetic rabble band.

Unlike the disruptions further east, the unrest in Tswana territory did not completely destroy tribes and scatter their members permanently, and today most Tswana still inhabit their traditional, pre-nineteenth-century lands. The same applies to the north-eastern Sotho areas, despite the presence in those parts of a desperate and reputedly cannabalistic band who, between 1827 and 1830, terrorised and decimated the local population.

THE PAST AND THE PRESENT

The story of Bantu-speaking people in Southern Africa probably takes one back some seventeen centuries; to tell the story of the present-day Bantu-speaking inhabitants of Southern Africa we must turn the clock back at least nine hundred years, to the eleventh century.

For some eight hundred years these people were spared large-scale war, content, it seems, to live, love and squabble on the sunny plains they called home. It was during this time that a society developed in the interior which could boast steel articles imported from Europe, and the great stone towns of the highveld were linked by a network of trading paths. And, in the absence of a written language, a rich oral history developed, reaching back twenty to thirty generations into the past.

The *Mfecane* brought an end to all this. When the storm broke, three quarters of the people living in Natal at the beginning of the nineteenth century, fled south into modern-day Transkei, and many clans ceased to exist. The central Transvaal and Orange Free State areas became totally depopulated. In 1829 two traders, McLuckie and Schoon, on their way to visit the Ndebele monarch, Mzilikazi, reported that in six weeks of travelling they had seen no human being, only the burnt-out ruins of villages and skeletons. The only remnants of the once large population were a few cannibals, who lurked hungrily in the valleys and forests of Natal and the highveld. An atomic holocaust could hardly have been more effective in clearing the country.

But there was a difference in this situation from the aftermath of a nuclear war: the people were not dead; they were simply absent, having fled, mainly to the south, where they waited to return to their homes when the disturbances had come to an end.

By some quirk of fate, it was at this precise time in the history of the subcontinent that the white man plunged into the interior in search of land. The wagons of the Great Trek rumbled north in 1837-38 across apparently empty plains and hills. Bold, fiercely independent pioneers, these early whites needed no second invitation: they settled.

PAGE 37   A new bride of the Ngwane people of the Natal Drakensberg appears at a party or any gala occasion wearing a splendid cape of coloured cloths, edged with fine beadwork. All her bead ornaments are typical of her home area and her full, black, greased leather skirt is the sure sign of her married status. Traditionally, the married woman's apron is red or pink. Her manner of sitting shows respect for her husband's family, and when standing she must lean on her beaded stick with head slightly bowed and eyes downcast, for the same reason.

The clover-like pieces of beadwork on her headdress are known as butterflies or aeroplanes, while the forehead bands are respect tokens. The headdress is the contemporary derivative of a much more elongated form (see overleaf), evolved, it is said, to avoid height problems when travelling by motorcar or bus.

Traditional dress is anything but static, and adapts according to the dictates of fashion and to the availability of materials. Here a Mpondo man wears beads, which have become available only within the last century or so in sufficient abundance for the manufacture of beadwork destined to be worn by the majority of people in a community. The beaded felt hat and blanket are likewise European introductions, which have been incorporated into traditional life and given social significance as indicators of social status.

PAGE 38 A Zulu married woman of some thirty years ago. The tall, red-ochred hairstyle is worn with pride. It is a phallic symbol and is an explicit statement of the woman's marital rights. The head ring formerly worn by married men had similar, complementary connotations.

A fringe of beads above the eyes was and still is a respect token, as are all bead bands. Knobs of large red beads over the forehead announce that the marriage is blessed with children.

Ear plugs were skilfully devised of wood, ornamented with paint or with mosaics made from slivers of coloured combs or toothbrush handles. Beads were plentiful and worn in profusion on gala occasions. Yellow and black beads used alternately denoted a certain grasshopper whose prolonged mating symbolised marital ties.

THE KING AND HIS COUNTRY

THE traditional political units of the Bantu-speaking people of Southern Africa are usually termed clans and tribes, the latter being ruled by a chief, and indeed defined as a group by his existence. Historically, the original group was the clan, or kinship group, led by the senior male. With time, the conquest of one clan by another, the acceptance by a clan of refugees and so on, the tribe, a political group, emerged and became the object of a man's loyalty. The clan, often with members in many tribes, is usually of relatively minor importance, especially among the Sotho, whose clan ties are not as strong as those of the Nguni.

A tribe might be composed of two, three or four classes of individuals. First, there are the nobility, the members of the dominant clan, which is that of the chief. Second, there are the commoners, who are members of the clans which have long been part of the tribe and loyal to the lineage of the ruling chief. The 'foreigners', though of similar status to the commoners, are relatively recent arrivals and thus not yet accepted as full members. The fourth group, rare at all times and virtually extinct today, are the unfortunate vassals. Since the defeat of their own tribes, perhaps centuries ago, these people have been the servile clan or clans, barred from ownership of property.

THE CHIEF IN TRADITIONAL SOCIETY

A look at the traditional chief and his realm is today essentially a probing into the past. For this reason I have largely used the past tense for the rest of this chapter — this despite the fact that in many areas, notably Transkei, Botswana and Lesotho, many facets of the old political institutions discussed here still survive.

The traditional African chief has been called a 'limited autocrat'. Such a term describes his position rather well, but he was much more than that. To understand the nature of the traditional chief and his society, one must appreciate the meaning of existence to the traditional African. The African was largely conscious of his identity and wholeness as a member of his group; it was through the group that he felt and thought and his identity was closely linked with that of his people; and, essential to the cohesion of this group — tribe or clan — was their chief.

The person of the chief was the very embodiment of his people and the expression of their unity. He was venerated, loved, honoured and feared by his subjects. He belonged to a unique class. Any usurper not of royal blood did not have the divine mandate of the one who was king by birth or by selection from within the ranks of royalty by a predecessor or the tribal councillors.

Despite his eminence, however, the life of a chief and his family was not markedly different from that of his subjects. Though this was certainly the most complex household in the tribe, his huts were the same as those of his subjects. In almost all groups, his people cultivated several fields for his household, but his wives often had to work just as hard as the wives of commoners. One of the main privileges of his office was a comparatively large supply of meat and beer to supplement what would otherwise have been an average diet. The chief was also the wealthiest man in the tribe, owning a disproportionately large herd of cattle and well-stocked granaries. Both these forms of wealth, however, were not personal, but were expected to be distributed to the needy.

The position of chief depended, too, on the nature of his realm and on his personal strength of character and ability to command obedience. A great king, such as the leader of the Swazi, Pedi or Zulu in days of old, boasted many more of the frills of kingship. Bryant has left us with an account of the various individuals who attended to his majesty the king of the Zulu (mainly with a view to protecting his person — and therefore the tribe — against magical attack):

> Inside his hut, crosswise before the doorway, lay at night his valet (appropriately called by the Zulus, his *inTsila*, his 'Dirt'), whose duty it was, within the hut, to receive upon his body the royal nasal and throat discharges, and who by day dressed the king's hair, bathed his body, and adorned it with its finery. The *inTshasa* (chamber-man) was responsible for the cleanliness of the royal hut within, and the *umLindankose* (king's guard) kept watch on it without; while the *mSindabiso* (anus-wiper) accompanied his Majesty to the stool. The principal duty of this latter was to keep a good look-out against prying *abaTákatí* (secret evil-doers) and to hide away from them the royal excreta, a much valued acquisition for evil magic.[1]

A Mpondo married woman, as shown by her finely twisted and oiled hair. A married woman must always wear either a headcloth, or alternatively a beaded ring, as a token of respect for her husband's family. The facial scarification is associated with the ancestors.

First Fruits Ceremonies

The importance of the king is impressed on the people by the practice of various rites which, as they survive in varying degree to this day, are described in the present tense. Among the most important of these, in some groups, is the periodic rekindling of every hearth with coals from that of the king, and the annual first fruits ceremonies. When a Pedi paramount chief weds his principal wife (the mother of his successor), the embers from a fire generated in her hut are used to kindle every fire in the land, which should all have been extinguished in anticipation of the great event. First fruits ceremonies — the official eating of the harvest by the king — also emphasise his unique and apical position in the tribe. Before these rites, it is an offence to consume even a crumb of food prepared from the new crops. If a junior royal lineage has at some stage usurped the power of the 'great house' and become established as the power-wielding lineage, the ancient royal lineage still retains its ritual supremacy and 'takes the first bite'. A Pedi chief in this position is aptly called a 'pumpkin chief'. The oral traditions of the Sotho tell of how one of the earliest significant splits in the nation resulted from a dispute as to who among a group of royal brothers would have the first bite.

The Nguni tribes of old celebrated a great first fruits festival which today survives among the Swazi, several Natal tribes and the Bhaca. The Swazi festival certainly is the greatest event on their annual calendar, a symbol of the tiny nation's unity under their popular and capable monarch. The significance of this ceremony for King Sobhuza II, longest reigning monarch in the world today, lies in the reaffirmation of the principles of the only traditional African state left on the continent.

The Swazi Incwala

As the Swazi first fruits or *incwala* ceremony is well documented,[2] it is only briefly outlined. The *incwala* ceremony is held only when there is a reigning king on the throne, and therefore did not take place during the 25 years of Sobhuza II's minority. The traditional history of the ceremony is intimately interwoven with the history of the tiny nation and expresses, in the person of their king, their unity and wholeness.

The ceremony is divided into two parts: the 'little *incwala*', and the 'big *incwala*'. The start of the 'little *incwala*' is determined by the sun and the moon; the former must be approaching the summer solstice position (16 December).

The nation maintains a special group of diviners whose only function it is to preside over the *incwala*. These noble personages set off in two groups, one, of lesser importance, to certain great rivers to the north and the other, more noble, on a pilgrimage over the Lebombo mountains, across the thorny plains of Mozambique to the coast. Today, however, those who go to the coast use a car! The purpose of both these journeys is the ritual collection of water, which is carried back to the royal village of the queen mother. The water vessels are two sacred calabashes, which are freshly covered each year with the plaited skin of a sacrificial black ox, and anointed with its gall, thus securing the blessing of the royal ancestors.

Tradition tells that early in the history of the nation, when the royal Dlamini clan still lived near the sea, the queen mother ran away with her son, who was later to become king. Brian A. Marwick, a Commissioner when Swaziland was a British colony, is of the opinion that the collecting of sea-water is linked with this legend. The water is 'alive', and essential for the rejuvenation of the king and nation for the new year. The sea-water must be only the 'living' foam of the surf, while the rivers at the time of the *incwala* are in full spate, and therefore full of life and virility. The mission of these travellers is so important that they are privileged to demand gifts from any person they meet. On their return trip to the royal village, a beast is sacrificed at every homestead in which they sleep, and the gall bladder and tail are attached to a calabash.

These expeditions are timed so that the travellers arrive back at the royal village when there is no moon. Their return signals the withdrawal of the king into a special hut at the top end of the huge royal cattle kraal; he will emerge from the hut with the new moon. While in the hut, early in the morning, the king takes the first bite of the season's crops — the traditional sweet-reed and a certain type of gourd (*luselwa*). This leaves the people free to eat the year's harvest without fear of coming to any harm. To eat the crops before the king is not only an affront to his supremacy but is also highly dangerous, and anyone attempting this must be treated with protective medicine.

The biting of the first fruits is celebrated by dancing and singing of special *incwala* songs. These are said to have been sung by the legendary runaway queen mother to her child prince and even today they are cloaked in an aura of sanctity. No traditionalist, for fear of disastrous consequences for himself and his nation, will sing these songs at any time other than during the *incwala*, or at the funeral of a king. Among other tribes, remarkable features of similar songs and praises are the derogatory, aggressive and frankly libellous statements about the monarch.

The 'big *incwala*' begins somewhat less than two weeks after the 'little *incwala*', when the moon is full. It lasts for six days, characterised by great dances and the singing of the sacred songs. The glamour and magnificence of this affair, and its important role as a symbol of the unity of the nation, is such that few Swazi men have not attended at least one 'big *incwala*'.

The commencement is marked by the departure of a large group of pure young men (those who have not had contact with a married woman), each of whom must fetch the branch of the *sekwane* tree. The journey is on foot and takes a day and a night. After this marathon the youths are required to join in energetic dancing for many hours. The purity of these youths is of great importance and indeed the entire ceremony is surrounded by sex taboos to prevent any harm befalling the king or nation as a result of ritual impurity.

The tree the young men seek is sacred to the Swazi and tradition has it that it was one of the two foods that the runaway queen mother and her son had to eat. The other food is also from a small tree and the branches of this are collected. The branches of both trees are then plaited together around the king's special hut in the cattle kraal.

This is followed by the dancing of the warriors, who are dressed in finery kept especially for the *incwala*. This is soon over and the young men then don loincloths, for the time has arrived for a central feature of the *incwala* — the killing of a black bull. This animal, together with several others, is driven into the chief's hut, where he touches it with a switch to imbue it with virility and anger. Waiting outside the hut are the almost naked warriors. In the past when the bull emerged it was grabbed by the tail or legs by a mob of daring young men, wrestled to the ground and pummelled almost to death before being dragged back into the special hut. Today, however, the pummelling is omitted and the bull is killed by the diviner, who makes a deep incision in the thorax, reaches in and tears the trachea.

A further 'biting of the first fruits' ceremony then takes place; dancing ensues and the king receives medicines to renew his strength or 'shadow'. This takes the ceremony up to its sixth day. The end is marked by the burning on a pyre of all uneaten remains of the black bull, as well as all blankets and other items belonging to the king, thus destroying the past and setting the scene for the beginning of a new year.

Even a cursory glance at this series of rituals highlights its vital importance. In the first fruits ceremonies, strength is given to the abstract unity of the group and status given to the individual who is chief, as the manifestation of that unity. The symbolic rebellion, in the form of derogatory songs, serves to defuse feelings of antagonism and resentment towards the chief. The very fact that such rebellion takes place within, and needs the tacit approval of, the nation itself as expressed in the king, serves to reinforce the loyalty of subjects to the nation and therefore to the king.

Not only is the individual who is king secured as the embodiment of his people, but as provider. His symbolic biting of the first fruits frees — actualises — the new crops for his people. On the emotional level, it appears as if he controls not only the crops but time itself: it is only with his blessing that the new year comes into being.

The Medicine of Power

Medicines were — and are still — a principal factor in the making of a chief. A traditional chief had at his disposal the most exotic, powerful and dangerous arsenal of medicines in the land. As a result of his use of these medicines, the chief was endowed with a 'shadow' (see p. 53) of quite awesome power and magnitude, which made him especially feared. Even if an ordinary mortal had access to these highly secret medicines, however, he could not imbue himself with the power and aura of a chief; to a commoner, medicines of such strength are highly dangerous.

Thus the chief was not only an autocrat, he was an autocrat with a 'strong shadow' or great magical power. In addition to being the symbol of unity within the tribe, he ruled by the African equivalent of 'the divine right of kings'. In relating to the African 'divinities' — the ancestors — he played a very important role. Although the ancestors of a clan were of significance only to that lineage, those of a chief — as befits their position — had the interests of the whole tribe at heart. The chief was therefore also the link with this important group of shades.

Praise Poems

In ancient times, when the Pharaohs ruled Egypt, their subjects wrote poems about their rulers' exploits and recited these in their honour. The same reverence was accorded the African chiefs. 'Praise poems' were the traditional poetry of the Bantu languages, and the composers of such 'praises' (which may be in honour of events, cattle and important men, as well as chiefs) were the only professional artists of traditional society. The great chiefs of old had praise-singers similar to court jesters, who constantly lauded the greatness of his royal majesty in rather beautiful verse. Bryant's description of such a praise-singer is illuminating, if unconcerned with the poetic content of his creations:

> From our experience of one or two of these specimens, we should say that these men were, not exactly mentally deficient, but mentally abnormal. They lived in a chronic state of vociferous delirium; though otherwise quite intelligent. They would keep up a continuous harangue, addressed to nobody in particular, and so to say, for hours at a time, whether sitting at home or marching alone across the veld. They had the gift of 'speech' in a most extraordinary degree; and extraordinary memories too. They made it their business to know everything that the king and all his ancestors ever did or ever had done; then to frame the several events into terse phrases,

Mpondo man with facial scarification inflicted during early childhood according to the customs of the ancestors. Incisions on the chest were made in order to administer medicine at another time. The finely plaited hair is typical. The bead ornaments are love tokens and may be interchanged with those worn by his girlfriend or wife.

mostly simply commemorative, but frequently disguised by metaphor or even humorously satirical; and finally to recite their compositions before king and public, by loud incessant shouting whenever opportunity occurred.[3]

The King and his Duties

Superficially, it might appear that the chief was given *carte blanche* to do what he willed in his state, Lilliputian though it may have been. This was not the case. Ideally, the monarch was far from being a dictator, but found the restraining hand of his people on him in all affairs and at all times, exerting pressures in different ways. He, as a person, was just as responsible for the sanctity of kingship as his people, who were loyal to the office of chief rather than to the individual. The duties and obligations of a chief were many. He always had to put the affairs of state before his personal affairs, and could not postpone any tasks which confronted him as king. Decisions were not made by him alone, but together with the council of select elders and nobles, who had to be consulted regularly. He had to be strong enough to maintain law and order, and to be just without being harsh. He could not show favouritism. According to the Zulu proverb, the chief was the 'breast of the tribe'. It was his duty to help those in need and always attempt to provide for his people, and to protect them from aggressors.

The individual who was monarch was coerced into this role of the 'ideal chief' by various constraints. A chief who persistently made unpopular decisions in the face of his councils lost support. The Tswana chiefs, in particular, had little chance to be despots, for at regular intervals the whole tribe gathered (and still does) in popular assemblies where the chief was open to criticism and answerable for his actions. The Nguni chiefs, on the other hand, were much freer to become despots; the people gathered only on occasions such as the annual first fruits ritual. Chiefs who were consistently self-willed lost their following; subjects left to pay allegiance to other more flexible chiefs. This was a grievous threat as people were the wealth and military strength of a tribal subsistence community. A brutal, intransigent chief might, despite the traditional sanctity of his person, be murdered, often by a royal sibling. Laws which were disliked by the whole tribe were often simply disobeyed, and the chief found himself with no power at his disposal to enforce them. 'A chief is chief by the grace of his people' is an apt African proverb: few chiefs succeeded in being completely autocratic — even notable tyrants like the warrior-chief Shaka were murdered after comparatively short reigns (which, incidentally, were not without parallel in Europe).

Traditional States

The anthropologist, Dr Basil Sansom, has divided the African states of Southern Africa into two broad categories — those in the west, and those in the east.[4] To the west, the people tended to concentrate in large villages and towns, often housing an entire tribe; other examples were the Pedi in the north-eastern Transvaal and some South Sotho. In the east, however, especially in Nguni territory, individual extended family units were dotted about the countryside amidst the lands where they grazed their cattle and planted their crops. These two different modes of organisation are thought to be due primarily to divergent weather and vegetation systems: in the west, for instance, the rainfall is erratic and unevenly distributed and it is thus provident to place one's fields at widely separated points around a central town (also easy to defend), in order not to have all one's eggs in one basket.

Sansom has also described the two different ways in which the chief provided for, and held, the allegiance of his people in these two types of state. In the scattered, eastern type, where people lived on their land and had a fairly secure usufruct over them, as well as a strong cattle culture, the chief had great power as a kind of cattle 'reserve bank', levying fines and receiving tribute in cattle, as well as distributing largesse and aid in the same form. The power of the western-type chief, whose people were agriculturalists rather than pastoralists and who did not live on their land but 'owned' widely scattered plots, lay in giving or withholding this land as he saw fit. It must be reiterated, however, that the power of the chief went far beyond his material resources. The chiefdom was the traditional Southern African state, and a people were a people by virtue of their unity under a chief. The position of the chief was, therefore, secure, and both divinely and magically protected in the eyes of his subjects.

The hierarchy of authority below the chief was in two or three or even four tiers, depending on the size of his clan or tribe. The living units or home-steads of an Nguni tribe were divided into groups of five to ten, which were controlled by a headman who, along with the others, was answerable to the subchief of the district. The latter dignitary would be responsible either directly to the paramount chief, or to a higher chief who ranked just below the paramount chief, or king. In the eastern (Nguni) system, a group was associated with an area, and their subchief likewise. On the other hand the lesser royal dignitaries of the western (Tswana) system were in charge of divisions or wards of the big, rambling towns, each of which contained more or less related people.

The degree of control of a king over the subdivisions of his tribe or state varied. The Zulu kings after Shaka and others seldom made use of the traditional rulers of component clans but preferred to appoint loyal headmen who owed all to their king but little to their charges. The Pedi of Sekhukhuneland, on the other hand, formed a much looser federation. The different tribes within the federation are still conscious of their dual identity — for instance, the Kwena, 'who are also Pedi'. Each component group has a good degree of autonomy, though they pay tribute to and, in the past supplied warriors to, the ruling clan.

To summarise, the traditional chief was given a fairly liberal mandate to wield power in his realm and over his people. The precise meaning of this was dependent on the particular group. However, he was strictly controlled by a system of restraints and the need to retain the loyalty and allegiance of his subjects. Bearing in mind the importance of the group as opposed to the individual in traditional thought, it may be said that the chiefdom, in its true sense, was the African democracy. Nevertheless, this system of government is as vulnerable to tyranny and other political perversions as the various European systems have proved to be.

THE CHIEFDOM TODAY

It is inevitable that, with the subordination of chiefs to a higher government — in Southern Africa and other territories — much has changed. Today, with the political leader of a country as effective paramount chief of all component groups, the chief finds himself answerable not to his people and the royal ancestors, custodians of the law, but to the central government. It is now the political leader who must be treated tactfully in order for the chief to remain in office. Inevitably the chief has lost a great deal of his power. No longer can he determine foreign policy. The chief who passes the death sentence is a murderer. His whole relationship with his people has changed, and likewise his ambitions; no longer does he achieve fulfilment in his role of father and provider for his people. Many a chief, unable to fulfill his traditional role without clashing with political superiors, now allows his own personal interest to come before duty, and the wealth that accrues to him by virtue of his position is used largely for himself, which creates impotent discontent among his people.

I recently followed the plight of a couple trying to obtain a house on land controlled by a certain (government-recognised) subchief. The amount of string-pulling and palm-greasing necessary to obtain land in his area was illuminating. Dr A. Vilakazi, a Zulu himself, reports on the attitudes towards chiefs in the Valley of a Thousand Hills not far from Durban, where they are often referred to as 'boys of the government'.[5] Indeed, the traditionalist, while retaining his essential religious beliefs, is shifting from traditional political concepts to the various ideological systems imported from beyond the borders of his continent.

The new leaders of the black man are the politicians. Transkei has a Western-style constitution; Lesotho had one until Chief Jonathan seized power. Swaziland, too, found itself with a Westminster constitution at the time of independence but this has been repealed by Sobhuza II in favour of a constitution based, as far as possible, on traditional political principles. The writing of a constitution of this type that would be able to weather the modern politico-economic climate is a long and difficult task. The modern traditional state finds itself in a very different environment from that in which the original patterns of government evolved. In the past, political horizons were narrower and demanded different qualities from a government, and there was little need for legislation. Today, new laws are constantly needed.

The old African world moved relatively slowly and the groups involved were small. Shaka, at the height of his power, held sway over two hundred thousand people — one thousandth of the present population of the United States of America. The early Nguni and Sotho clan chiefs, those doughty adventurers who wove the early, half-forgotten history of Southern Africa, counted their followers in dozens. Today the groups are far larger, living in a dizzy world where traditional constraints are no longer effective. The unstable political situation characterising many erstwhile colonies is to be expected until a new equilibrium is reached.

LAW AND JUSTICE

The traditional law was of course an unwritten code. Stable yet dynamic, it was passed on through the centuries and exposed to contemporary analytical thought. It was an ancient code; the entire fabric of the society was intimately entwined with laws and customs sacred to the traditionalist.

Always looking over the heads of the people was — and is — the stern presence of the ancestors, ever ready to chastise the transgressor. It was this that maintained the spirit of the law, keeping it relatively constant even in the face of modifications introduced by the chief and his council. The coming of the European has, however, necessitated the creation of a large body of new laws and alterations to the old.

Perhaps the most obvious difference between the Western legal systems and traditional law is that in the latter the 'spirit of the law' took precedence over the 'letter of the law'. In addition, precedence played an important role in deciding a difficult case and experienced elders could be called on to compare the situation with previous cases. A further point in appreciating traditional law was the absence of the Western ideal of a self-evident right to individual freedom and the supremacy of the individual. For the traditionalist, the meaning of life was couched in terms of one's membership in society. Enforcement of the law was seen as the means of easing tensions in the social network rather than of upholding a legal code; as restitution and reparation, rather than retribution. A stolen object had to be replaced, and a consideration had to be given to the chief and the court. Murder (not clearly discriminated from manslaughter) was most commonly punished by a heavy cattle fine. People were the 'gold bullion' of the tribe; the loss of one person was enough, so why make it two?

Crimes against the state, however, were considered in a serious light and capital punishment often followed. Though no official discrimination was made between civil and criminal law, in effect this did exist. All crimes were seen as crimes against the chief, for an offence against a subject was an affront to the chief. Punishment took the form of fines — usually in cattle — and the supreme penalty, with occasional corporal punishment. Imprisonment was unknown in traditional society and regarded with abhorrence.

The courts that dispensed this law reflected its nature. Apparently imprecise, haphazard, and lacking a rigid outline, they nevertheless served their purpose admirably. The vast majority of breaches of the laws or customs, or interpersonal disputes, never reached a court but were resolved within the extended family or clan. Those that were beyond settlement at this level were considered by the local subchief or headman's court. Here all men could attend, gathering out of doors under a tree, smoking and gossiping.

Procedure was similar to but much looser than in Western courts. With the arrival of the headman or his representative, who was respectfully greeted, the case commenced. First the plaintiff stated his case, followed by the defendant, and then anyone who felt he had something to contribute. No one swore to tell 'the truth and nothing but the truth' and everyone rambled on, eloquently dragging in masses of irrelevant detail and often relying heavily on circumstantial evidence, which was quite acceptable. While an impassioned witness was holding forth earnestly, a quite different conversation might be started between two members of the audience/participants, even across the gathering — but they were sure to be silenced quickly. Interjections were of course common.

The court was judge was well as jury and the decision the chief and his advisers reached was usually a reflection of what the court regarded as the just and fair outcome. A hierarchy of courts existed, however, and should the decision not prove satisfactory to either party, the case was carried to higher and higher courts until, eventually, the court of the tribal chief was reached.

Here much the same procedure was followed and I quote Soga on the Xhosa, a description which can be applied equally well to any other tribe:

> In what we may call the Supreme Court trials, that is , trials coming before the supreme chief and his councillors, we see the Xosa at his best. His mentality, his mental equipment, his cleverness in cross-examination, his wonderful grasp of all the points, material and immaterial, truth and falsehood, and his summing up, are testimony to the possession of an intellect of a high order.[6]

The efficiency of the body of custom and law which were evolved to maintain order in society, and the responsible, moral, well-considered manner in which this operated without recourse to the printed word, are a proud heritage and showpiece of African culture.

No system is perfect, however. While painful gaps exist in Western justice — 'crook lawyers' and 'technical loopholes' — the hiatus in the Bantu-speakers' traditional system of justice was contained in a single word: witchcraft. In a witchcraft case the law could be completely bypassed. Gone were the well-deliberated decisions and the justice of the wise men, meaningless the legal system; a man could be accused of witchcraft and condemned without recourse to any court. In days gone by, the old men of today assert, it was a lucky man who became very wealthy and lived to a ripe age, unless he were a special friend of the chief or of someone in power. After all, it was the chief who received the spoils when a man — and his family — were executed for witchcraft . . .

However, the traditional magical world was — is — anything but sordid, and provides a fitting topic for the next chapter.

A district headman wearing the now-vanished husband's headring, symbolising conjugal rights, which is traditional in Zululand and Swaziland.

BELIEFS AND RELIGION

L IFE demands explanation. Nature is cruel and fate capricious, the world lonely. Man has evolved systems of faith to explain the life experience, to justify behaviour, to reassure himself of his power and significance in an otherwise vast and alien universe.

From another angle, a society conceived of as an entity can be said to present its members with a world-view designed to stimulate behaviour-patterns that will perpetuate it.

Westerners — the writer of this text and most of its readers — have been reared on a world-view very different from that presented to the traditionally brought up Bantu-speaking Southern African. For this reason, it is impossible to describe the manifest religious and magical beliefs of Africans without some prior perspective both on the context of such beliefs and on Western perceptions of these beliefs.

Professor W.D. Hammond-Tooke, a leading anthropologist, has said of the traditional black Southern African, '... it must be stressed that there is a substantial knowledge of nature and its workings that is essentially non-magical and empirical .... If he did not have this expertise he would be unable to survive. It would be incorrect to describe this knowledge as "scientific", if by this one meant that he explains these properties in terms of explicit theories which postulate logical connections between phenomena.'[1]

It is in this statement that one sees the basic difference between the Westerner's world and that of the African. The African reality is a loosely defined world which, in the absence of 'explicit theories' can easily accommodate magical concepts. One could characterise such a world as a 'magical materiality'.

By contrast, the Western comprehension of reality has for centuries been in varying degrees split between reified 'mind' and reified 'matter', God and Science, with each (no matter refinements and names) absurd in its isolation and yet irreconcilable one with the other. The Westerner looks at African culture to find a strange Pandora's box of weird and wonderful beings and beliefs. Yet, all too often, in the name of 'science', he reduces these African beliefs to the context of some social or psychological jargon which suitably enshrines his dualistic thinking. This patronising approach avoids alternative, possibly more logical and successful approaches to theorising.

Traditional magico-religious concepts can be divided into four categories:

the Creator, various nature-spirits, the ancestors of a clan who interact with the living, and witches with their magical powers.

A characteristic of traditional thinking is its pragmatic nature — involved theologies and mythologies are all but absent. 'Supernatural' powers have relevance only in so far as they affect the living. Thus both the Creator and, in varying degrees, the different nature-spirits/demigods are of limited significance to the traditionalist. His concern is with the ancestors and the witches/sorcerers who have power over his life.

THE CREATOR

All Southern Africa's Bantu-speaking peoples believe in a God — the Creative Force — which pre-dates the Creation and is all-powerful. To the Zulu this monotheistic deity is *uNkulunkulu* or *uMvelinqangi*, to the Venda he is *Raluvhimba*, and to the Swazi *Mkulumnqande*. The Sotho people describe their deity as *Modimo*, while the Xhosa term is *Umdali* or Creator (from *ukudala*, to create, to form) and the Mpondo word is *Umanzi* (derived from *ukwenza*, to make.) The last three terms particularly emphasise the impersonal nature of the deity, which is conceived of as a primal, distant and disinterested force, rather than as a personal and imminent being like the Christian God.

Traditional religion is not centred on God. Vilakazi states: ' In all my experience as a Zulu, living among Zulu . . . I cannot remember a single instance when I heard a prayer by a traditionalist offered to uMvelinqangi.'[2]

This statement could just as well have been made by any member of any other tribe.

Occasionally, however, appeals and responses are made to the deity. The Thembu *Umtendeleko* ceremony is their supreme form of worship and is resorted to only when the people are in dire straits as a result of drought, an epidemic or some other disaster. This appeal to *Umdali* is clothed in the utmost reverence and for a week prior to the *Umtendeleko*, all who are to participate must meditate on goodness, purity and love. Bitterness, quarrels and sexual relations must be avoided. The ceremony, conducted beside a pure spring on an open hillside, bears a remarkable resemblance to the Christian Holy Communion. Consecrated beer and maize are consumed, following a spoken prayer and a song, recorded by Professor B.J.F. Laubscher:

> Please *Umdali* hear our prayers as you have heard and granted the prayers of our ancestors who, through many long years now gone, have prayed in this manner to you.[3]

This song is followed by symbolic gifts of white beads and an exhortation to the supplicants to be patient. The ceremony may be repeated, in abbreviated form, on several successive days.

The Venda appear to have a more personal relationship than most with God — *Raluvhimba* — who is seen as the orchestrator of the phenomena of nature — the sun, the winds, the stars. He is spoken to by the chief, and occasionally one of his more spectacular phenomena will provoke a response by the general populace. In 1914 the shock wave of a small tremor shook a mission station in Venda territory and was, according to the resident

Reverend MacDonald, greeted with loud shouting and ululation from all points of the compass as the people greeted their God.

The origin of the Zulu and their *uNkulunkulu* was a bed of reeds: first came *uNkulunkulu*, followed by man, the firmament, plants and animals. The Sotho people similarly claim descent from an ancestor who emerged from a bed of reeds at Ntsuanatsatsi. (This myth became confused with sundry biblical epics. One hybrid maintains that the Sotho are descended from the people who hid in the rushes when the Jews were fleeing Egypt.) The Tswana 'first people' are said to have emerged from a hole in the ground at Lowe near Mochudi, where their footprints are still to be seen in the rock. The Lobedu's *Khuzwane* also left footprints in solid rock. The Pedi *Modimo*, after he had created the world, left the creation of man to his son Kgobeane.

THE WORLD

Traditional concepts of the world thus created are similarly vague and liable to be idiosyncratic. Zulu tradition regards the sky as a blue rock dome inside which the heavenly bodies are arrayed. The sun, which daily travels the sky, plunging into the sea at night, is a great chief, and when he emerges again in the morning, after his death beneath the sea, the stars pale in his august presence. Traditionally, the moon dies each lunation and the new moon is literally new. When Armstrong took his 'giant step for mankind' on the moon, I described the event to an old Zulu man. He looked up at the pale orb in the early evening sky. *Gangile!*' he said sternly. 'They are up to mischief!'

According to traditional Venda belief, the world is a flat disc afloat on water and covered by a blue dome called the sky. The sun, *duvho*, behaves similarly to the Zulu sun. The moon is head of the stars and when it waxes, with the horns pointing upwards, it contains all the cold wind as in a basin, which it empties over the earth when it is waning and the horns point downward. To tell a traditionalist with little Western contact that the earth is round would be regarded by him as an attempt to confuse; that it is flat is perfectly obvious to any sensible-minded person.

There are three categories of being that cannot be reconciled with Western concepts, which are therefore described as occult or 'supernatural'. These are the ancestors, symbolic of the socialised or benign supernatural; the various nature-spirits and demigods, which constitute a neutral or morally value-free, though possibly mischievous, aspect of the supernatural; and the powers of witches and sorcerers, which symbolise antisocial forces. Each of these three categories of being/force can be described through African eyes as a picture of one aspect of African reality. Alternatively, they can be described in terms of Western concepts of social reality. For Westerners, this may be the most meaningful way of looking at the African pantheon, although it all too often leads to a narrow, patronising attitude — regarding these various concepts of African magic and religion as wholly explicable in terms of social or psychodynamic models. Rather, their symbolic nature should be emphasised, and along with it, the transcendent nature of the symbol, which is not amenable to a dismissively complete incorporation into any model of 'reality'.

THE ANCESTOR RELIGION

To describe this religion, I shall emphasise traditional concepts of the dead and then try to evaluate these in social terms. However, to appreciate traditional ideas of the ancestral dead, one must first appreciate concepts of the living.

The Zulu, like all the tribes from the Venda in the north to the Southern Nguni, conceive of man as possessing, besides his physical body, qualities called breath or air, and a shadow or reflection. The South Sotho, according to E.H. Ashton, recognise these two additional parts of man but do not differentiate clearly between them.[4] The breath or life principle is said by the Pedi to be unevenly distributed in the body, being concentrated in the lungs, sex organs, head and hair. The shadow corresponds to the visual form of the spirit self and in sleep wanders in the same way as does the 'astral body' recognised by occultists. This shadow is a very real part of a person and a Venda who is foolish enough to let his shadow fall on a crocodile could very easily be pulled into the water by it. The Pedi claim that a drunk man's shadow is not firmly attached to his physical body: 'This friend of ours isn't one, they are two'.[5]

The prestige of a person and the strength of his shadow are closely linked. An important, commanding person is said to have a strong shadow; a chief has a very strong shadow and it is in this that much of his power resides, drawing the respect of his subjects. Much of the medicine associated with the position of chief is aimed at strengthening his royal shadow. It is the shadow and the breath of man that leave his body at death. These two qualities together constitute the spirit. Without the breath, or life force, not only does a person not exist in the flesh but he could not exist as a spirit. Many a Venda traditionalist will swear that a corpse does not cast a shadow (this is probably mainly due to the fact that most burials are held when the sun is down). Some South Sotho say that the shadow of a dead man may be seen out of the corner of the eye, usually at dusk. (Psychics in the West say that second sight is much clearer in the peripheral vision and in poor light.)

Traditional concepts of the dead and their abode are vague, however. Concepts encountered tend to be idiosyncratic; and one of the few ideas common at least at one time or another to all tribes is that the dead live under the earth, an idea given substance by an alternative Zulu word for the dead, *abaphanzi*, those below.

Not all the dead become ancestors, the beings of practical interest to the living. It is principally the socially significant dead who achieve ancestor status — an indication of the social nature of the religion.

Individuals are vague as to the fate of those who, according to traditional belief, are not named ancestors. The dead who are retained as named ancestors vary with tribal affiliation, but they certainly represent the body of the family dead. The South Sotho and Pedi, among others, must perform a rite to send a person to a spirit land, but later bring him or her back as a member of the clan. The Zulu-speaking people have a similar bringing-back rite traditionally performed for individuals who, while living, passed through the ceremonies marking their acceptance as fully social beings.

With variations from group to group, the commoner family remembers its significant ancestors for some three to six generations. Among the ancestors, the same social hierarchies and positions pertain as in life. In general, it is the household heads and important people who are appealed to in the land of the shades. Among the strongly partrilineal Nguni tribes and the Sotho, the ancestors of the male lineage are the important ones and those to whom appeals are made. A wife is concerned with two sets of ancestors — those of her own lineage and the adopted shades of her husband's family.

Another feature which gives a clue as to the social nature of the ancestor religion is the practice of calling an aged person 'ancestor'. Despite his or her continued corporeality, such an individual is a member of this social category. In view of this, it is not surprising to find that 'worship', 'reverence' and 'veneration' — words usually associated with religious observance — are quite inappropriate to the relationship of the traditionalist with his lineage ancestors. The word 'respect' is a better description of the attitude of the living towards the ancestors and this is a word much used to describe the relationship of the living with the living in traditional society. The respect stems largely from the ancestors' status as representatives of the traditional morals and values and from their power to protect their descendants or to chastise them with minor illness or misfortune. They must be placated by means of offerings and ritual sacrifices of goats, fowls and cattle. They remain, however, essentially human and the relationship between them and the living is a human one.

For instance, if ancestors are persistently negative in their attitudes and actions, their descendants will 'scold' them and accuse them of not doing their duty by their people. Dr H.A. Stayt relates that the Venda, as a last resort, even have a method for eliminating a particularly troublesome ancestor. The spear of the wicked ancestor is tied to the neck of a black goat which is weighted with a stone and thrown into a deep pool.

The ancestors, then, are a category of persons who, but for their physical absence, are real in every respect and in some ways more real — they have mystical power and vision. They serve to provide an emotionally satisfying explanation of his fate, as justly deserved, to the traditionalist. The ancestors are also the conservative custodians of traditional morals and customs.

As the lineage dead, the ancestors demand attention on a personal level, and in a broader context they demand obedience to the group's morals. Psychologists researching in Western society have found that misfortune is frequently perceived by both onlookers and victims as the just deserts for transgressions of cultural mores. This, but for the absence of a clear symbolism, is no different from the invocation of the shades as the active policemen of traditional African morals.

Another interesting characteristic of the ancestors is their desire to possess

PAGE 55 A calabash with curly handle takes pride of place as a drinking cup or dipping spoon. This Venda mother, dressed in the traditional and popular salempore cloth, kneels in respect for the traditional brew she is drinking.

Around her neck are a series of beads and amulets, often very old, each of which is associated with an ancestral spirit. These are passed down through the generations as a sacred trust and to part with one is to risk immediate retribution from the ancestral realm. Ill fortune, always attributed to some cause in traditional thought, may well be diagnosed by the priest-diviner as the result of the displeasure of an ancestor, and the relevant bead is pointed out so that the appropriate placatory ritual may be performed.

Barbara Tyrrell

All things are reversed in the ancestral realm: light is dark and gall is sweet and attractive to the ancestors. Here, novice priest-diviners inflate the bladders of sacrificial goats which are to be worn as those already on their heads.

certain living individuals. This possession (described more fully in the next chapter) leads, after appropriate training, to the status of diviner — the mouthpiece of the ancestors among the living.

A point to note is the terminology used to describe the ancestral spirits: Zulu — *amadlozi*; Southern Nguni — *amathongo* or *isi(imi)nyanya*; Lobedu — *vadimo* or *zwidajani*; Tswana — *medimo* or *bodimo*; Venda — *midzimu*; Sotho — *badimo*. These are all plural forms, and it is as a corporate body demanding respect and obedience that the ancestors have their greatest significance. The Mpondo, when appealing to their ancestors address them *en masse*, but the Nguni to the north-east will recite the names of individual lineage members. Frequently, however, contact with the ancestors will involve a specific shade.

Ancestor religion is therefore not a religion in the sense of Christianity, Islam or any of the proselytising faiths. It is not an abstract system of beliefs and articles of faith to complement a faith in materialistic science, nor is it regarded as a pathway to heavenly fulfilment. It can be described with some accuracy as a symbolic system of cultural morals, which accommodates and explains both mystical experience and 'commonplace' events in the life of the individual and enforces correct behaviour. There are no adherents eager to convert the world and to find confirmation of their beliefs in another's acceptance of the same dogmas. As already emphasised, African religion is not one pole of the divine-material dichotomy: it is reality.

PAGE 56 A Mpondo married woman on her way to a party is dressed in her finery. She purchases a white hen on the wayside from a married woman in everyday dress.

Ceremonial wear is rendered 'white' by the use of prodigious amounts of commercial washing blue. Although the net result is undeniably blue, it is always known as white. A coronet of beads indicates married status, and the red ochred blanket and skirt are daily wear. The white fowl is probably destined for use as a sacrifice. White is always associated with the ancestors as a symbol of goodness.

A traditional home abounds in signs of the ancestor religion. Here, in a hut in the Natal Midlands, hanging in the *umsamo* or place of the ancestors, are various items associated with a typical traditional family's recent dealings with the ancestors. On the left is the mesentery, that is, the fatty membrane peeled from the outer stomach wall, of a sacrificial heifer, hanging to dry before being ground up as medicine. Behind is a square of cloth soaked in the blood of a sacrificial fowl and wiped on the limbs of the homestead head before being hung in position. This procedure was carried out under the direction of a 'prophet' of a Zionist sect, who amalgamate ancestor beliefs and Christianity, in order to cure the homestead head of a tendency to lose money. The corn cob is some seed for next year's garden that is receiving protective treatment, as is the commercially obtained pumpkin seed in the packet behind. The piece of paper hanging on the wire bears the names of the homestead members in an appeal to the ancestors for protection against evil.

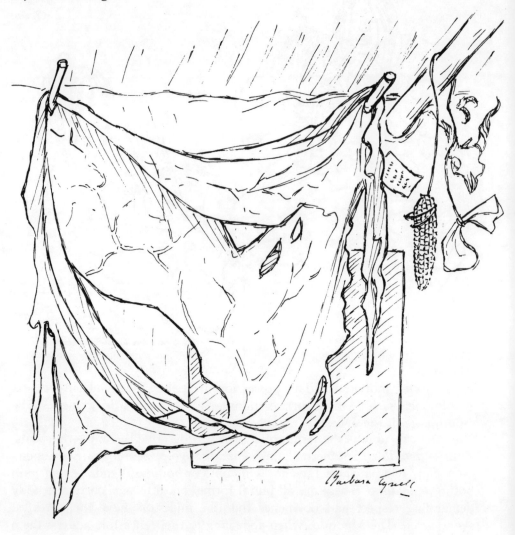

To be born into traditional society is to be convinced of its reality and truth, to live in a religious world where the intangible and the physical are simply different aspects of the same reality. There are no Sundays and no churches counterpoised against everyday life and living. Every day is Sunday, and the ancestors cluster with the living about every hearth — very real both in their presence and in their influence for good or ill. It is for the ancestors that a Pedi will pour the dregs of his gourd of beer on to the ground; for them the South Sotho leaves a little grain on the threshing-floor when the day's work is done; for them the Nguni woman prepares that small extra pot of beer which is stored in the *umsamo*, or place of the spirits, in the hut. In this day of readily available bottled drink, many people still pour the first cupful of every new bottle of brandy on to the floor as an offering to the shades — 'so they don't think we are forgetting them and take away all our drink'. Not only do the living supplicate the ancestors and the latter protect and chastise the living; an important feature of the relationship is communication by the shades to the living. This may take the form of visitations in dreams, messages passed through a diviner, or omens. Ancestors are thought to appear in the form of animals on occasion, certain species of snake being noteworthy representatives of the ancestors.

Important Venda lineages have a sacred bull which represents the ancestors. Those who cannot afford such a luxury have to be content with spirit stones half-buried near the huts. In addition to this, every male member of a lineage who dies is represented by a spearhead. Nguni families may keep a beast in the herd sacred to and representative of the ancestors. This animal can be recognised by the fact that, unlike the others, its brush is never cut. Sacred herds are to be found among several tribes, including the Venda, Bomvana and, formerly, the Xhosa.

To summarise, ancestor religion is particularistic — its deities are concerned with closely defined groups of persons. In so far as a lineage's ancestors represent the morals of society at large, they administer these within a very restricted context of social responsibility and obligations. Ancestors with a wider arena of concern are those of the tribal chief who, in addition to protecting the living of their lineage, are concerned with the whole tribe.

NATURE-SPIRITS

The nature-spirits are peripheral to society and of limited importance. Various groups conceive of spirits that live in the wild. However, these spirits are mischievous and capricious rather than evil. Thus the traditional South Sotho belief tells of the spirit of the spring, which must be propitiated by a handful of herbs before one drinks from the spring. The penalty for neglecting this observance is an irritating gush of water in the face.

The two most important nature-spirits or groups of nature-spirits are *Nomkubulwana*, the Corn Goddess of the Zulu, and the River People or *Abantubamlambo* of the Xhosa. *Nomkubulwana* is a typical personification of the spring and her presence is ritualised as such. The Xhosa *Abantubamlombo* are an interesting category of beings who live under rivers and are sometimes described as having long fair hair. They are visited by trainee diviners who live among them for some days, this being symbolic of the diviner's contact with the foreign, asocial natural world on behalf of society. The water symbolism is also significant: water is a universal symbol of the unconscious and of the spiritual or 'paranormal' aspect of life. When Laubscher tentatively asked a diviner whether 'under the water' didn't actually mean 'beyond the sky', the diviner confirmed this insight with surprised pleasure.[6]

WITCHCRAFT AND SOCIETY

Like the ancestors, witchcraft can be regarded as a social metaphor. But again, as in the case of the ancestors, this analysis in terms of one component of the dichotomous Western reality does not exhaust all its meanings. However, for present purposes, it is the social significance of witchcraft that is most meaningful.

Primarily, the witch is the embodiment of evil, and witchcraft can be used as an explanatory medium: incidental minor ailments are cheerfully given an organic origin; more persistent minor illness or misfortune is the work of neglected or offended ancestors; serious illness or calamitous misfortune is ascribed to witchcraft. Witchcraft accusations are the legitimate channel for the expression of negatively valued emotions such as fear, jealousy, anger and so on. One thus expects and finds a high incidence of witchcraft at stress points in the social system, most of which occur within the extended family, but today also extend to other environments, notably between individuals in competition for jobs.

Witchcraft accusations are not confined to specific interpersonal situations where some evil motive can be ascribed to the accused but can take the form of scapegoating. Here, the potential and actualised evils of society are given substance and focus in the person of a witch who, whether she admits guilt or not, becomes the scapegoat for the evil inherent in society. It is not surprising to find that individuals thus accused have always been those who stand out from the mass, whether through being social misfits or from extreme wealth.

I remember attending the purification ceremony following the death of a child near Cato Ridge in Natal. The death was believed to have been caused by sorcery, and suspicion rested on a member of the homestead. It was immediately apparent who this was: a young man stood framed in the doorway to his hut, the whites of his eyes bright against the gloom within and, on his face, the lonely pain of the socially ostracised.

It stands to the eternal credit of Moshweshwe that, on his own initiative, he banned witchcraft accusations in 1855. Today witchcraft accusations are outlawed by the various administrations controlling traditional law.

No law can remove suspicion or efficiently prevent allegations, however, and people are still accused of witchcraft. An informant has described how alleged witches are killed by having thatching grass forced up their anuses, or being chopped with cane-knives. Intermittent reports of the murder of suspect witches indicate the continued existence of these beliefs. Two well-publicised cases were the mass witch-burnings in Lebowa homelands in 1976 and two deaths by burning near Port Elizabeth in 1981. Old men may sometimes be heard bemoaning the suspension of the death penalty for witches and blaming many of the ills of modern society on the freedom granted these malevolent people to continue perpetrating evil.

Should a person suspect that a witch is magically attacking him, he will do his utmost to put a distance between himself and that witch — either by forcing the witch to leave or by leaving himself. These days, with many people living in permanent houses, a man may have to face the difficult decision whether to remain in his house at the mercy of a witch or leave.

The distinction between witchcraft in a limited personal context and that in a more general context is not given a name by all tribes. However, the Pedi and Lobedu discriminate between day witches or sorcerers, and night witches or true witches, and the Mpondo and Bhaca differentiate between 'witches that bewitch with medicine' (sorcerers) and 'witches that have familiars', the true witches.

It is indicative of the essentially pragmatic concerns of witch lore that people are much more afraid of 'sorcerers' than of 'witches': the social reality of a hostile and potentially dangerous relationship is much more important than the abstract and mythologised presence of evil in the human mind and society.

The meaning of African witchcraft is often clearly explicable in the terminology of a Western system of witchcraft: psychoanalysis. Accusations of witchcraft constitute, in many cases, instances of projections where the negatively valued emotions one feels are simply projected onto their cause. It is jealousy that finds the wealthy man guilty of witchcraft; it is fear of jealousy that causes the man with a bigger hut to fear magical attack by a neighbour, fear that victimises the social misfit — and ensures a standard hut size.

In general the witch beliefs are macabre to the Westerner. However, the fantasy of Africa, for its objectification within the African world, is neither more grotesque nor more logically dubious than that of the West, relegated as it is to a reified 'unconscious' of uncertain status. Thus any interpretation of African magical beliefs can be regarded as an operation of 'revealing' or 'explaining',*only* if these terms are interpreted as denoting no more than its translation into a more familiar idiom.

The concept of the day witch or sorcerer is perfectly straightforward — that of an ordinary person who uses magical medicine to achieve evil ends. In the use of this magical medicine, however, traditional belief gives him enormous power and he may wreak havoc with his medicine.

In contrast to certain other traditional societies, where the correct wording of the spell is all important, Africans consider the secret of success to lie in the nature of the medicine. Sympathetic magic, too, is widely used (as it is throughout the world) and a person may be bewitched via his or her body waste such as scrapings of skin or nail-parings. A Zulu king of old had a servant whose sole job it was to hide the royal faeces. When Zwide, the Ndwandwe chief, won his epic battle against Dingiswayo (see p. 29), setting the young Shaka free to pursue his destiny, Zwide's success and the capture of his opponent were attributed to painstaking magical preparations involving the gift to Dingiswayo of a daughter of Zwide who had been instructed to procure Dingiswayo's intimate 'body dirt'. This was used to concoct a powerful magical potion which sealed the fate of the king.

A man who wishes another dead can buy an appropriate medicine from an unscrupulous herbalist and, by blowing this medicine in the direction of his opponent and saying, 'you must die', achieve his desire.

It is impossible to say how much witchcraft (sorcery) is actually practised today (as opposed to accusations of witchcraft made). However, given the tempting possibilities offered by African magical lore, and the regrettable failings of the human heart, it would be surprising indeed to find that witchcraft was not practised.

Even if the medicine used has no pharmacological effect and it is assumed — characteristically by Westerners — that causation is confined to the material model of the universe, the *psychological* effect of knowing oneself bewitched can be devastating, not only for the traditionalist with his belief in witchcraft, but also for the white man who is in a susceptible state of mind — as I discovered for myself.

I had been alone for four days on Mount Mulanje, a misty rock massif rising from the plains of Malawi to an altitude of more than 3 000 metres. As I was descending via a narrow path through the rain forest, I noticed an object in the fork of a small tree beside the path. On examination, I found it was a very neatly constructed cone of twigs about 3 centimetres long, containing what looked like a piece of dirty underwear. At first I was filled with a feeling of revulsion for what I assumed to be the evil motives of the person who had placed it there, and decided to throw it away lest an African passer-by see it and think himself bewitched. However, it then occurred to me to retain it as a keepsake and I put it in my pocket. But those four days alone among the rain forests and bald granite domes of the mountain had made me susceptible to tricks of the mind, and the further I walked, the more conscious I became of the unpleasant object in my pocket and the more fears and apprehensions welled up from the depths of my mind. A kilometre or so further on I finally threw the object away, heaving a sigh of relief.

At home, a month later, I discussed the incident with my mother, bemoaning the loss of such a treasure. Secure in familiar surroundings, I found it difficult to appreciate the vague but threatening shadows that had overcome me on that distant mountainside.

Traditionally, the true witch is the quintessence of evil and the focal point of a body of belief notable for its infinite and colourful variety.

In order to leave unnoticed at night to go about their foul work, Venda and Lobedu witches charm their families into a deep sleep and leave behind some hideous creature as a bedfellow for their nearest and dearest. Alternatively, as in the Nguni territories, witches may leave their own bodies to travel about in the shadow body. For those who roam in their own bodies, it would be dangerous and embarrassing to be caught at dawn while still far from home. Against this contingency, witches in Lesotho will have their companions cut a deep incision between the buttocks, into which is rubbed a magical medicine which causes fierce itching at first cock-crow, and gives the witch time to get home before the family awaken. Should this ingenious method fail, however, and a witch be caught about her dreadful work, she has another trick up her sleeve: she will simply turn into any one of a whole variety of animals, or she may even become a walking stick.

There is no real protection against night witches, as they have the ability to enter a hut through the tiniest crevices to perpetrate their evil. Though most traditional homesteads are protected by a comprehensive magical defence system (see p. 232), their inmates still suffer the consequences of witches' nefarious visits. A Lobedu man may awake one morning feeling ill, and later die; a witch paid a visit and poured blood over him. Perhaps he will awaken feeling tired and worn out, because a witch made him work all night in her garden. Apart from being the agent of a great deal of sickness and death in tribal communities, the witch also steals seed from newly planted fields, harms crops, dries up the milk in cows, prevents successful churning of butter, blocks the fermentation of beer to produce a vile gelatinous mess, and is the perpetrator of innumerable other misdeeds.

Like attracts like, and witches come together in bands for macabre all-night parties, during which they carouse and feast on the flesh of fresh corpses probably procured by less senior witches at the command of their more powerful fellows. A newly covered grave should be very carefully examined against the depredations of witches.

Witches have trials of strength. Especially dramatic are those between specialists in sending lightning, which can be aimed at some prearranged target or even at one another. (These witches should not be confused with the 'lightning doctors' or 'heaven herds' found in kwaZulu and extensively described by Dr I.A. Berglund.[7]) To acquire this accuracy training is necessary, and during a thunderstorm in Lobedu country, teacher and novice can be found at the top of a lonely hill, the latter aiming lightning bolts at any aloe his teacher might select.

Witches' Familiars

True witches maintain one or more magical familiars and the possession of a familiar is the sure sign of a witch. Much of a witch's evil is perpetrated by his or her familiars — which may be one of a vast and rather grotesque collection of creatures. Familiars may be any animal but are typically those that arouse a natural feeling of fear or revulsion. The Venda and Lobedu familiars are predominantly snakes, owls, or the mongoose. The *impaka* or wildcat is a well-known familiar in Zulu territory. Recognisable by its large size and short tail, it is kept in a pot in its owner's hut and occasionally let out on an evil mission. She may take it, concealed under her clothing, to a beer-drink where she will await an opportunity to release it for some dark purpose. The baboon and hyena are familiars that enjoy universal popularity as the mounts of witches. The witch always rides facing backwards and holding on to the tail with one hand. She may be heard asking where the animal is going or admonishing it, 'Go easy over the stones'. In Indaleni township near Richmond in Natal, there are times when the entire canine population sets up a clamour which lasts all night. An examination of the local roads the following morning is said to reveal the tracks of a baboon.

The Southern Nguni are noteworthy for their collection of familiars. A feature of these is their sexual relationship with their owners, who are usually women. A characteristic of witchcraft throughout Southern Africa, in fact, is the feminine gender of most people accused of being witches. This has been explained in psychoanalytic terms as the result of a male guilt complex operative in this patriarchal society, because of which men attribute to women the antisocial emotions they — men — would feel if dealt the hand they deal women. In other words, women, as an unjustly treated sector of the community, are perceived as a threat. This perception is given symbolic reality; witches ease their sexual frustration in their illicit relations with familiars.

Thikoloshe

The most notorious of these familiars is *thikoloshe*, a hairy little dwarf, somewhat less than a metre tall, whose most outstanding characteristic is his penis, which is so long that he carries it slung over his shoulder. This preposterous little dwarf who, apart from his role as familiar, lives naturally in the wild, is found throughout Nguni territory and in Lesotho (where he is called *tokoloshe*). On his own, *thikoloshe* appears to be mischievous rather than evil, and is a popular playmate of children, whose company he enjoys. In this role he is a typical nature-spirit, not overtly threatening to society and accessible only to children because they are not fully social beings.

As a familiar of women, however, he can become the agent of evil for his mistress. He serves as her sexual partner and his right hip can often be seen to be worn away as a result of frequent sexual intercourse. A woman who has *thikoloshe* is frigid and unattractive to men — the (perceived) rejection of the power-wielding male is accepted with a hostility which manifests itself in the form of witchcraft accusations. Among the more innocuous of *thikoloshe*'s activities are the sucking of milk from cows, scratching their udders, and replacing the milk in gourds with water.

Ichanti

Other familiars in the tradition of *thikoloshe* are the magical bird, *impundulu*, and *ichanti*, 'the snake of women'. An informant described *ichanti* to me:

> *Ichanti* is a snake made of medicine obtained from a witch. It is used by women, especially in polygamous marriages. One wife sees she is not liked as others are and goes to get this snake to gain (magically) her husband's love. When she goes to the witch she tells him her troubles — the number of wives. He says he can give medicine and gives her two drugs, and instructs that when she comes home she must not tell anyone, she must dig a square hole and put ashes in it.
>
> Early in the morning, before talking to anyone, she must grind medicine and boil it and *phalaza* [vomit] into the hole. She is told how many times, and she must do it for five days, but she must cover it each day. She must vomit only into the hole; and in only the one hole. On the sixth day she will see something small and beautiful in the hole. It moves slowly and changes each day and on the eighth day is making colours, all different colours, in its skin. She must keep on vomiting as it grows and when it fills the hole she will move it to a big river and there it grows quickly. And she must visit her 'friend' every day, rain or shine, have a bath where it is because when she is naked in the water it wraps around her and has all things like a man and acts like a man. But she must come to it before her husband or it is jealous and will come, angry, to the top of the house and blow opposite where he sleeps and the top of his head will disappear inwards. If she obeys these rules, her husband will last . . .
>
> Such people do not have children. When there are already children,

---

PAGE 65   Among the Xhosa peoples, smoking among women was the privilege of the married who had also borne a prescribed number of children. This young woman, unmarried as shown by the fact that she is not wearing the white apron of marriage, smokes because she is modern and defies custom. The white, beaded bag suspended from her waist contains her smoking equipment.

Her bead collars are traditional, however. The necklace of hair is a health charm. It is made by a priest-diviner who plucks the tail hairs of a sacred cow kept at the homestead for this and other ritual purposes, which will not be sold under any circumstances. A boy leaving for circumcision school will be provided with such a necklace to guard him throughout those rigorous months.

PAGES 66-7   In many areas of Southern Africa winter brings aloe blooms in bright profusion and variety. Where aloes occur they are inevitably used for various purposes. A mother might smear the bitter sap of aloe leaves on her nipples when the time comes to wean her child. The dry leaves on the stem of certain species are ground for snuff. As is the case with many plants, the various species of aloe are to make many different medicines against disease and mystical conditions: in Natal, for instance, both the gravediggers and their implements must be treated with medicine compounded from an aloe.

they die. The woman cannot get rid of it. There are many among the amaKhuze clan. They are fond of these snakes because men there have an average of five wives.

There is also the story of two wives of a five-wife house. One had a herbalist father and a snake. She took the second, also unpopular, wife to the river, stripped her, rubbed her all over with fat, during which time she had to keep her eyes shut. However, she opened them when she heard the snake in the water and ran frantically home, naked, and fainted in her husband's hut. He sent her home for a cow as fine because she had shamed all his people by running naked among them.

I know all these people. They are Ntshontsho's wives. The snake owner became popular with her husband but not the runaway.

When *ichanti* is three feet long, in the hole, it tries to come out and the woman has to bind it under her skirt like a band.

On one occasion, when drinking, the snake owner became drunk and was dancing and perspiring. The snake dislikes heat and perspiration. It fidgeted and fell. All present were startled at the strange snake — and she disowned it. Then they killed it and she cried as if a baby had died.

But when a snake is big, about nine feet long, coming from the river with anger, it kills men. When it opens its mouth it is just as if you see lightning and when you try to stab it, you slip — and the spear slips and does not penetrate.

The snake can kill all and it goes back to the river to die only when it has done great damage and killed people. It kills men, not women. This happens only if its owner doesn't go every day to visit. Then it comes out to kill.

Ichanti and *thikoloshe*, when you have accepted them, cannot easily be got rid of. They take possession.

MEDICINE AND MAGIC

Traditional magic, with all its witches, familiars, and diabolic contrivances, is also a world of good and socially acceptable practices. For example, whereas a Zulu will use most love potions with a clear conscience, a Tswana traditionalist feels that their use is antisocial and his society condemns them. A Zulu who treats his field to improve his crops must inform his neighbours so that they can perform the same magic, thus ensuring that he does not 'steal' their fields' fertility.

Throughout the world and the ages it has been recognised that the very

---

PAGE 68   In many areas, notably Natal and Zululand, priest-diviners of both sexes may be recognised by their beaded hair, surmounted by bladders and feathers, strips of animal skin across the torso, and the switch made from wildebeest or cow's tails. This lady boasts her financial success by wearing a splendid array of beadwork and profusion of cloths. The ancestral spirits approve of one who earns much money by her attention to their instructions. Bright chiffon serves to adorn her head and she carries a small ceremonial shield. The 'sjambok' switch of hippo hide is used to drive away evil spirits. On her ankles dancing rattles are made from the silvery cocoons of a moth. Today, however, dancing rattles are more frequently made from bottle-tops strung together on a length of wire.

key to a full life is good health, and man has focused his energies upon the search for soundness of body for himself and his fellows. Bantu-speaking Southern Africans are no exception: no volume could possibly list all the remedies and procedures available to the traditionalist. There are medicines and magic for literally every possible purpose, and the *materia medica* for the treatment of human disease comprise a very large part of magical lore. The natural recuperative power of the body is not held in high regard. Injuries and ailments must be healed by medications, and the appropriate conciliatory or countermeasures must be taken for diseases caused by ancestors or witches, respectively. As in sorcery, there is no discrimination between magical medicines and those with some obvious effect recognised by medical science. Of the medicines used, the vast majority are herbal (eighty per cent in the case of the Lobedu).

An example of a very practical medical procedure is that for setting broken limbs. In 1835, when Gardiner visited the Zulu, he found them using an ingenious method for setting broken arms. The arm, with hand open and fingers spread, was placed in a hole, which was then partially filled with clay. Several burly men lifted the patient perpendicularly until the arm was pulled out of the hole. It was then wrapped in a secure 'splint' of bark.

This does not mean, however, that the healing of bones is without its magical side. The South Sotho have a medicine called *thobeha* to facilitate healing in both man and beast. This wonder drug is used in the following way: an impression of the limb is made on sandy soil and this impression is then cut deeply with an axe. *Thobeha* is placed in this gash by the diviner and covered up. Such is the power of this medicine that the patient, man or beast, soon recovers. The most remarkable characteristic of *thobeha* is that if a beast cured by it is later slaughtered, and the healed bone is split open, inside a black lump will be found — the *thobeha* which was originally buried in the ground.

A wide variety of simple folk remedies are used in traditional society, and the Zulu word *amakhambi* is equivalent to the English 'housewives' remedies'. The term covers many simple but helpful infusions, herbal ointments and poultices of crushed leaves for everyday swellings, boils and bruises that come the way of any housewife. Of course, every person or tribe knows a 'cure-all' patent medicine, such as the Sotho *lelibe* which, during an epidemic, was distributed free to all comers.

Apart from being taken orally or applied externally, medicines may be administered in various ways. The patient can be smoked, steamed, given snuff or medicines to induce vomiting, or medication can be rubbed into incisions. Many treatments are rather prolonged and involved. Stayt has described a Venda procedure for combating pneumonia which is reminiscent of an alchemist's recipe, and includes the dried blood of a magical bird among the medicines applied during the course of the protracted ritual.[8]

Magic can also be applied for purposes other than the curing of bodily ills. For instance, there are two medicines which are useful in fighting court cases. The first is *itshe ijaji* or 'stone of a judge' — a scented, multicoloured stone, apparently used by those who judge major cases in court, but also obtainable by ordinary people who use it to gain the judge's favour. The second, more potent, is called *icala ka lithethwa* or 'the trying of a case'. An informant describes its use:

Take the leg of a fowl and salt, and boil it and put one teaspoon of this medicine on it. Give the meat to one in prison. If he eats it he wins the case. They [the judges] say, *'Kulega'* — greetings — and go, and it really works. You can get this good medicine at Dukuduku in Zululand. You do not need a big lawyer. It is a lawyer itself. The judge cannot judge this case. I know two people who have been judged in this way.

Medicines may be even more exotic than this, and the more distant their origin, the more varied their nature, the better. Some of the more rarified substances put to use include lion's fat or vomit, and the powerful potions concocted from these can achieve great things. The potions are used throughout an individual's life to protect him, his crops, cattle and home against virtually anything — witches, lightning, pests, hail, sickness, other medicines.

The traveller, too, has certain magic and medicines at his disposal. A Venda setting off on a long journey may place a round stone in the fork of a tree. The sun becomes identified with this rock and is therefore similarly trapped in the tree, thus allowing him to reach his destination in daylight. On one occasion, when transporting priest-diviners on a long journey, my van had to be 'doctored' beforehand. A Pedi will similarly bless his travels by placing a root of the *morarwana* tree in his car — a rabbit's foot, African-style. Should he be going to a soccer match, a Pedi will hope that his team has used powdered root of *moraro o mogalo* in order to ensure that the ball is always repelled from the home goal and is attracted to that of the opposing side. Indeed, many African soccer teams that venture on to the field bolster their chances of winning with magical medicine.

The Pedi *moraro o mogalo* is also known as a love-charm and is but one of a veritable arsenal of potent methods and medicines designed to assist in all manner of romantic situations. These useful medicines may do anything from unleashing in a favoured member of the opposite sex an unquenchable appetite for oneself, to removing all competition by bringing sickness to a wife's illicit lover.

Black and White Medicines
The older and more traditional magical remedies and rites fall into certain categories. Two important classes among the Zulu and other Nguni people are the black and white medicines, which are used in conjunction. Black medicines are used to counteract evil in the form of personal characteristics (which may cause an employer or girl to dislike one), or to remove the taint of a close brush with lightning. These medicines are used both in washing and as emetics. After taking an emetic of black medicine, the patient will build a fire of dry aloe leaves, which must then be extinguished by vomit. He must then vomit on the paths so that others passing by may take away his evil. Use of this medicine brings on a state of ritual impurity which must be removed by the use of white medicines of the *ubulawu* class, which are also often used in conjunction with the shades.

A class of medicines which has grown in importance with the advent of the European is made up of those designed to secure the indulgence of an employer. The European, too, has brought with him his interesting selection of patent medicines and these have been an instant success in Africa. Most popular is a whole range of 'blood purifiers' and laxatives which the traditionalist may take in enormous doses.

Ritual Murder

Worldwide, ritual murder has been with humanity a long time and seems set for a long stay yet. Africa is no exception, with many real and rumoured examples of this crime. The motive is, of course, the acquisition of powerful medicine, which is generally compounded from the fat, internal organs, foetus or genitals. In order to retain their magical essence, these items should be removed from a living individual.

With its poor communication system and remote mountain areas, Lesotho can be called the home of ritual murder, although the incidence is in fact countrywide, and has been known to occur in the cities as well as in the rural areas. Ashton notes that at least 60 ritual murders were reported between 1940 and 1952. In addition he lists 27 ritual murders which came before the courts, of which 6 were committed simply to obtain medicine for routine requirements, 10 to provide medicine designed to help men to better positions in the administration, 4 to make magic for use in court cases, and 7 to make medicine for undetermined reasons.

Ritual murder is by no means confined to Lesotho. It is said in Natal that no first-fruits ceremony can be complete without the use of medicine from ritually murdered human beings. A human skull is reputed to be used as a vessel from which certain medicines are drunk. Some years back it was rumoured that my home village, Richmond in the Natal Midlands, had been chosen to supply these necessities. The frightened gossip certainly ensured that few ventured out after dark and alone, and this caution would appear to have been justified — there was at least one ritual murder during this period.

RITUAL IMPURITY

The concept of ritual impurity is a vital component of traditional thinking throughout Southern Africa and is evocative of Old Testament images of the Jews. It is associated with certain human conditions and states: menstruation and childbirth, sexual intercourse, contact with death or lightning, the sight of (for a man) a naked woman or an old woman's buttocks, and contact with other impure persons or even clothing. Unless it is a condition which wears off, a person who is ritually impure must undergo a purification ceremony.

Various taboos are associated with the condition. A person with any form of ritual impurity must avoid, among others, the sick lest their condition become worse. Women between puberty and menopause are not allowed into the cattle kraal and should not have any association with cattle. Thus, when the Zulu warlord Zwide, much against the will of his mother, was about to set off on one of his many sorties, she put paid to his plans by running naked into the cattle kraal where he was sitting with his councillors. To have set off in the teeth of such a blatantly evil omen would have been courting certain disaster.

Closely allied to the concept of ritual impurity is that of 'heat' and 'cold': the former is an unclean, undesirable and impure state, while the latter is correct and desirable.(Heat is also associated with biological functions and can be regarded as a type of impurity.) Witches are hot. A method used by the Zulu and Lobedu for keeping witches out of the homestead is the burial of a cool river stone beneath the entrance; this takes away all the malevolent visitor's heat. A person must be cool to participate in religious activity, and the ancestors are attracted to cool materials and people. The coolness of beer is invariably a part of religious ceremonies and serves to lure the ancestors.

In addition to the river stone, there are other medicines and methods for inducing coolness. The bulb of the creeper *modipidikwa*, which the Pedi consider to be particularly cool, is used to treat barrenness in women, a condition said to be caused by heat in the blood.

TRADITION AND THE TWENTIETH CENTURY

The above is a brief description of the traditional beliefs and related practices, all — or virtually all — of which still flourish today to some extent. The question is: to what extent? But this question alone is inadequate and must be qualified by another: do the traditional beliefs and practices still have the same relation to one another and mean the same things to the individual and his society, both in their presence and in their absence?

A West African academic I heard questioned on the subject of African religion, called the Jewish religion 'an enormous and beautifully structured superstition' and referred to Islam and Christianity as 'the two greatest living superstitions in the world', continuing: 'As long as these superstitions exist, why can't lesser-known ones go some way to satisfying the psychological well-being of their adherents?'

It should come as no surprise to learn that the traditional religious and magical beliefs of Bantu-speaking Southern Africa continue to flourish in both the urban and rural settings. Professor A. Mafeje wrote in 1975: 'Whether Zionist or high-Anglican, all Africans in Langa [a black township outside Cape Town] share an implicit belief in ancestor-cult and have held on with varying tenacity to their *amasiko* [customs].'[9]

That not only the ancestor religion, but traditional witchcraft beliefs continue to flourish in both rural and urban settings is illustrated by two quotes. The first is from a 1977 issue of *Drum* magazine:

> Fourteen people have been brutally burned to death after being accused of witchcraft at Gamphahlele near Pietersburg. 150 people have been arrested for the gruesome murders, which need never have been.
>
> Lt. Philip Moloto, chief of the cops at the Lebowa capital of Lebowakgomo, is at his wits' end. How do you take preventative measures against such killing when people explicitly and foolishly believe in witchcraft?
>
> So is Dr Cedric Phatudi, chief minister of Lebowa, who believes that people must be educated to outgrow superstitious beliefs. Pietersburg tribesmen and women are gripped with fear. They fear being bewitched and struck with lightning or being smelt out as witches. Burning alleged witches at the stake should have ended with the Middle Ages, but it didn't.
>
> Something has to be done about the rot that has set in in Pietersburg.
>
> For this reason *DRUM* issues this challenge to all witchdoctors: There is a quick R5 000 waiting in our offices for you if, during March 1977, any one of you can strike Stanley Motjuwadi dead with lightning. If you can't,

let everyone know that the pretence of being able to control lightning is silly, murderous rubbish

So, you phoney witches, start bubbling your cauldrons. We dare you to take up this challenge.[10]

The second extract is taken from the *Cape Times* of Saturday, 30 April, 1977:

A Guguletu [a black township near Cape Town] resident, Mrs Phyllis Mdudu, 38, told the court that on February 23 this year a crowd of 40 children arrived at her home and demanded the bodies of their 'comrades' killed during the riots last year.

'They threatened to kill me and burn down my house because I was a witch and had enslaved their dead comrades.

'The next day a crowd of more than 300 youths arrived and started throwing stones through my windows and shouting, "Kill the witch — kill the cruel mother for raising the dead".'

. . . She estimated the damage to her four-bedroom house to be R80.00.[11]

The extent of involvement with traditional belief is shown by figures gathered by various researchers. In a study published in 1972, the Reverend Moller found that just over 80 per cent of Soweto residents believed in the reality of the ancestors, while half (49.9 per cent) performed rituals to appease these beings. In addition, more than a quarter of his subjects had had experiences which they considered to be connected with the ancestors; two-thirds had consulted a diviner or medicine man; and three-quarters believed in the reality of witchcraft and sorcery.[12]

In Grahamstown, Hammond-Tooke found in 1970 that his Xhosa informants attributed 72.8 per cent of cases of misfortune to witchcraft and sorcery, and 7 per cent to the ancestors.[13] B.A. Pauw, Professor of Anthropology at the University of South Africa, discovered that among the members of three churches in Port Elizabeth, 89 per cent of members believed that the ancestors could influence their lives, while 70 per cent cited experiences in their lives for which the ancestors were allegedly responsible.[14]

Among members of a Johannesburg Dutch Reformed Church congregation studied by Dr A.G. Schutte, 45 per cent had sacrificed to the ancestors, 43 per cent prayed to them regularly, and 77 per cent considered that sacrifice to the ancestors was not sinful. This congregation's traditional belief was even stronger — 91.3 per cent of the informants recognised the existence of witchcraft, 67 per cent were prepared to consult diviners, and 57.9 per cent paid regular visits to them.[15]

These figures and news reports signify little, however, unless one considers what these beliefs *mean* or represent to the individual living today, be it in the country or in a large city. One cannot simply locate the individual Bantu-speaking person on some hypothetical traditional African-Western continuum.

Mafeje, in the same article from which the quote on page 73 was taken, wrote: 'Strange as it may sound virtually everybody is *nominally* a Christian in Langa'.[16] Which gives some indication of the complexity of the situation.

Without claiming to be exhaustive, it is possible to go some way towards accommodating the second question I asked by arbitrarily defining five

Barbara Tyrrell

broad ways in which a Bantu-speaker may respond to the twin faces Western society presents to him, the secular and the religious.

The first way of responding is to continue to hold largely unexamined traditional beliefs simply because that is the cultural norm — an approach for which there are many parallels in Western society.

A migrant labourer away from his family and lonely in the impersonal city may take great comfort in the presence of his ancestors. But it is equally true that his ancestors will disapprove of his living in the city and add to his problems. The absence of the familiar ways of living and people, together with the imagined desertion by the ancestors, can make the individual from the country feel very vulnerable to magical attack. This vulnerability may be symbolic of fear of the city; psychiatrists tell us that the move of any tribesman to the city is accompanied by an increase in anxiety.

Even where traditional belief has been overtly abandoned, it tends to persist at a deeper level of the mind. S.G. Lee has demonstrated that for the Zulu social mores expressed in Zulu dreams lag some fifty to one hundred years behind the overt adaptation of the individual to Western ways.[17]

Individuals whose attitude can be summed up under this category of more or less conscious acceptance of traditional belief are in an unenviable position in the urban setting. They are confronted by a dominant society imposing its own similarly entrenched beliefs. If such an individual runs into psychological difficulties and finds himself in the power of psychiatrists working from the more or less consciously accepted Western viewpoint, he has troubles indeed. To illustrate this point, consider the following quote

On the stockade around the cattle kraal hang the remains of animals sacrificed during the 'coming out' or gradua-tion ceremony of a Zulu priest-diviner. On the left are goat-skin bands and bracelets to be worn by the priest-diviner.

concerning ancestor possession taken from a well-respected book on transcultural psychiatry:

> It is easy to see how this possession experience prepares the individual to accept a healer's assurance of improvement, as well as his directions with regard to ways of making satisfactory adjustments. The anxiety and panic that are associated with loss of usual defences induce the individual to try to understand the experience, which cannot be readily understood in commonsense terms. The cognitive dissonance that is engendered in the possessed, and in those who witness them, genuinely behaving as if in the control of outside forces, cannot fail to impress everyone involved with the validity of whatever theory is immediately at hand to explain the phenomenon.[18]

This passage is, itself, manifestly 'a theory immediately at hand' called up in response to the need for an explanation within the context of a particular concept of humanity.

This passage calls to mind a train journey I made some years back, from Beira in Mozambique to Blantyre in Malawi. The train was packed as usual with black Malawians on the last leg of their long journey home from the gold mines of the Witwatersrand. My travelling companion was the only other white on the train. In the carriage next to ours was a man who had lost his senses in Johannesburg. He was completely demented, frothing at the mouth, writhing, screaming. He sat in the aisle, his hands bound behind his back and to the legs of a bench. He struggled vainly to get free for the greater part of the 36-hour journey. But it was whenever my companion or myself appeared before him that he really went berserk; cowering, but grimacing with fear-filled malevolence. I wondered about the circumstances of his life in Johannesburg.

Today, with fifth-generation townsmen a part of black society, this sort of attitude is not common. For most blacks, the contrast between the power-wielding Western culture and traditional belief necessitates the development of a lively awareness of both. And the attitude of deliberately embracing traditional belief and custom — in part at least — constitutes the second type of response to culture shock.

This approach by most traditionalists, urban or rural, can best be described as a survival tactic, the alternative to self-alienation. From the beginning, the established Christian denominations in South Africa have, like their secular counterparts, imposed on African society an incongruous system of European middle-class values. Enmeshed in this ethical system, churchmen have been unable to see the Christian message in any other context. Thus the African has been challenged from the first to reject his culture's values and customs, his self, to embrace a foreign and, to him, unreasonable system

PAGE 77   This Ndebele woman wears the now-unfashionable narrow, beaded hoops. Pierced coins hanging over her forehead were a fashion until outlawed. The rectangular beaded pendant of stiffened cloth is still fashionable today, as are carved wooden beads. Letters of the alphabet, used either correctly or reversed, are favoured in the designs for beadwork or murals. In this instance, shaved in the hair is the mirror image of a portion of the registration number of a Pretoria boyfriend's car.

Barbara Tyrrell.

which he perceives as a subterfuge on the part of the society that subjugated him. It is a deliberate and conscious act of self-preservation to remain a traditionalist or 'pagan'.

My third category includes those individuals who reject their traditional beliefs for either the secular or the Christian alternatives offered by the West. In opting for the secular stance, they are taking the more popular step but, as statistics show, their materiality is often bolstered by some reliance on traditional belief or a synthesis of traditional and Church belief. The implicit belief in the ancestors which may characterise individuals in this category, but which is not accompanied by appropriate religious observance, is in interesting contrast to the observances of a deliberate traditionalist (category two), whose outward practice of custom is very often a statement of identity rather than a response to the requirements of traditional religion.

I recently met an artist, Harry Magagu, who, having lost his traditional religion to a secular attitude, had through his mystical experiences been led back to the ancestor religion. Today Mr Magagu is a successful artist, combining technical skill and inner vision to portray the symbolism of his culture.

Rejecting traditional belief to embrace the religious component of Western culture, the Christian Church is perhaps a more popular choice in rural areas where the missions offer education and medical services which may otherwise be scarce. Whether or not the motivation of the early converts was the Church itself and its system of ethics, or the material advantages of being a Christian, their descendants, raised in the Church tradition, have experienced the African-Western alternatives differently and may continue in the Church tradition untroubled by self-alienation. In Transkei, for instance, one can distinguish two quite distinct communities, the 'red people' or traditionalists, and the Christians.

A way out of the dilemma of having to reject one's cultural values in order to embrace Christianity is provided by various Christian sects rooted in the African ethic. Identification with these is the fourth alternative. Most characteristic of this category are the so-called Ethiopian churches, which reject both the white man's church and traditional religion.

My fifth and final category, as an obvious alternative to the above, is the deliberate synethesis of traditional and Church belief — a popular choice, both in and out of the urban setting. The several thousand so-called Zionist sects admit to the existence of ancestors and commonly invoke them for healing and sacrifice, but in no way feel that this prejudices their relationship with the Church deities. This is in fact *explicitly* believing what many Christians covertly believe. When Schutte questioned the members of a

---

PAGE 78 A Zulu trainee priest-diviner from Natal calls up the ancestral spirits. Essential for this purpose is an aromatic herb — *imphepho* — which is burnt in a fragment of broken cooking pot. In the beaded box is special snuff, which clears the head to receive the voices of the ancestors. The clay pot contains a 'cool' frothing medicine, *ubulawu*, very attractive to the ancestors. It is said to froth heavily as illustrated only when stirred by a good-natured and benevolent person.

The line drawing shows the *umsamo*, or part of the hut opposite the doorway allocated to the ancestral spirits. Suspended here for ritual purposes are certain organs taken from sacrificial animals.

Witwatersrand Dutch Reformed Church regarding ancestors, one replied, 'If you love Jesus, He will allow the Diviner's medicine to work for you. Otherwise it will be ineffective.' Another of Dr Schutte's informants justified his continuing communion with the ancestors by pointing out that whites remembered and prayed to their ancestors regularly — at barbecues!

Though this categorisation is simplistic and an artificial imposition, it brings home the necessity of realising that a system of belief, be it Western or traditional African, is manifest at various levels, from the abstractly intellectual to the concretely practical, from the deeply unconscious to the wholly articulated, and that such beliefs or practices cannot be characterised as independent entities, but are amenable to discussion only in terms of a socio-political and physical environment. The real range of attitudes and combinations is infinite and, rather than being locatable on an African-Western dimension, they will be understood by Western man only if he is willing to step outside his culture's world-view, to appreciate it from the standpoint of another, equally valid, perspective on reality.

A Natal Midlands priest-diviner's hut that embodies three disparate worlds. On the thatch are hung the skulls of animals sacrificed to the ancestors, while a medicated peg in the floor guards the hut against witches. The cross is an acknowledgement and supplication of the Church deities, with the secular West represented by the injunction to respect privacy.

THE HEALERS

NO society in the world is without its healers — of body, of mind, and of rifts in the social fabric. The integrity of society depends not only on the tangible benefits to be derived from the talents of these people but on the sense of security engendered by belief in their powers.

In a culture where the boundaries between 'fact' and 'fantasy', medicine and magic, are diffuse, where the divine is completely accepted as a part of life, it is not surprising to find that the work of healers encompasses a wide spectrum of activities, ranging from the mundane to the miraculous. A healer will set a broken limb, but will with equal self-assurance supply a client with deadly magical medicine to use against an enemy said to be sending ill luck or death to the home. He may dose an ailing patient with herbal medicine which, with luck, may have a beneficial pharmacological effect, but almost certainly his diagnosis of the disease will take into account the displeasure of a dead relative or the machinations of a witch.

Traditional healers can be divided loosely into two categories: herbalists, who provide medicines of herbal and animal origin according to knowledge they have acquired; and priest-diviners, who function in both the religious and the magico-medical spheres.

PRIEST-DIVINERS

Priest-diviners occupy a jealously guarded position in traditional society as official communicants with the ancestors and the interpreters of their wishes. They smell out witches and also diagnose and provide treatment for diseases caused by witches (and a witch's familiars) or displeased ancestors.

The role of Nguni priest-diviners differs from that of the inland peoples in that theirs is a calling: they are led to become *isangoma* (Zulu) or *igqira* (Xhosa) healers by the ancestral spirits they represent and who provide them with all the information they require. They are thus clearly distinguishable from the herbalist, and the large majority are female. In contrast, the priest-diviners of the inland peoples, while claiming supernatural access to knowledge, are predominantly male and *learn* their techniques and medicines (bone throwing, for example) from practising priest-diviners (as opposed to Nguni priest-diviners whose training consists in making the novice a vehicle for the expression of the wishes of the ancestors). The dividing line between priest-diviner and herbalist is thus blurred among the inland peoples. Today the greater mobility of people and culture contact in the large urban centres, notably Johannesburg, have led to the spread of Nguni-type priest-diviners to various Sotho groups, notably the South Sotho and Pedi, and the adoption of bone throwing by some Nguni priest-diviners. The situation is thus complex and fluid, defying criteria and classifications.

Many Western students and missionaries have vested psychological interests in their own particular world-views, and therefore dismiss priest-diviners' talents as being no more than chicanery, which exploits the gullibility of their clients. Priest-diviners' powers are also often put down to a thorough knowledge of local gossip. In answer to this, I quote Adrian K. Boshier, one of the few Europeans to qualify as a priest-diviner:

> Earlier I spoke of the popular misconception that the witchdoctor's power comes from his knowing everyone in the area. Some time ago I was at the Museum of Natural History in New York where they had a section on African witchdoctors. It stated there that the witchdoctor is a person on whom all gossip falls; thus when a patient comes in and sits down, the diviner divines, already knowing the nature of his complaint. Perhaps this could be accepted if one had only the small village witchdoctor as an example. But in Soweto, where thousands of people consult hundreds of witchdoctors every day, one must recognise that the power of these diviners is impressive — unless, of course, we believe that each diviner is familiar with all the gossip of this vast urbanised complex![1]

Certainly, wherever one encounters human beings, one finds indisputably valid experiences of the psychic side of nature. The Bantu-speaking peoples are no exception — indeed, with a culture accepting so completely the powers of the supernatural, they are a living laboratory for the study of parapsychology. However, it is true that many a priest-diviner relies at times — if not always — on trickery, and can be aided and abetted in their deceptions by the attitude of many of their clients. Dr Kobus Reynecke, an authority and author on Tswana witchcraft, informed me that, after some twenty years spent among these people, he had yet to see a valid demonstration of psychic ability. The traditionalist is concerned not with the Western myth — the scientific verification of fact in a rigid conceptual framework — but with the more holistic meaning of events and people and their interrelationship in the mind. For those little exposed to Western materialistically based thought-patterns, the external appearance of an event or its more superficial relevance is easily eclipsed by its numinous quality — its intense inner meaning.

Smelling out or Divination

The supernatural knowledge to which the priest-diviner claims access is considered to be held by the ancestral spirits, who pass it on. In more familiar terms, the priest-diviner is a point of contact or interface between our familiar phenomenal world of personalities, time and space, and the numinous or divine world, in which lie the cause, meaning and morality of the phenomenal world. Western psychologists have invented several terms for the different forms of manifestation or awareness of the numinous. The priest-diviner speaks of different types of spirits, which are also more or less

'powerful', in other words, a priest-diviner may have greater or lesser contact with the numinous.

Communion with the spirits may occur in many ways. Dreaming is a common channel of communication used by all ancestors and priest-diviners. All Nguni priest-diviners attempt to induce a state of semi-trance by dancing, which they stop at irregular intervals to announce whatever information the ancestors have imparted to them.

Most Nguni priest-diviners follow a characteristic pattern in answering a client's questions. The priest-diviner will make statements relevant to the subject at hand, which are answered by the formalised responses of the neophyte (*thwasa*). These exchanges increase in frequency and excitement until the priest-diviner enters a state in which he or she can communicate easily with the ancestors. In practice this is often no more than a guessing game of 'hot and cold', with an informed neophyte accomplice or gullible clients giving away the information and their views on the matter simply by the enthusiasm, or otherwise, of the response. This technique, used in conjunction with another popular method, whistling spirits, is illustrated in Appendix 1. Whistling spirits are regarded as very powerful. A priest-diviner with such spirits is respected. Whistling is firmly rooted in traditional thinking as a means by which the spirits communicate with the living. I discovered its significance when transporting a vanload of priest-diviners (*izangoma*) and their neophytes: I was requested to refrain from whistling as it disturbed the attendant ancestors who, as everyone should know, regard it as their special language.

The concept of 'whistling spirits' is encountered throughout the world. Spiritualists of our own society claim that, in addition to using knocks and bumping and voices, spirits — those still learning to communicate with the living — use whistles. Whistling as a means of spirit communication takes place on the other side of the world, too. Sir Arthur Grimble, Governor of the Gilbert Islands during the early part of this century, reported whistling family spirits, whose twitterings were interpreted by a diviner and the findings employed to plan family affairs.

The highest manner of 'seeing' supernatural information or of any

Accompanied by a diminutive novice beating the drum, a Zulu priest-diviner sings and dances her way towards a homestead where she is to commune with the ancestors on behalf of her clients.

communion with the ancestors is the gaining of knowledge without any ritual or trance induction at all. The class of powerful spirits called the *Lozi* (as opposed to *Nguni*) are often said to be involved here. I spoke to a young male Pedi priest-diviner practising in Soweto who claimed to have three classes of spirits working through him; the two mentioned as well as the *Ndawu*, possession by whom is a growing phenomenon in the Transvaal (see p. 93). On his forehead he wore a cow's horn standing vertically. This, his own personal innovation, allowed him to 'see' using the *Lozi*. (In addition to this formidable panel of spirits at his disposal, this young man claimed to be an *iProfiti* (prophet) or representative of *Modimo* (God) and had worked in a Zionist sect.) In Transkei, a special term is used for those priest-diviners with a highly developed contact with the numinous. They are the *iisanusi*, as opposed to the more numerous *igqira*.

Many (it is impossible to say how many) divinations can be categorised as elaborate games of hot and cold and would, according to Western ways of thought, be described as fraudulent. Perhaps the most striking feature to emerge from these divination procedures is the fact that they are acceptable to and paid for by the clients. Confronted by their unquestioning acceptance of the symbols and bogies of their culture, one is reminded of Western man and his obeisance to his particular catchwords such as 'science', 'progress' and 'I.Q.'

In cases where guesswork is used and the priest-diviner appears to have no psychic ability or contact with the ancestors, she can still serve a very meaningful role in that, by invoking the ancestors, custodians of the society's codes, she gives weight and certainty to what she gathers to be the popular opinion on a matter. Such a system, though it is potentially very harmful to the unfortunate accused of being a witch, serves to stabilise the community as a whole and can even be termed democratic.

However, it would be a mistake to believe that all traditionalists are simply gullible. The common observation is that, while fraudulent priest-diviners do exist, there are just as certainly those who are very gifted psychics whose contact with the numinous is fostered within the context of, and used to the benefit of traditional culture.

Bantu-speaking psychics are usually drawn into the calling or profession, but only those who are good become well known unless they have a particular gift for showmanship. I could cite the case of the priest-diviner living near Richmond in the Natal Midlands, who accurately located a cat which had been stolen and taken to Durban, 100 kilometres away, or of the woman who requires her clients to arrive at her house at five o'clock in the morning to drink a magical concoction and stare into a mirror. This certainly sounds a fairly off-beat procedure but a friend who did this in searching for a lost dog swears that she saw the image of the animal. Whatever the case may be for others, my own experience in consulting priest-diviners leaves me in no doubt at all that, while there are charlatans (and probably always have been), their ranks do contain some highly developed psychics and talented psychologists.

Until a few years ago there lived near Greytown, not far from Pietermaritzburg, an old woman whose powers were famous throughout the Natal Midlands among black and white alike. In her time she located keys, stolen cattle, several engagement rings and even (when the client was of the right beliefs) identified witches. One of the more amusing answers she provided was for a part-time farmer. This (white) man was kept too busy by his business to live on and protect his farm and the day came when he discovered that a large number of new tyres had disappeared. Frustrated in his efforts to discover the culprit, he fetched this famous woman to his home. She had barely arrived and had certainly been told nothing of his problems when she spoke:

'Those things that you seek,' she said, 'you will find on the feet of those who work for you.'

Sure enough, an investigation revealed that one shrewd and industrious labourer had made sandals from the tyres to sell to the surrounding population!

Divinatory Bones, Dice and Bowl

Unlike the Nguni, the Sotho/Tswana and Venda priest-diviners tend to rely on physical techniques for divination. The most popular divinatory implements are bones or dice. The former are popular throughout the interior, and now also among the Zulu, but are a recent introduction to Nguni priest-diviners. Divinatory dice, which are of Karanga (Zimbabwean) origin, are used to some extent by the Venda, Lobedu and other tribes of the north-east.

Bones

The smaller 'bones' may consist of a variety of objects, including sea shells and even buttons, but they are based primarily on a universal and clearly defined 'core' set which can be supplemented by additional bones. This set is usually composed of four bones (two pairs): the 'big one' or 'male', and the 'female' are carved from the hind hoof of an ox and a cow, respectively, and the 'male *phalaphala*' (horn, trumpet) and 'female *phalaphala*' from the horns of an ox and a cow, respectively. The rest of the set consists of the hindleg anklebones of sundry animals, especially those which are the clan totems of patients. The 'male' and 'female' each have four sides which can face uppermost when the bones are thrown — they can be 'walking', 'standing', 'covering', and 'dying'. All other bones in the set have only two possible falls: 'walking' or 'dying'.

The two principal pairs are the most important and the fall of all the other bones serves only to embroider their central revelation. Like the ancient Chinese oracle, the I Ching, these principal bones can give 64 different answers and, also like the I Ching, each answer or 'fall' of the bones is described by a 'praise' (which is fairly standard but not unaffected by the poetic whim of the priest-diviner). When consulted, the priest-diviner will often hand the bones to his patient, who breathes on them to 'infuse' them with his breath before throwing them. The fall of the bones is determined by the shades, as are the finer, inspirational points of their interpretations which, like those of the Tarot cards, is fixed yet dependent on the 'clairvoyance' of the interpreter. The praise to describe the combination 'male-walking, female-dying, male *phalaphala*-walking, female *phalaphala*-dying', which denotes a man who has lost his wife for a barren woman, is called the 'Swimming of Rangoaka' and may take the following form (as recorded by Joas Mapetla and translated by F. Laydevant):

> Rangoaka is crying
> He is crying on account of things forgotten,
> On account of losing a child's kaross.
> It is not lost, it has been seen
> On the border of other people's fields.[2]

These basic meanings can be considerably elaborated on by the additional objects in the set. An example are the bones of Rosy, a young Xhosa priest-diviner working on the Witwatersrand. As well as the basic set and dice (see below), she had a cowrie shell which, depending on its fall, indicated money in the future or otherwise, a cone shell which indicated either happiness and laughter or the need to brew beer for the ancestors, and a group of assorted shell-fragments whose fall indicated what the future would unveil in the sphere of the home and possible accidents. A limpet shell indicated distant ('over the sea') journeys: upside down, affirmative; right side up, no travel. Assorted small bone-fragments warned of evil (in the form of *thikoloshe*), or some called 'the thieves' told whether anything had been lost or stolen and hinted at its location. A small white plastic leopard served to indicate whether the client was proud of some achievement, which it did by standing (as it occasionally did) when the bones were thrown. A pair of tortoise-shell segments, cut from the collar of the living animal completed the set, which can be regarded as typical.

Dice

The divinatory dice of the Venda correspond closely to the bones — two pairs of marked ivory or bone, domino-like objects engraved with triangular or circular markings. The pairs are those of the old man and old woman, and their young counterparts, paralleling the two basic pairs of divinatory bones. The dice, too, are thrown together with a collection of other objects including sea shells, which amplify the meanings of the 16 possible combinations. The ancient Western mantic system, the counterpart of the I Ching, also works on the format of 16 possible basic answers.

A set of bone divining dice. There is a blurred distinction between 'bones' and 'dice' and the latter, especially, are often characterised by a wide and imaginative selection of oddments, including sea shells, stone, claws and even fragments of dolls. [Arthur Smit coll.]

Divining Bowl

The Venda priest-diviner, who uses only bones as a means of divination, is not considered as talented a psychic as the one who uses both the dice and the 'divining bowl' (which, in the Republic of South Africa, is peculiar to the Venda as a means of divination). The divining bowl is a shallow, wooden basin, carved on the base and on the edge with numerous symbols and figures. In the centre of the bowl is a cowrie shell. Such a bowl was excavated at Zimbabwe in the last century and was for some time believed to be an African representation of the Zodiac.

As in most common divinatory methods, the principal purpose of the bowl is to ascertain the identity of the witch who has caused ill-fortune, sickness, or death in the family. When consulted, the priest-diviner fetches the bowl for his clients but must keep it wrapped in its protective skin until he has treated their eyes with a medicine compounded from the droppings of a kingfisher. Should an ordinary person look at a divining bowl without taking such precautions, he or she will go blind. For use, the bowl is filled with water on which about five seeds of the *murutu* tree are floated. The priest-diviner exhorts these to float towards the appropriate symbols. The approach towards, or touching, of symbols by a seed indicates, depending on the sequence, the family of the guilty witch, that of his/her father and so on. The exhortations of the priest-diviner as he leans over the bowl, and his blowing of a whistle made from the wingbone of a vulture, give him considerable control over the movement of the seeds. Divining bowls are often passed from priest-diviner father to priest-diviner son, and may be of great age.

Lest my descriptions of these traditional divinatory systems should be taken as being critical or supercilious, let me mention the 'ephod' and the 'Urim and Thummim', both divinatory systems frequently referred to in the Old Testament. These appear to have been used to elicit answers — the 'will of God' — expressed in a 'yes/no' framework. And, just as in the case of the Bantu-speaking people, these answers justified catastrophe or blessing in terms of the relationship of mortals to the 'God of Israel' — the 'ancestors of the lineage' in the present context. One is reminded, too, that early in the Old Testament the word God is used in the plural. In addition, like 'the ancestors', the 'God of Israel' had 'prophets' who gathered together to sing and dance and divine 'His Will'.

The calling, training, and initiation of the Bantu-speaking 'prophets' of the ancestors is our next concern.

The Ancestors' Call

I cannot overemphasise the power and the significance of the ancestral spirits in a priest-diviner's life. It is said that the ancestors 'brood' in priest-diviners, and it is from their ancestors that they gain their knowledge. Especially among the Nguni, one cannot choose to become a priest-diviner (*isangoma*); one is chosen by the ancestors and 'called' to be their servant — a call not easily refused. (From this point until p. 93 the term *isangoma*, plural *izangoma*, will be used, as this section deals specifically with the Nguni.)

This call comes in the form of a sickness called *ukuthwasa*. The sufferer becomes ill and is plagued by dreams. The nature of the illness is not defined in detail, although there are certain set symptoms, including body pains and peculiar dreams. These pains are generally confined to the upper back, the neck and the shoulders, for this is the area of the spirits. (A friendly pat on the shoulder is anathema to an *isangoma* because it disturbs the spirits clustered there.) The diagnosis of the ailment known as *ukuthwasa* is made by an *isangoma* and usually comes as no surprise, especially if other family members have also suffered from it, because the ailment is said to run in families. The consultant *isangoma* also reveals the identity of the ancestors who are attempting to use the individual. A man is often 'brooded in' by his patrilineal ancestors, while a woman may be used by those of either her father's or her husband's clan.

Women consititute by far the majority of Nguni *izangoma*. Different theories have been advanced to account for this preponderance of women over men. It is notable in Western society, too, that the majority of 'fortune tellers', 'crystal gazers' and mediums are women. The reason may lie beyond a mere desire on the part of women to escape the role of 'second-class citizens'; it may be some aspect of feminine psychology that facilitates the

Barbara Tyrrell

A Nguni priest-diviner's hairstyle can be a nuisance and today many wear a wig. Here a woman makes such a wig, using an old milk can as a mount. Loops of white beads are strung onto a strand of wool and then wound onto several strands, which are then attached to the crocheted woollen skull cap. Note the woman's facial scarification and hairstyle worn by some Zulu women as an alternative to the built-up, ochred head-dress (see page 38).

manifestation of psychic gifts. Pythagoras said: 'Women as a sex are more naturally akin to piety'.

The individual suffering from *ukuthwasa* has two courses open to her (in the following account I have used the feminine only on account of the prevalence of female *izangoma*). She may either accept the call of the spirits and be initiated as an *isangoma*, or she may wish to bar them and return to health. Very few people welcome the call of the spirits or wish to become an *isangoma*. The initiation is long, hard and expensive — and few desire a life as the servant of the brooding shades.

Barring the Shades

The barring of a shade involves recourse to both 'black' and 'white' medicines (see p. 71). Black is useful for the removal of a particularly stubborn shade. (A really determined shade, however, cannot be forced to leave.) The barring of a shade also involves a sacrifice, usually that of a goat. Barring can become expensive, for the shades do not leave one alone for long and their illness returns at intervals. For years now, a Zulu woman of my acquaintance has been plagued by *ukuthwasa* but remains unwilling to become an *isangoma* and is yet undecided in the face of the determination of these supernatural beings to make a servant of her. She has persistent symptoms (which medical examination suggests are caused by pressure on the brain), and such is the 'power' of this woman's shades that she cannot enter a church. Should she try — much against the will of her shades — they will cause her to sweat and have hysterics.

Acceptance of the Call

If a person accepts the call of the shades, she must either choose or be referred to an *isangoma* of standing. The call is almost always dramatic and the called one will go crying into the night. By morning, or (more usually) some days later, she finds herself at the home of her teacher. She may take a taxi not knowing her destination, and be driven by someone as much in the dark as herself. This is no problem, however, as the vehicle is steered by the shades to her final destination, which may be hundreds of kilometres from her home. Many novices walk off not knowing where they are going and arrive unannounced and unknowing at the home of their instructor-to-be, claiming that they have walked under several rivers.

The references to rivers and water appear to represent a 'psychic world', and the entrance into a river or under it, entry into this realm. This is reminiscent of the universal appearance of water as a representation of the psychic realm in dreams and philosophies.

A sign of *ukuthwasa* is prolific dreaming by the sufferer; the novice will dream of medicinal plants and set off in search of them. A novice who does not spend days and nights wandering, apparently aimlessly, in the mountains in search of medicines which have been revealed in visions and dreams, is not considered genuine.

The most important dream, or series of dreams, in the life of a novice is that of her visit to the river to obtain the white medicinal clay with which she smears herself during her training. To obtain this she must enter a river and descend to the bottom. There, lying on the white clay, she will see a snake. It must be approached, and persuaded to allow the novice to take her share of clay. The novice will also encounter, and be required to capture, another animal during her wanderings or in the dream state (there being no strict differentiation). The animal usually encountered and captured is a snake, but this snake has to be 'in the flesh' in order to convince the people of the novice's courage and of her faith in the shades, as well as of the reality of their intervention. Those who claim to have encountered and conquered the slightly less likely and now rare lions and leopards, are usually required to produce the snake as well.

Training of an Isangoma

The life of the novice is not easy. She is extremely vulnerable to the effects of any form of ritual impurity, including that which arises from sexual relations. Understandably, this makes husbands loath to allow their wives to undergo the training. This problem is often circumvented, however, by the sacrifice of a goat, or simply by a small payment to the *isangoma* instructor. A Mpondo neophyte is careful to use only running water that she has collected herself for her ablutions, and her fire must be lit with a match, for fear that the live coal she would otherwise use might have come from a fire at which a ritually impure person had warmed himself. A great deal of time is spent in taking various medicines, washing in them, and vomiting to clear the head so that the spirits can work in it.

The finer points of an *isangoma's* training vary as much as do the individual *izangoma*, but the fundamental aims of this training are twofold. First, the novice should be cured of the physical ailment which was the first sign of *ukuthwasa* (this may or may not be achieved, and some diviners remain ill for the rest of their days, but bear their afflictions in much the same way as St Paul bore his). Second, training allows the shades to brood in the novice and live in communion with her (a relationship hopefully manifested in her psychic abilities), while, at the same time, protecting her sanity. Uncontrolled brooding by the shades leads to insanity. In different, more familiar terms, uncontrolled contact with the numinous can result in its taking over the mind, resulting in psychosis. The mind must therefore be disciplined and trained to maintain contact with yet not be swamped by the numinous. Individuals who, in Western society, would have taken their problems to the psychiatrist, find themselves as *isangoma* novices. Laubscher has found that a large proportion of his mental patients in Transkei suffered from *ukuthwasa*. The bodily pains which are one of the diagnostic criteria for *ukuthwasa* are also neurotic symptoms. Further evidence that psychiatric disturbance often leads to training as an *isangoma* is the fact that many novices do not practise when they have qualified — presumably because they lack 'the sight', or the lively intellect necessary to convince their clients.

Though the whole process of the *ukuthwasa* sickness and training is not recognised in Western society as it is among the Africans, a similar pattern might occur. Edgar Cayce, famous American psychic, suffered loss of voice which was cured only when he went into a trance and prescribed healing methods. This was the first of many thousands of psychic diagnoses. Even the great Professor C.G. Jung as a boy suffered a debilitating neurosis and was conscious of another 'self' or personality. A growing school of thought in the psychiatric profession maintains that a person should grow through a psychosis rather than try to avoid or suppress it. The similarity of this debate between psychiatry's two schools of thought to the choice that faces a traditionalist suffering *ukuthwasa* need hardly be emphasised. *Izangoma* certainly claim that training as an *isangoma* will cure mental illness, where that is a symptom of the *ukuthwasa* condition. I have met apparently sane novices and *izangoma* who claim — as do their acquaintances — that when they first started training they were quite mad.

An important part of an *isangoma*'s training is learning to dance. This dancing is of a kind peculiar to novices, known as *ukuxentsha* — a strange, rhythmic shuffle in which the feet are stamped hard into the ground, ball first, heel following. Dancing is accompanied by clapping or beating on a rolled-up cowhide or, today, on a drum copied from the bass drum used by European bands. This performance is usually held inside a dimly lit hut, crowded with spectators and seething with dust and the sweat of the dancers. The novices dance with fierce, vacant energy, stopping at intervals to confess dreams. The ritual can best be described as an attempt to stamp themselves into an oblivion of rapport with their shades. The more verve and ecstatic abandon an *isangoma* exhibits in her dancing, the more the audience is impressed with the power of her spirits and the expressions on the faces of *izangoma* dancing are a study in grimaces of abstraction. An important part of the dance is the twitching and shaking of the surface muscles, particularly those in the shoulder regions. This is indicative of the brooding presence of

At a gathering of her kind, a Nguni priest-diviner dances herself into rapport with her ancestors before a clapping, chanting group of colleagues.

the shades, and a sign that the novice is ready to qualify.

Another indication of the brooding of the shades is the ability of the novice to 'know' medicines which she discovers during her wanderings in the hills. The *isangoma* differs from the herbalist in that the latter does not have any supernatural knowledge of the properties of medicines.

Traditionally and properly, it is the instructress who decides when her trainee is ready. Today, however, in some instances, the trainee makes up her own mind when she has had sufficient training and is ready to go out into the world. The criterion of readiness is that one's head be 'soft'. This does not equate with the flippant Western expression of 'softness' in the head, however. To say that a traditionalist's head is soft, is to say that her life is lived as an expression of the will of the shades, and that she has largely done away with her personal wishes and desires in order to live a life of service to her unseen masters.

The duration of training may be anything from three months to four years. In the past training took many years to complete and was followed by stiff tests of the prospective *isangoma*'s psychic ability (the locating of hidden articles) before she could qualify. At the other extreme I met a young man who trained novices for only three months. He certainly was a gifted psychic and told me a great deal about myself (before informing me that I should undergo training myself, and offering to be my mentor!).

During her training, one or more sacrifices are performed for the novice. She may dream of a particular animal which is then said to be selected by the shades. Her relatives will go to great lengths to obtain this creature in order to sacrifice it as an appeasement to the shades. A special sacrifice is performed to affirm the novice officially as a trainee or *thwasa*. Today this ceremony frequently takes place at the beginning of the training period, but traditionally it occurred only after some months of training. The animal killed is a goat. Two rings of skin are cut and one suspended from each shoulder and wound around the body so as to cross in front and at the back.

A novice priest-diviner chews medicinal bark from a stick. In her hair is a snuff-spoon: the taking of snuff is practised to 'clear the head' for the ancestor to appear. On her torso and arm she wears the skins of sacrifical goats. The forked sticks in the foreground are used like antennae to listen to the ancestors.

These are the essential marks of an *isangoma*; traditionally both rings should not be donned at once but at two different stages in the training.

The Isangoma's Graduation

The final 'coming out' or graduation ceremony of an *isangoma* is held at her home in order to reintroduce her and her retinue of ancestral spirits to the living and dead of the homestead. A full description of the graduation ceremony of a young Zulu male *isangoma* is included in Appendix 2.

Briefly, the ritual and ceremony on these occasions are directed at the establishment of the new *isangoma* and her panel of spirits as a recognised social reality in her home district and at the testing of her psychic powers. This last part of the proceedings is sometimes not included today but takes the form of a 'hot and cold' search for some hidden article.

Ritual focuses on dancing and the sacrifice of animals, including cattle, goats and fowls. The fowls have an interesting experience immediately before death; they are placed carefully on the head of the dancing graduating *isangoma*. Should they fall, this indicates the disapproval of the ancestors and the graduation must be deferred. However, despite being witness to this ritual on several occasions, I have yet to see this happen. The completely disoriented birds appear to concentrate all their will on maintaining their unusual perch in the noisy gloom of the hut. Quite often, a bird thus placed will celebrate its last defecation — an event welcomed with great enthusiasm as a good omen.

While the newly graduated *isangoma* and other diviners present on such occasions place utter reliance on their ancestral spirits, it is not too unusual to spot a crucifix among the beads and cloths and bladders of the ritual dress. My questions concerning the significance of this item on one occasion elicited the following reply: 'Yes, I believe in my ancestors', the *isangoma* assured me, 'of course I do. But you must admit the Church of Jesus is strong, so I am getting some of that as well.'

POSSESSION CULTS

Among the interior tribes to the north-east and in the central Transvaal, the Pedi and Lobedu for instance, a spirit possession cult similar to *ukuthwasa* has become more and more popular this century. During this time it has moved southward from Zambia and Zimbabwe to the territory of the Venda, northern Sotho and Tsonga. Like the *ukuthwasa* sickness, this cult involves the presence of a spirit (of the *Ndawu* class) and features ceremonies to integrate that spirit and allow it to express itself. The cult is favoured by women, possibly because (as with the *ukuthwasa* sickness) it allows the initiate an enhanced social standing. Unlike the graduate *thwasa* or priest-diviner, the person possessed by a spirit of this cult is not expected to divine, and neither is she, according to E.J. and J.D. Krige, of the nervous, psychologically disturbed type. Initiates are in fact quite normal people and carry on normal activities.

The initiation takes the form of a dance, which is supervised by a past initiate and may last for as long as two days with little rest. It reaches its climax when the initiate finally collapses from exhaustion, allowing the possessing spirit to speak through her. This spirit always speaks in a foreign tongue, which must be translated by a past initiate. After this experience, the initiate is always different — slightly superior — a fact which is emphasised to her relatives and friends by occasional trances, dances and utterances by her spirit and by the fact that she wears red and white, colours favoured by the *Ndawu* spirits.

HERBALISTS

Unlike the priest-diviner or *isangoma*, the herbalist (or most herbalists) pretends to no supernatural powers. He (most herbalists are men as theirs is a profession rather than a calling) learns his craft at his father's knee, or by buying formulae for powerful medicines from herbalists of repute.

Everyone uses medicines and a man may gradually accumulate medicines and a reputation for success which enable him to live by herbalism. Usually, however, training under a reputable herbalist is required. The pharmacopoeia of herbalists is quite spectacular. In my home town, Richmond in Natal, there are two dark little shops tucked away in between larger stores in the bustling Indian section of the village. From my youngest days I have been fascinated by the colourful and convoluted mass of powders, leaves, roots, bulbs and bones piled up in the windows. When I ventured carefully into the dark interior of either shop, I would be confronted by an even weirder collection, and then by the owner himself. What always amazed me was the discovery that this purveyor of crocodile's eyes and hippopotamus fat would be a quite ordinary-looking, middle-aged man, dressed in tatty European clothes. I subsequently learned that the drabness of these little shops was by no means a reflection of their economic success, for they had a thriving business whose clientele included diviners from all the surrounding districts. Nowadays, for the layperson or diviner who prefers to remain at home, there are mail-order herbalist companies, notably one, in Johannesburg — which gives the name to the building in which it is housed — Muti (Medicine) House! The large scale of the 'muti' business is causing concern in conservation circles, because many of the medicinal animals and plants, once common, are becoming increasingly rare.

The following extract, translated from Zulu, has been taken from a circular put out by a mail-order company from Durban, and shows the wide-ranging mixture of medicines for traditional and modern ailments.

Oh kind of people whom I love,

I have listed for you on this paper below, my medicines, medicines that have come out of the waters of the sea. I obtained them there after I had been taken by the Sea Dwellers with whom I stayed for a year and a half. I emerged with full knowledge, having been taught by these people. This may sound incredible, also because I am a female.

I have tried to select your special medicine which is apart from other people because mine is of the waters of the sea, although I know the other, outside medicines.

PAGE 95   The taking of snuff is essential to a priest-diviner's performance. It is a special blend used exclusively for clearing the head in order to receive the voices of the ancestors. Among the Zulu and affiliated tribes, long beaded hair denotes the priest-diviner, the white beads being a protection against evil. The many bladders and feathers from sacrificial animals constitute an advertisement and a boast but are, unfortunately, no guarantee of psychic powers. The cow's tail worn on her back is from the beast sacrificed at the coming-out or graduation ceremony which ended her training. The beaded knob on her forehead reveals this to be a married woman from southern Natal.

The line drawing shows a learner seated in the appropriate attitude of respect for her instructress.

PAGE 96   This priest-diviner is said to have 'died' while working in Johannesburg. She was brought back to her home in Natal apparently in a coma and there she received the 'call' to become a priest-diviner from her deceased paternal grandfather, who appeared to her in a dream.

Her wig is atypical, the red and white beads showing the influence of the *ndawu* possession cult imported into the northern Transvaal from Zimbabwe earlier this century and now passed on to her in the cultural melting-pot of the metropolis. In a Natal priest-diviner's dress, red may also symbolise the evil of the magical *mamtsotsi* bird, which is vanquished by the inevitable white — good — beads. The wildebeest tail switch is used in calling up the spirits of the ancestors, who direct the priest-diviner in all his or her treatments of the sick and troubled.

The line drawing of the priest-diviner's hut shows the sacred place of the ancestors, or *umsamo*. A low wall jutting out into the hut conceals her medicines and incense, and serves as a place to hang items of ritual dress.

If you wish to know a lot from me, your Mother — and my remedies, write privately that which you alone know. This is the road to use for your order . . . (address follows)

MEDICINE OF HOME CONTROLLING
For stoppage of evil spirits . . . R10

For catching evil spirits . . . R15

Sending back of disease-causing medicine so that your home is free from spells . . . R29

Of trapping any witchcraft from disturbing your home . . . R27

Of causing the quarrelsome person to be insane or his house to catch fire . . . R20

For court cases — to be found innocent all the time . . . R11

For removing poison in your body . . . R12

To protect against poison and guard yourself that it cannot enter your mouth . . . R11

For increasing the annual harvest in your field . . . R11

For increasing your stock . . . R11

MEDICINE FOR GOOD LUCK AND FINDING EMPLOYMENT
For finding work anywhere . . . R10

To make your white master love you as his own child and pay you well . . . R11

Induna (headman). To be an induna either at work or even a Big Chief's induna . . . R25

A spell. To cause a person to lose his job . . . R11

To relieve tiredness when engaged in very heavy work . . . R6

To improve your image and inspire respect in strange company . . . R12

For strength to load heavy freight or to work the machinery under-ground . . . R12

To open your brain at school and to pass school exams . . . R12

PAGE 97   Like their counterparts in the Zulu-speaking areas, the Southern Nguni priest-diviners wear much the same dress — predominantly white, as illustrated — with the male having a slightly shorter skirt. White beads guard against evil and those wound around the right wrist are ritually placed there after the dream that informs the person that he or she has been 'called' to become a priest-diviner.

At the end of the training period, a novice must enter the forest and the skin of the animal first encountered there must always be worn on the head and elsewhere. The 'sjambok' switch is traditionally of hippo hide and is used for driving away evil spirits. Smoking is a national habit and a smoker's bag is always tied to the person, as is the 'doctor's bag' of medicines.

PAGE 98   The Zulu 'teacher' or head priest-diviner is attended by her apprentices. Here her hair has been washed and is being combed and braided, later to be strung with white beads. At all times she wears the cross-over bands of goatskin from sacrificial animals, and her married woman's skirt. Her trainees are in the early stages of their training, as indicated by the whitened faces and bodies, the white (or red, in certain schools) being said to protect from evil and cold. Bladders on their heads and goatskin bracelets are from animals ritually sacrificed at various stages of initiation. Red medicine in the bottles worn on the necklaces, protects against the dreaded magical bird, the *mamtsotsi*, which can assume any convenient shape in order to perpetrate its evil unnoticed.

The Shangana are re-
nowned herbalists. This
young woman of the
northern Transvaal
wears many of her
medicines on her
person, in gourds and in
the form of wooden
beads and seeds.

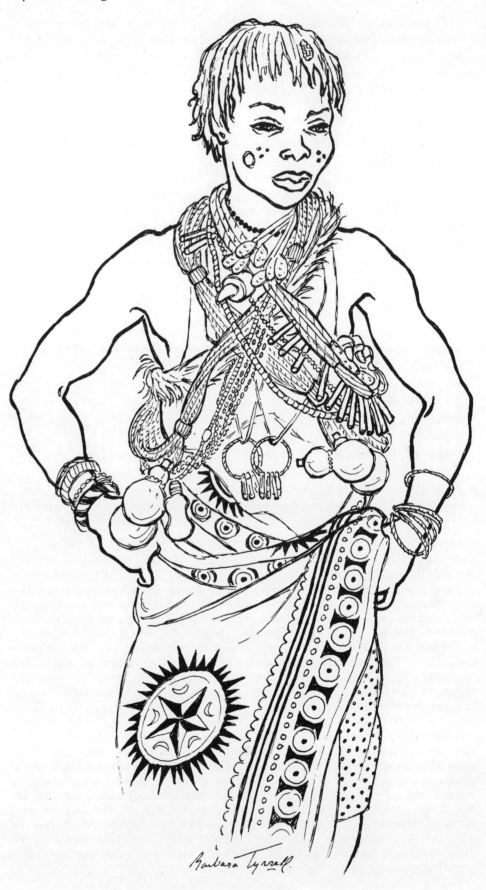

To make you a great boxer or when using sticks to confuse your opponent
  so that he is unable to see . . . R11

FOR YOUNG MEN TO BE DESIRED BY GIRLS
To discourage Don Juans so that in a crowd of suitors you will walk out
  with the girl . . . R12
Abandon mother. She will even desert her mother to follow you . . . R11
To stop your wife from promiscuous behaviour and become true to you
  alone . . . R10
To unite your wives if you are much married and promote harmony in the
  home . . . R12

ASSORTED MEDICINES
To bear children if you are no longer conceiving, open fertility . . . R13
To cure painful feet due to having walked over a spell . . . R6
and so on.

The closing footnote reads:

> My things I put plainly, those which I am allowed to write, and I say that
> health is in your own hands. If you do not order you will die, yet health is
> being held in your own hands. Do not forget, I am your Mother. I have
> sympathy and knowledge of my child. Do not be afraid. Tell me all that
> afflicts you. I shall put it right. There is NO MOTHER who forgets her
> child, also no child who forgets his mother. Mother's breast has no sores
> and is sucked perpetually. I send greetings to you my child. Please do not
> die. Order from your Mother.

Diviners and herbalists are among the most travelled and knowledgeable of
traditionalists. For example, I came across a herbalist, who hailed from
Johannesburg, in the market at Monkey Bay at the southern tip of Lake
Malawi. He had also practised in Durban and spoke five languages well:
English, Afrikaans, Zulu, his native South Sotho, and the local langauge,
Chichewe. Before him on the dusty ground of the market-place was spread a
variety of interesting-looking potions and herbs. Seeing my interest, he
quickly summed me up and was not long in selling me the dry, brown sprig
of a tiny plant which, when placed in water, has the seemingly magical
property of swelling to look green and healthy within a few short hours.

The further away a priest-diviner journeys from home, the greater his or
her powers and influence, both when travelling and when home again.
Around Richmond (and in other parts of the Republic) the Shangana/Tsonga
diviners are surrounded by a dark aura of power and awesomeness. Any
farmer in Natal wishing to protect a crop against pilfering does well to
employ the services of such a fearful personage. The priest-diviner or
herbalist who returns home after a long journey to collect medicine (Ashton
mentions a South Sotho herbalist who undertook a 500 kilometre round-trip
on foot to the sea and back) will be rewarded for his trouble by the many
customers who come for the exotic and therefore powerful substances.

Herbalism is an imaginative and progressive profession and herbalists
have not been left behind by the miracles of modern medicine. One man I
know who has kept his finger on the pulse of current methods in a most
admirable way is involved in follow-up treatment: any person who has

visited a local doctor for an infection is advised to visit this man for 'after care' treatment to ensure the effectiveness of the white man's medicines! I'm told he is a very talented practitioner with a high success rate and a healthy wallet. His one wish is to acquire some hypodermic syringes in order to do the whole job himself!

PERSPECTIVE

In Western society the equivalent of the priest-diviner's role is shared by many different professions, including those of the medical doctor (healers of the body), psychologists and psychiatrists (healers of the mind), and even the clergy, as the apparent custodians of man's spiritual self.

Before the Westerner considers the reality which the healers of another culture claim to represent, he should acknowledge the tentative nature of his own healers' theories, and the arbitrariness of the materialism on which medical science is based. The reality that priest-diviners represent or deal with on behalf of their culture is very different in kind. I do not suggest that either the reality or the methods of these traditional healers are perfect or better than those of the West — far from it. What I wish to emphasise is that because the African's traditional healing art has evolved to tend to a culture quite different from that of Western man, this does not mean that it is laughable or contemptible or even less successful (at least in treating psychological problems) than that which has evolved in the West.

And if it is certain that the traditionalist benefits from the hard-won expertise of modern medical science, it is just as certain that the Westerner can benefit by clothing some of the time-gleaned wisdom of Africa in his own symbolism and using it in the healing of his sick.

A switch is an essential part of the Nguni priest-diviner's equipment. Ideally, the switch should be made from the tail of a gnu, but that of a white cow may be used, provided that it is specially treated in the *umsamo* of the priest-diviner's hut.

BIRTH AND INFANCY

CHILDREN, who perpetuate the group, are of fundamental importance to the traditionalist. Children are an economic asset and will carry the memory of and give reality to their parents as ancestors.

CONCEPTION AND PREGNANCY

Theories of conception are fairly uniform. The Nguni people believe that during pregnancy the menstrual blood brought by the ancestors of the woman's lineage is used to build up the child, who is shaped by the man's ancestors in association with his semen. One of the reasons given for the strict exogamy practised by the Nguni is that, if two people with ancestors of the same clan were to have intercourse, the ancestors of the clan, on meeting their fellows, would fight instead of cooperating in the creation of a child.

Most Sotho see the blood in the same role. They say that the womb moulds the child, the semen supplies the vital energy, and the sex of the child depends on the relative strengths of the male and female contributions. The Lobedu, though aware of the concept held by other tribes that continued intercourse is necessary to provide enough male semen to mould or vitalise the foetus, realise that conception can take place after a single union. On the other hand, Professor I. Schapera noted in 1940 that some Tswana were so convinced that continuous intercourse was necessary before conception that many amorous young unmarrieds thought it necessary to abstain only every third night in order to fool nature.[1]

In Zululand the early months of pregnancy are characterised by many dreams which may tell the mother the sex of her child. A green and black snake or a buffalo heralds the birth of a boy, while a girl is announced by a dream of a puff-adder or the crossing of a full river. A pregnant woman has the means at her disposal to alter the sex of a child by taking a medicine made from the forked roots of the lily *Gloriosa virescens*; should she use a root resembling the male genitalia, her child will be a bouncing boy, while a girl will result if she uses a root formed like the female genitalia. The Swazi doctor will give man and wife each a different medicine to drink to assist the ancestors in the production of a child of the desired sex. While a Zulu mother-to-be is happy to dream of a flooded river if she wants a daughter, a pregnant wife of the Fakudze clan in Swaziland avoids crossing a full river lest she have a miscarriage. A Sotho woman can miscarry if she eats meat that has crossed a river — it is said to kill her foetus and in addition cause her intestines to rot.

Food taboos for the pregnant woman are many and varied. For instance, a Bomvana mother-to-be will not eat the flesh of a beast which has aborted or died while giving birth. In Swaziland, the wife of a Dlamini man, whose clan may not eat sheep, also practises the avoidance out of respect for the unborn Dlamini within her womb. A Zulu girl, even before she becomes pregnant, will avoid guineafowl, as they will cause her child to have a head like a bird — long and flat! Hot food is avoided by expectant mothers in some tribes for fear it will scald the unborn child. A Zulu woman may believe that standing while eating will cause her child to stand while being born and emerge feet first. The Venda woman may not eat any vegetables while pregnant, and some Bomvana clans also place a taboo on a whole range of vegetables.

The world is full of additional dangers for the mother and her unborn child. Among these, lurking witchcraft and evil must be countered. Paths especially are said to abound with magical impressions left by animals and witches. One of the effects of these, according to the Zulu, is to cause the sinking of the fontanel. This can be avoided if the mother keeps with her the *umkhondo* plant when journeying far from home. In Lesotho a woman is expected to stay at home as much as possible in order to avoid the influences she will almost certainly encounter on the paths she takes. A pregnant Pedi woman will not cut her hair (where breath is said to be concentrated) in order to conserve all her 'breath' or life-force for the sustenance and protection of her child.

As the carrier of a perpetuator of the tribe — an unknown quantity, destined perhaps to be a great person in the future — the pregnant woman becomes a highly valued member of society. She is fulfilling what is considered to be her most important function. A pregnant Venda woman must be saluted by all male visitors to her hut and by the chief himself. In most tribes, depending on the availability of a substitute worker, the mother-to-be works until the sixth or seventh month of her pregnancy. She is treated with concern and, within reason, her husband will try to provide for her wishes. When a Bomvana woman becomes pregnant, she gathers for herself a supply of wood for use in the period when she will be unable to work hard.

Many of the Sotho tribes, the Venda and some Nguni (excluding the Zulu) send a woman who is pregnant for the first time to her parents' home for the birth of her child. In Lesotho, the traditional family receive their pregnant daughter by carrying out a particular rite: her eyebrows and forehead are shaved, all ornaments are removed and a mixture of red ochre and fat is smeared on her head, face and torso. To cover herself, to keep her child warm and to protect herself and her baby, she should be given a sheepskin similarly smeared; a sheep should be slaughtered for her, its gall sprinkled on her and its bladder placed round her neck. (Gall is associated with ancestor rites.) Round her neck a small medicine-horn and a piece of metal, usually a key, are suspended.

Some of the Southern Nguni tribes — the Thembu, Mpondo and Bhaca included — set up a sympathetic relationship between the foetus and a plant, in which the growth of the latter reflects that of the former. This plant, usually a euphorbia, is planted before or at birth, and a good, fat-stemmed, healthy specimen is hoped for. Death of the plant presages or accompanies that of the foetus or child.

BIRTH

In a society where male and female roles are very distinct, the birth is exclusively the affair of the woman. As a female function, the birth of a child renders those articles associated with the birth ritually impure, in addition to making the mother and her offspring particularly vulnerable to magical attack. Thus the birth process must take place in absolute seclusion from the rest of society.

Officiating at the birth are two or three midwives — usually older women, past their menopause and consequently untainted by any ritual impurity which might harm the child. Many women, notably the Venda, are afraid of the rough treatment meted out by these midwives and prefer to go to a hospital, or even to face childbirth alone. Positions for giving birth vary with the different tribes, but this is mainly left to the individual. In Swaziland, if a woman has a difficult labour the men are called upon to assist, but they are not allowed to enter the hut. Instead, a rawhide rope is tied round each of the woman's ankles and passed out through the grass walls of the hut to the men, who pull on these according to shouted instructions from within. A Zulu woman having difficulties would have her husband enter the hut and sit down nude beside her in order to facilitate the birth.

Sympathetic magic may also be used in childbirth. In Thembuland the women in the vicinity of a birth may have to loosen their clothing in order to facilitate the process. Among the South Sotho the expectant mother is treated with a medicine concocted from the afterbirth of a mare (which gives birth easily). Should labour prove extremely difficult, a healer — priest-diviner or herbalist — may be called in to assist, and may be quite proficient. He may also use medicines, or even dice, to discover the cause of the trouble. The root cause may be believed to be infidelity and, until the unfortunate woman confesses in full, she cannot hope to deliver her child . . .

As soon as the baby is born, the umbilical cord is cut. In Transkei this is traditionally done by means of a split piece of thatching grass. The placenta of a Venda woman is buried inside the hut and boiling water is then poured on the spot to prevent the mother having afterbirth pains. In addition, the baby is given special medicine to drink and medicine is also applied to the area of the umbilical cord to dry it out. A Pedi newborn baby is immediately bathed in cool water to remove the ritual heat associated with birth. Similarly, a Zulu baby is bathed in a basin scooped in the *umsamo* (place of spirits) at the rear of the hut, where the placenta and umbilical cord are also buried. A certain clan in Zululand, who venerate the crab, give the afterbirth to these creatures which, it is claimed, know in advance of the coming feast and are ready for its arrival. All the procedures described above vary from tribe to tribe.

RITUALS AFTER CHILDBIRTH

Part of the full traditional ritual associated with childbirth among the South Sotho and Bomvana is the lighting of a ritual fire as soon as the child is born.

This fire is not allowed to go out as long as the period of confinement lasts. Much of the medicine administered to the newborn is intended to 'make it firm' as it is considered to be 'soft' (not fully formed) immediately after birth. A Zulu baby may be given medicines made from the leopard's whiskers, salamander skins and lion's claws, as well as (if it is obtainable) an important traditional ingredient — crushed meteorite.

Another Zulu treatment which has now died out was to combat the malady inherent in all people called *isiGwembu* — an itch causing undue sexuality and lecherousness. The procedure followed was to rotate the stem of a castor-oil plant in the baby's anus until it bled profusely, sometimes with fatal results.

A widespread practice to make babies strong and to protect them from the ever-present threats of black magic is 'smoking'. The child is passed several times through the smoke of a medicinal fire. While the child is passed through the smoke, its mother will sing a song; today the smoking may also be accompanied by the administration of various patent medicines obtained from the trading store.

First feeding
The tribes differ in the ritual first feeding of the infant (apart from the medicine). The South Sotho give the first food in a little ceremony called *lelimo*, meaning mouthful. The mouthful is not of mother's milk but constitutes an introduction to the ancient and traditional food of many Africans — millet porridge. This is given to the baby by someone whose personality the parents would like transmitted to their child. A Pedi infant, after limited suckling at its mother's breast, is put on a diet of porridge for three days before it is returned to the breast. A Zulu baby is kept away from its mother's breast for the first few days and instead is fed cow's milk, thereby relating it to the family cattle. The South Sotho believe the first of the mother's colostrum is bad for the child and some is squeezed from the breast before the child is allowed to drink. The introduction of a Thembu child to the mother's breast is a time of trial for her, as the child of a witch is known to refuse to drink. A witch's child can also be recognised in another way: in contrast to a normal child which, if thrown against a wall, hits hard and falls to the floor, the offspring of a witch lands softly and clings like a bat. One wonders how often it is deemed necessary to use this test!

Telling the world
The happy occasion is announced to the world in various ways. The South Sotho father is traditionally informed of a son's arrival by being tapped on the shoulder with a stick, while a daughter is announced by a sprinkling with water. The Pedi also adhere to these rites, although one of the first actions of the midwives after the birth is to run out of the happy hut and shout lustily — once for a boy and twice for a girl. The taboo against entering the birth hut is proclaimed among some Sotho groups by a stick or reed placed across the hut entrance or, among the South Sotho, stuck in the thatch. One reed indicates a girl, while two are for a boy. The significance of a reed is its connection with Ntsuanatsatsi, the bed of reeds from which, legend says, the South Sotho originated.

As biological birth is the introduction of a child to the world, so his or her début in society is marked by the emergence of the mother and child from their period of seclusion. The time separating those two events is often measured by the time it takes for the umbilical scab to dry and fall off. The ceremony marking the end of the seclusion is then performed. In general the period of confinement may be much shorter than it was in times past, and varies from three to ten days.

The Thembu ceremony of emergence of a mother and child is called *ukufukama*, meaning purification (from the state of uncleanliness associated with birth). Every woman in the homestead gives the mother two white beads, saying as they do so, *'Camagu'* and repeating the procedure with the child. After this, the mother is smeared with a mixture of fat and red ochre. A sheep or goat is then killed in order to ensure good health for the child in the future. The end of the seclusion of a Bomvana mother and child is also marked by a sacrifice called *qaba imbala*.

These ceremonies are only two examples of the introduction of a child to his father and society. The Zulu version is a joyous family affair, with perhaps a sacrifice to the ancestors if the child is a boy, and certainly plenty of beer to thank the midwives. The Venda seclusion is ended by a visit from the herbalist who gives the baby the protection it needs by rubbing medicine into incisions made all over its body.

Unusual Births and Infants

Twins are given a mixed reception. Traditionally, one of Zulu twins was killed, as also happened among the South Sotho and Pedi. The latter drowned the unlucky one in a pot of water. Venda and Lobedu twins were both killed. Among the Xhosa, Bomvana, Thembu and Mfengu, on the other hand, twins are welcomed as being lucky (as indeed they are when born to these tribes). A pair of euphorbia trees are planted near the home to grow along with the twins, but woe betide them should one tree die, because (it is said) the twin with whom it is identified will suffer a similar fate.

All groups ascribe supernatural powers to twins. Zulu twins are said to be song composers, weather prophets and good mediators; Lobedu twins are noted for their powerful 'shadow' which makes them dangerous, especially to sick people. Among tribes which abhor them, the very existence of twins threatens society as a whole and cannot be tolerated. The concealment of twins by parents is an offence against the people. Thembu, Xhosa and Mfengu twins share experiences throughout life, and when a boy who has a twin sister is at initiation school and being circumcised, his sister will be symbolically circumcised with him. Similarly, the boy must undergo part of the procedure of his twin sister's *intonjane* initiation rite.

Other children considered to be undesirable or dangerous to the community are those who are obviously deformed, those born feet first or with teeth, and those whose upper teeth emerge first. In such cases the child would be killed and most studies agree that these killings still occur. Dr H.O. Mönnig points out that in traditional communities few twins or people with congenital defects are encountered.[2]

Naming

The time of the emergence of a child from seclusion is also often the time when he receives his first name. A Venda infant is named by the father's sister or brother, and is often given the name of an ancestor, who is invoked thus: 'You have arisen now, we ask you to come and live in this child, and we call him by your name.' (Similar appeals are made to ancestors by some West African tribes, whose members ask the ancestors to arise in or as a child, even before it is born. At first sight, this seems to suggest reincarnation beliefs, but this would be an inaccurate interpretation.) The Zulu child is named during a small family gathering held a few weeks after birth. A Bomvana child, however, is given a name only when it begins to walk.

In addition to ancestral names, a baby may be called after a person associated with the birth. For instance, I visited the home of a Zulu *isangoma* at the time of the birth of his son and the child was given my Zulu birthname — Mandlankosi (strength of his father).

Just like European children, young Africans acquire suitable nicknames from their playmates. Giving names, to adults as well as to children, is in fact a popular African pastime. For instance, my birthname has been replaced by the more appropriate but less flattering *'Nhlahla umute ashlali isinyoni'* (the tall tree that the birds don't roost on), or *'izinyoni azimi'* for short.

The first name is only a beginning. When a man attends initiation school he will receive another, most often that of his age-regiment. Among many tribes (the Zulu and Swazi for instance) this is the proper form of address for him thereafter, though his friends may still call him by his birth or childhood name.

Children are often given unattractive names. This is to confuse any malevolent force, spirit or witch into thinking that the child is not highly valued, with the result that it will be spared a possibly evil fate. This is especially important if a child has arrived after a long period of barrenness; it may be called anything from 'Vile thing' to 'Dog's tail' or 'Human excrement'! Little notice is taken of this unfortunate child — also a ruse designed to foil malignant influences. Where a son and heir has arrived after several daughters, he will often be given a girl's name, and even treated and dressed like a girl in order to confuse a contrary force.

Since the advent of Europeans, a whole range of names and random words has become available and been put into use. An additional incentive for adopting European names has been the use of derogatory terms such as Sammy and Sixpence by employers unwilling or unable to pronounce the African name.

Rites Associated with Childhood

A Venda infant, after its emergence from seclusion up to the time it cuts its first tooth, must be held upside down and shown the moon every month in order to prevent sickness. The moon features prominently in traditional thought and this ceremony, together with similar ones performed by the Tsonga, Swazi and Pedi, seems to be the remnant of a strong moon cult among the ancestral Bantu-speakers. A Bhaca child who is sickly or otherwise not developing properly must have vertical incisions made in its cheeks during a ceremony conducted at full moon, and the gall of a sacrificial goat must be rubbed into the wounds. This custom, which harks back to ancestral practices, is also found among some Xesibe, Mfengu, and various Natal clans. It appears to have been picked up by early Nguni who entered Natal

Ear-piercing of young children is common in Nguni territory, where it is said to open the ears to understanding. The ears of this Mpondo boy were recently pierced and the hole is kept open with a piece of reed.

via Mozambique and brought it with them to Natal, and later to Transkei and the Ciskei.

Xhosa and Thembu children who are difficult to toilet train have the top phalanx of the fourth finger on the left hand amputated — a custom apparently learned from the Khoikhoi (Hottentot). The male descendants of an individual who has had this operation performed usually undergo similar treatment. Laubscher believes that this sacrifice of a part of a finger is performed in the hope of a reciprocal grant of health for the body as a whole. Ojibwa Indians of North America may perform a similar amputation to promote the appearance in dreams of a personal mentor.

THE INFANT AND SOCIETY

The early years of a child's life are characterised by the use of many medicines. The body is given no credit for being able to grow of itself, and it is regarded as vital that the infant be propped up with medicine at every step. There is a traditional Tsonga saying: 'A child grows by medicine'. Despite this, the first few years of an African child's life are warm and happy. Much of his time during his first year is spent tied to his mother's back — today, with a cloth or blanket, but in the past with the skin of an animal slaughtered ritually at the time of his emergence from seclusion. Where mother goes, baby goes — down to the waterhole, to the trading store, to a beer-drink, to a dance (in which mother participates with baby bouncing and jerking violently, yet sleeping peacefully). A mother with a child on her back is a familiar sight, even in the cities. The child can also be carried on the back of an older sister, female relative or friend.

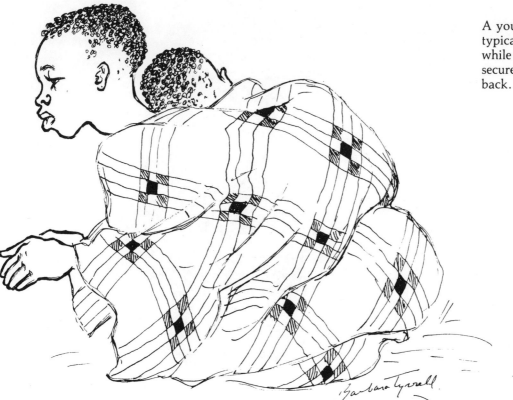

A young Zulu girl in typical resting posture, while an infant sleeps securely fastened to her back.

One word sums up the attitude towards the infant and toddler: indulgence. The little one is never sharply rebuked and need not look too far to find a comforting elder or his mother's breast. At first the child is not expected to control its natural functions, but with age it must leave the hut and kraal when nature calls.

The feeding of newborn babies varies from tribe to tribe. In Lesotho, the food given for the first six months is mainly mother's milk, while among other tribes (the Zulu and Lobedu for instance) this is supplemented by porridge, which the child is literally force-fed: one hand is cupped over its mouth to form a funnel; this is then filled with porridge which is pushed down by the other hand. Only when the little belly is round and hard like a football is the baby considered fed. Right through life this individual will associate satiation with that feeling of utter fullness which was forced on him in his babyhood. The Kriges reported that children have been choked to death by this forced feeding. Such a death is of course blamed not on a careless nurse or mother but on the machinations of a witch.

The child is generally weaned at about two years of age but this can vary from one to three years. A boy of four or even five years old may rush up to his mother for a drink before running off to do his day's work with the herds, and return for more when his job is done. Weaning a child is achieved by rebukes from his elders and through the ridicule of his peers, not to mention bitter aloes or some other bitter herb which can be smeared on the nipple for the child who does not wish to learn. In most cases, by the time of weaning, the physical dependence on mother's milk is low and the breast-feeding has primarily a psychological significance, minimising the trauma of leaving the security of an indulgent mother to rely more on the wider society of the homestead or group of homesteads.

A Ntwana girl's doll, dressed as a young girl with the short, red-ochred hair, grass necklets and apron with small buttons, a favourite form of adornment.

GROWING UP

THE GROUP

AS we have seen, early childhood is a happy time with little discipline. With weaning — perhaps in the third year — the child finds itself comparatively free and is encouraged to join the larger group of children of a similar age in the village or cluster of homesteads. He discovers the world, in which the term for mother is also used for his father's other wives, and in which their children are his brothers and sisters as much as are his biological brothers and sisters. In this group he must learn to mingle happily. Parental control is remarkably lax, and he quickly learns to subdue his personality and to merge with that of the peer group.

Though a parent may protect him from gross injustices, seldom will any action be taken that may stimulate a child's pride in his individuality. This goes for punishment as well. Children work out their young lives as a group, and punishment is meted out in an offhand and uncomplicated manner, discouraging any sense of self-importance. The selflessness and community spirit of these youngsters is quite remarkable, particularly in the more remote areas where the traditional way of life is followed; only near main roads does one see snatching and fighting for hand-outs from tourists and travellers.

Not long ago, while walking in the mountains of Lesotho between Mokhotlong and the Orange River, I stopped for my lunchtime snack, watched by a shy group of children. I took a bar of chocolate and carefully divided it, placing equal portions into ten pairs of hands. Finding myself with a sizeable piece left over, however, I held it up, expecting to be stormed by eager takers for whom sweets are a rare delicacy. To my surprise, after a short consultation among themselves, the tiniest of all was pushed forward for his large piece. He had apparently missed out in the first round because he was shy and afraid.

LEARNING

Traditionally, apart from the various initiation schools (see p. 119) the child received no formal education to mould him for his role in society. Today the ancient pattern has changed, with many children attending a Western-type school. Traditional education for the individual constitutes a gradual absorption into society and the acquisition of certain skills and behaviour patterns.

The society in which the traditional child finds himself is very different from that which confronts his Western counterpart. Western capitalist society, with its emphasis on large-scale, dynamic growth, sophisticated technology and diversity, benefits by stimulation of the individuality and ambition of its members. As a result, people in Western societies tend to exert themselves to the maximum in order to fulfil personal ambitions, thereby also promoting the good of their society as a whole.

The traditional society of Bantu-speaking Southern Africa, on the other hand, revolves around very much smaller and more isolated social and economic units, and its members are therefore much more directly concerned with the fundamental occupations of food-gathering and production. This means that, economically speaking, the individual is of the greatest value to his group, not as a unique combination of interests and talents, but rather as a human being capable of working alongside his fellows and providing for the group. The identity of the traditional African is absorbed into that of the group to which he belongs, and the primary emphasis in bringing up the African child is to impress upon him that his significance, his safety and his prestige rest with the group. Instead of being encouraged to express himself and use his individual abilities and talents to achieve and acquire for himself, he is made to conform. A precocious child is liked by neither his parents nor his peers. The greatest ambition of each child must be the eventual assumption of the stereotyped duties of adulthood.

WORK

Learning to fulfil his role as a worker starts early for the child. As an accepted, useful member of society the child soon takes a pride in performing the traditional work of his or her people and discovers a real sense of meaning and belonging. This fosters a desire to be integrated further and, later, to perform willingly the tasks required of an adult.

Little boys aged four or five years become herds, starting with the sheep and goats. Today, unlike times past when cattle had to be defended against predators and raiding parties, the tiniest boy can also tend cattle. The herds have hours upon sunny hours in which to observe and absorb nature and they acquire a knowledge of plants, animals, birds and weather which is quite remarkable. One of the games played by children in Lobedu country is to test one another's knowledge of trees, birds or animals. The Kriges cite a Lobedu boy aged 15 who could name 200 different plants growing around his home.

In sharp contrast to her brother, who is out in the country with a crowd of boys exploring his manliness and independence in a world away from parental supervision, the little girl is always under the wing of the adult women of the home and is drawn more and more into what is often called the drudgery of the traditional woman's life.

At four or five years of age the girl is helping her mother, accompanying her to the waterhole to fill a tin or gourd and carry it back to the home, where she receives generous praise. As she grows up, she becomes a very real asset to her home. The pots that she carries increase in size, and the journeys to the waterhole become more numerous. She fetches wood too, and I have photographed a small Natal Nguni girl carrying a four-metre pole on her

A typical clay ox made by young black children. The large horns and hump survive as a memory of the traditional sanga cattle, which have in reality been absent for a long time owing to interbreeding with European imports.

A young Venda girl and infant. In the traditional setting, the preparation of food and care of babies are two of the responsibilities of even very young girls.

head — more than three times as long as herself!

Baby care is also learned by the girls at an early age. Tiny seven- and eight-year olds (and often even younger girls) can be seen carrying infants on their backs. A mother going off to hoe in the fields need not look far for a baby-sitter if she does not want to take her baby along. Heavy tasks, such as hoeing in the fields, begin when the girls are about 12 years old and physically strong enough to keep pace with their elders. This work certainly requires strength — I have hoed alongside these people in the fields and marvelled at their stamina and energy when I was more than ready to quit.

GAMES

Leisure hours are generally spent in play. The games traditional children play under the slow-moving African sun are many and natural to any children of similar age. Youngsters in modern-day kwaZulu and Lesotho enjoyed skipping with plaited grass ropes long before Europeans had arrived in Southern Africa. All over Southern Africa children play 'touch' and, particularly in Venda, they can be seen playing 'hide and seek'. A game of deft tossing and catching of stones similar to the 'jacks' played by European children is also popular.

A common sight today is a little boy running along pushing a skilfully constructed wire motorcar, giving vent all the while to the relevant engine noises.

The games of girls are not nearly as complex as those of the boys and, as can be expected, include various domestic activities. They may cook little pots of maize porridge over diminutive fires or perhaps, in areas where the marula palm grows, brew marula wine (for which the small boys are sure to come and beg).

While the boys are out learning to be the dynamic leaders of the group, the girls — the resilient heart of traditional society — are at home perpetuating the ordered, solid, unchanging, peasant way of life.

The gradual socialisation of the child is accompanied by various rites and ceremonies, which mark both the individual's biological growth and his mental and emotional maturation and consequent acceptance by society.

African children provide most of their own toys. Very popular are ingenious wire motorcars, very elaborately constucted and featuring such refinements as steering and suspension.

MUSIC AND DANCING

Music is fundamental to African culture. Perhaps one of the reasons for the remarkable sense of rhythm possessed by virtually every African is his early introduction to singing, music-making, and dancing. The tiniest children may be seen doing a jig to the handclaps and singing of their companions. Women will clap encouragingly for a dancing toddler, and at an adult dance there will often be a diminutive person on the fringes emulating his elders.

As time wears on, these talents blossom within the small African until they become a part of his very person, to be released and expressed as easily as turning on a tap. In Venda young girls spend hours beating the big *domba* drums, absorbing their rhythms and intricacies until they become a part of themselves. Dancing, often performed in groups, is another important facet of society.

Dr D.H. Reader, a well-known ethnographer, sums up the significance of dancing:

> It is contended that anyone who has witnessed these activities among the Zulu would appreciate their most salient and immediate quality, the fact that together they assert in the most forceful way possible the presence of a homogenous social group, imbued with the social value of its existence as a single-minded and independent organisation.[1]

PAGE 115　In a traditional community the woman not only bears many children but fetches and carries water, firewood and provisions, attends to all domestic duties, and hoes in the fields. Shopping often takes her many miles across the country via winding, narrow paths to return home laden sometimes beyond belief. A strong back and splendid carriage are her reward for this chore, which she commenced in early childhood.

This Bhaca woman's dress reveals that she lives with her man and bears his children, but is not yet wed. Only when the full quota of bride-price cattle has been passed on to her father by her betrothed, may she cover her hair with red ochre. If a marriage is long delayed and the older generation of men have all died, the bride-price will go to the eldest in the line of descent.

Barbara Tyrrell

HUNTING

Games are frequently educational. No rodent or bird is safe from the scheming squads of little boys, who catch or kill them, using an armoury of spears, bows, arrows, knobkerries, catapults, traps and bird lime. The boys become adept in all these hunting skills. Many a youngster can knock a bird out of the air with his knobkerrie, to roast it over a small fire and feast together with his companions. Stayt observed Venda children shooting birds with ingenious air pistols constructed from hollow twigs and using as ammunition pellets cut from maize stalks.[2]

A popular game in many areas is to throw assegais at a large bulb or tuber which is rolled between two rows of boys.

WAR GAMES

Games also serve to prepare a boy for warfare. Indeed, when a youngster first joins the herds, he finds himself at the bottom of a highly stratified society where grading is based on prowess in stick-fighting. With age and increasing ability, he gradually moves towards the top of his group, and may even become the leader. In Lesotho the head of such a group of boys makes them hunt and steal, bringing to him the fruits of their labours and escapades. He then distributes the spoil with great largesse.

Courage and skill among boys have distinct social advantages too, because the toughest of the group monopolises the best grazing for his father's animals and the latter also have first place at the waterhole. Apart from the prestige gained from achievements within the hierarchies, battle among themselves teaches the boys the virtues and skills of self-defence, and prepares them for adult life in the wider society which is based on a strict hierarchy determined by birth under the chief. Pedi youths use whippy sticks for their fights, but the Nguni, notably the Southern Nguni, use a knobkerrie for attack, and a stave, held in the left hand, for defence. Even a teenager learns a remarkable stoic endurance of heavy blows to the head.

Later, when different gangs fight one another to gain ascendancy in a district, the virtue of loyalty to the group is learned. With increasing strength and age, such battles become more serious and even hazardous to life and limb. In the past these were excellent training for warriors. However, the young person is not allowed to slip into the adult role unannounced: rites of passage are a central feature of the African's life, and those marking his recognition as an adult are perhaps the most important.

PAGE 116   Stick fighting, especially in Transkei, is an essential part of growing up. Sticks are not only treasures, they are individuals. When a youth goes away to work, any stick that does not accompany him is stowed away in a safe place to await his return.

This older man is likewise armed with a stick, and in this instance keeps a safe hold on it with his foot while he smokes the traditional, long Xhosa pipe. The smoker's bag is an essential item and in some Transkei areas the carrying of a whole series of heavily beaded bags is high fashion. The panel necklace, known as 'keeper of the heart', was given to him by his wife and explicitly reveals what sort of woman she is: this wife is joyous and given to much dancing. Other 'keeper' necklets tell of lazy women, gossiping women, hard-working women, as well as the number of children borne.

INITIATION

MEN

THE human experience can be divided into several distinct phases: birth, infancy, childhood, adolescence, early adulthood, the married state, parenthood, old age, and death. It is essential to the psychological well-being of the individual and his successful participation in society that he be fully aware of his status and role. To a large extent, this awareness can be promoted by appropriate rites of passage, which emphasise the irreversible nature of the changes associated with maturation.

The transition from youth to mature and responsible adulthood is one of the most important steps, as reflected by the initiation rites for both men and women. It has been said that the African goes through three births: biological birth; birth as an adult; and birth into the spirit realm through the transition of death.

In the strongly patrilineal tribal society, the birth of a man into the ranks of the mentors of the culture is of the greatest importance. The rites of passage into adulthood are basically divided into two parts: puberty rites — primarily a local or family affair acknowledging the biological maturity of the individual; and later, and more important, initiation (circumcision) schools, which operate with a group of initiates and are a tribal or district institution rather than a private ritual.

Puberty Rites
These rites for boys among the Venda, Lobedu, Zulu, some Swazi clans, and clans in Natal, mark the first nocturnal emission. As with other ceremonies, these observances have been greatly abbreviated over the years and are performed in varying degrees of completeness by the clans and lineages in the different areas.

Professor Eileen Krige has described the traditional (and abbreviated) form among the Zulu.[1] The boy awakens and leaves the homestead early in the morning following the discharge, taking the cattle and informing no one. When the homestead stirs, his and the animals' absence tells the story and the boys who have reached puberty, but have not been included in an age-regiment, set off to look for him.

Meanwhile, the boy has taken the cattle as far as possible and is hiding beside a secluded stream, in which he bathed before sunrise. When eventually they are found, he and the cattle are driven back to the homestead. At this stage the theme of birth is noteworthy, as it is in the circumcision: until the appropriate rites have secured his birth as a human being, the boy is a beast and is symbolically treated as one by being driven home with the cattle.

On his return the boy's father treats him with medicines if the latter is in a ritually pure state at the time; otherwise the function is performed by a substitute. Part of this procedure involves licking from his fingers a concoction which is boiling in a potsherd over a ritual fire in the cattle kraal, a gathering-place of the ancestors. After this he is secluded in a ritually 'clean' hut, usually that used by the boys, and may go out to relieve himself only if he is surrounded by a group of boys. In the hut he sits in the *umsamo* or place of the ancestors to introduce him in his new status to the lineage dead — a great honour. With the commencement of his first period of seclusion, beer is brewed and when it is ready, three to four days later, all the neighbours arrive for a party, which may last one or two days. There is also a sacrifice of a beast or beasts.

This phase ends when the boy's companions take him to the river for a second immersion. He is then given a new name which will be his for the rest of his life. On arrival back at the homestead he is dressed in new clothes in the seclusion hut, from which he and his fellows emerge dancing in single file. He gradually makes his way to the front of the group and eventually leads the procession. He has become a full member of the family and an adult. In recognition of this fact he is called *umakoti*, or bride, for, like a bride he is regarded as a new acquisition of the group. Relatives and friends shower him with gifts and good wishes to show their pleasure at his 'coming of age'. Such a procedure is obviously not possible if a family possesses no cattle or lives in a built-up area, situations common to many people. My information from the Natal Midlands agrees with Professor Krige's description: after his first nocturnal emission, the boy washes himself in the stream before dawn and returns home where he is secluded for the day; after medication the concluding feast is held on the evening of the same day.

The ceremony for Venda boys, which is held when a group of some six youths have reached puberty, is more rugged. Their mentors are the previous group to go through the procedure, the *midabe*, and human nature being what it is, the initiates can expect no mercy. After a dance every night for two or three days, they must 'beg, steal or borrow' livestock and firewood which the *midabe* will enjoy while watching their charges shivering in the river for three or four hours in the early morning. This torment is repeated every day for six days, punctuated by various punishments for real or imagined misdemeanours. The reward is the honour of new status and, presumably, the chance to torment the next group of boys!

Initiation Schools and Circumcision
Prior to the nineteenth century, adolescent males of virtually all Southern Africa's tribes had to spend time in an initiation lodge, where they would be circumcised and taught the requirements for the state of manhood: knowledge of the tribe, hardiness, tolerance, humility.

Immediately before the advent of Shaka, however, the initiation and circumcision lodge had begun to fall into disuse among the clans now forming the Zulu nation. During the *Difaqane* the same thing occurred among other Nguni clans of Natal, such as the Bhaca, Xesibe and Nhlangwini. Faku banned the custom of circumcision among his Mpondo people on pain of a heavy fine. However, one Mpondo clan, the Nqanda, still practise the custom; they were away in the south during the *Difaqane*, when the law was announced, and they returned much later to their home — and retained the custom. The practice was forbidden in Swaziland during the reign of Mswazi after a large number of men died in the veld during the Sekhukhune war, supposedly having caught cold through their genitals.

Apart from those mentioned above, all other Southern Nguni peoples — the Xhosa, Thembu, Mfengu, Bomvana, and Hlubi — still practise circumcision. Among the highveld tribes the situation is less clear but Krige has listed the South Sotho, Pedi, Masemola, Lemba, Ndebele, the Matlala of the north-western Transvaal, Mmamabola of Woodbush, Transvaal Shangana-Tsonga, Venda, Lobedu, Hananwa, Letswalo and Khaha, a list to which the Ntwana can be added.

The situation is not static, however, and in 1952 Ashton observed that in Lesotho, where initiation had been probably the 'most important ceremonial institution', it was rapidly vanishing. However, this tendency was to some extent counteracted by a new category of initiates submitting to the rites for nationalistic reasons.[2]

Similarly, circumcision at an initiation lodge has increased among the Venda, for whom it is not an indigenous institution but adopted from the Sotho peoples to the south. One of the contributing factors, oddly enough, was the construction of a railway line. In the early part of this century Pietersburg in the northern Transvaal was the railhead and in order to reach Johannesburg, the Venda mineworker had to travel past the Sotho tribes of the plains. These people held circumcision lodges whose inmates were so strongly convinced of their cause that they would kidnap and forcibly circumcise any man who had the gross effrontery to retain that offending part of his person!

In this century the young Bhaca and Mpondo men, especially those who attend Lovedale or some other college, have found it is worth their while to be circumcised in order to avoid the rejection and derision of girls from tribes which still practise these customs.

Lister Hunter, a well-known student of Xhosa custom, relates a story emphasising the importance of circumcision. Some years ago, just before Transkei gained independence, a large beer house in Umtata was forced to close when staff and clients marched out *en masse* upon discovering that the two young (black) book-keepers recently hired were still 'boys' — that is, uncircumcised. Normality and the shocked men returned only with the dismissal of both the offending employees.

The initiation schools of the Sotho tribes tend to be much larger than those of the Southern Nguni. Sotho schools are generally organised by a chief or subchief, and accept youths (sixty or more) from a fairly large area. Southern Nguni schools, on the other hand, can comprise as few as three or four initiates, but many young men of circumcision age try to be part of the same school attended by the son of a chief, and these schools can be large. Nowadays, with many men away working in towns and unable to take time off together for extended periods, Southern Nguni schools may be held with only a single initiate. Some years ago, I visited such a solitary Thembu initiate in his tiny hut, and wondered whether the loving attention from the homestead not far along the path and the magnificent green valley opening before his lonely home made up for the companionship and adventure that would have been his lot as an initiate in times past.

A notable feature of some circumcision lodges, especially those on the highveld, is that they cut across tribal boundaries, with Venda, Tsonga and members of various Sotho tribes attending the same school.

The underlying symbolism of initiation schools is of the rebirth of a whole group who, particularly on the highveld, become part of a brotherhood. With the abandonment of initiation schools in the last century, the Zulu and Swazi created brotherhoods of men — the 'age-regiments', groups of young men who were called up for service in the army at about the same time and shared similar bonds. It was the introduction of these groups, establishing age loyalties at the expense of loyalty to the clan, that was a stroke of genius ensuring the security and stability of the Zulu and Swazi nations.

The boy looking forward to initiation should have the correct approach — he must regard himself as being drawn into a new phase of life, he must be filled with anticipation, and should cast no backward glances. The Southern Nguni boy is expected to elect to join initiation school, although his father may hint to him that the time is ripe — 'Initiation might be an idea this year'. The youth of Lesotho is lured into the school with such stories as 'You will see your chief flying through the sky', or 'You will learn to bore through a mountain'. Should these inducements fail, he may be told that uninitiated people have a vile smell to initiates and will be treated accordingly. In extreme cases he may even be forced into a school. In areas or among tribes (such as the Lobedu and Pedi) where circumcision schools are held infrequently and serve a large area, the youth has no choice other than to join when a school is held.

The boys who enter a school usually know one another. They either come from the same district or, in the case of some Sotho tribes, have contributed towards the construction of their lodge or learned the songs of initiation for about a month before school began. Pedi boys entering initiation schools are already organised into definite groups under leaders and are required to work together before the school begins.

Leave-taking

When the Southern Nguni or Sotho initiate leaves home it is an important occasion, for it is his final leave-taking as a youth. He returns as a man. Before the departure his father, if wealthy enough, holds a sacrifice for him. A Thembu father throws the *isipika* (flesh of the right shoulder, which twitches for some time after death due to the presence of the ancestors) of the sacrificial animal into the dung of the cattle kraal, a place of the ancestors. His son is required to show enough humility to retrieve it in order to eat it and receive the ancestors' blessing. In Lesotho prospective initiates may be given a feast by their maternal uncle and are then free to take part in the sacrifice of a black bull. This is an exciting occasion, with dancing and the ululations of women building up to the climax, when the bull is killed. Its right frong leg is ripped off, cut into sections, roasted and treated with medicines and with the saliva of the men present. These chunks of meat are then skewered on a spear point and 'fed' to the initiates. This 'feeding', done by a famous warrior, entails thrusting the speared meat erratically before each initiate, who must attempt to bite it while kneeling with his hands behind his back. A similar procedure is followed by the Thembu.

The Caretakers
Caretakers of the young initiates are usually men of standing in the community. In Transkei a boy will find himself under the care of the 'father' of the school, a good, important man whose son is also being initiated. Under the 'father' are the *kankata*, or guardians, whose job it is to discipline the boys.

In Lesotho, initiates are looked after by the *babineli* — one for each boy among the Tlôkwa clan, but only two or three per school among other clans. The master and deputy-master of a Pedi lodge are chosen by the chief's inner council, while the boys have the vindictive post-initiates of a previous school as guardians.

Initiation Hut
The hut to which the initiates retreat is usually cut off from society, situated on some lonely hillside or in a quiet thicket, preferably near a stream. The Thembu initiates collect the material for this hut and place it in the vicinity of the chosen site (which, until the hut is constructed, is a close secret). Here the men eventually build the framework, and the women do the thatching. Once the women's job is finished, the hut is ready for occupation. Huts of Sotho initiates are built later than those of other initiates to coincide with the time of the circumcision operation, which, in all tribes, takes place shortly after the beginning of initiation.

Circumcision
The status of the 'surgeon' varies from tribe to tribe. Care is taken in the choice of this individual, as he has ample opportunity for the practice of witchcraft. Among the Southern Nguni a strong, good and respectable man is chosen for the task and he regards it as an honour. The Pedi, however, consider it a menial undertaking. They engage the services of a doctor from another tribe, who is also unlikely to have personal scores to settle by means of witchcraft. If this man is good at his job and no signs of infection or witchcraft are evident, his services will be retained for subsequent ceremonies.

The order in which the youths are circumcised is similar in all tribes. First to be operated on is either a man of low rank (among the Southern Nguni) or a headman's son (among the Venda) who 'wipes' the witchcraft off the blade of the assegai or other instrument used for the operation. Second is the chief's son, or the most important initiate, followed by the others in descending order of rank. This strict adherence to rank, especially among the Pedi, emphasises another change from boyhood to manhood: a man's place in the hierarchy is no longer determined by his martial skill or force of character but by his birth. The Nguni initiate, in order to shed the past before the operation, is required to sit in a river and, while cleansing himself by splashing, confess all his misdemeanours. Laubscher reports that the men who listen to these sins are often shocked and amazed at what they hear.

For a Pedi youth the moment of truth arrives suddenly: he is led to a rock nearby and made to sit; suddenly someone slaps him on the back and, as he looks round, his loincloth is removed and he is circumcised in one deft operation. Afterwards he is taken to stand in the cold, wintry river, which deadens the pain. A South Sotho youth is similarly taken unawares, unless he courageously indicates that he wishes to be circumcised with dignity. In this case he is sat down and the operation is performed without haste. Should he flinch, he will not find himself discredited. This does not apply among the Southern Nguni: the initiate must sit down with legs spread on his sheepskin kaross near the lodge, either beside the river or simply in the open veld. The men of the area gather around to watch him and he is expected to remain calm and unflinching throughout the ordeal.

Immediately after the operation, the wound is dressed with medicinal leaves and washed regularly. For the month before healing is complete, the initiates in most tribes remain in the hut and have to observe various food taboos — notably a ban on the drinking of water, and on the eating of fresh or green mealies and green foods. Lobedu initiates have greens brought to them during their three-month confinement, but these must be discarded uneaten. A common taboo concerns sour milk, which must not be taken for three days after the operation — a very thirsty time indeed, considering the taboo on water. Bomvana initiates are allowed to mix water with earth, producing mud, which they may then consume to slake their thirst.

The initiate, especially according to the beliefs of the Southern Nguni, is highly vulnerable to magical attack via his amputated foreskin. Each youth must secretly dispose of this item himself, possibly in an antheap, where it will quickly be consumed. South Sotho collect, burn and bury the foreskins of all initiates, while the Pedi keep them to make medicines for use on subsequent groups of initiates.

Rebirth and Life of the Initiates
The circumcision operation is the highlight of the rites of the initiation school and marks the boy's birth into manhood. In being circumcised he has symbolically shed a part of himself and parted with the mother-image. He is no longer a complete and self-sufficient being, but now definitely requires membership in society and union with a woman to attain wholeness. Yet, paradoxically, he has shed his dependence on women and is a man born into a patriarchal society, where he is treated as a newborn infant. The entire process resembles that of birth, and most tribes, in recognition of this complete break with the old life, and also out of respect for the society that is about to receive them, have their newly circumcised initiates use different words for various persons and items. The words for mother, father, spoon, and plate, for instance, are changed during the period of seclusion.

The need for humility is instilled by harsh treatment. Among the Pedi the first ceremonial beating, received before circumcision, is followed regularly by others. In addition, initiates of all tribes are beaten for a whole range of real or imaginary misdemeanours. The Thembu youth who angered a particular man in his younger days will probably be thrashed by him during initiation. In Sotho and Venda schools the initiates are taught the laws, customs and traditions of the tribe. These, often phrased in highly stylised and archaic language, must be repeated over and over until the youths are word perfect. A beating is the penalty for poor recollection. Tribal secrets

Each Transkei initiation school has its own uniform and this must be worn by the initiate during his wanderings away from the lodge. All these items must be burnt with the lodge at the end of the school to symbolise the start of a new life as an adult.

are also taught, and these may include the ceremonial disclosure of carvings and other sacred figures, as among the Lobedu.

When the circumcision wounds begin to heal, a sacrifice called *umdaga* is performed by Thembu initiates. Each boy has to sacrifice a goat and eat the *isipika* (twitching flesh in the shoulder region) and the entire right shoulder. In Southern Nguni lodges, when the wounds have all but healed, a single beast is sacrificed. This marks the freedom of the youths to go out hunting, and also releases them from the taboos on drinking water, eating fresh food (maize), and smoking. At this stage they are permitted to roam quite far, hunting for edible plants in the veld, or asking for food at neighbouring homesteads by standing in the cattle kraal until the inhabitants send a small boy to ask their needs. Should food not be forthcoming from a homestead, the boys are entitled — and expected — to steal. If caught, they are severely punished — not for stealing, but for being caught. Now, too, the boys are free to meet their girlfriends and to receive gifts from them.

The South Sotho initiates follow a similar pattern: a month of seclusion in the lodge during which food is brought to them, followed by a period of roaming, foraging, hunting, and stealing. Venda and Lobedu initiates go through several phases, the longest being the post-circumcision seclusion of three months for the Lobedu. Venda and Lobedu schools, and those of other Sotho tribes, have some association with a pole in the final phase. This is more than likely a phallic symbol. Venda initiates climb to the top of the pole, which is capped by a baboon skin and called 'grandfather', and shout triumphantly.

The fire in the initiates' hut is also an important feature among the North Sotho tribes. Among these people, it may take the form of a long line of coals, or each lineage will have a fire going in its portion of the hut, as with the Pedi.

PAGE 125   In Transkei, circumcision is the prerequisite of becoming a man. Until this custom is honoured, a male is always referred to as a boy and no self-respecting girl will accept his courtship. These two youths, members of a traditional circumcision school, have recently submitted to circumcision and are wearing the uniform of their group: two blankets of a specially chosen pattern.

In former times their cloaks were of animal skins, completely hiding the identity of the wearers. Initiates must be naked, their whole face and body daubed in white sandstone, to conceal identity and protect themselves against evil. Bottles of ready-mixed sandstone white are carried in special bags. The school is held during the winter months.

PAGES 126-7   In most traditional communities, adulthood is ushered in with ritual and acclaim. It is an important phase, when much must be learned and responsibilities recognised, so that the individual is fully prepared for a place in the adult community.

Domba, of the Venda community, is one of the more spectacular of the initiation schools. It is attended mainly by girls, but boys are also accepted. It usually takes place from autumn to the first rains, and involves preparation for adulthood and the revelation of the mysteries and secrets of the school. Initiates dance nightly to the deep tones of four traditional wooden drums, around a ritual fire kindled by a priest-diviner at the commencement of the school and kept burning until it ends.

Conclusion of Initiation

In Transkei, conclusion of the initiation lodges is marked by the washing off of white clay, which symbolised their pure state, in a river (in preparation for birth into society) and the burning of the lodge with all the impedimenta of initiation, representing a complete break with the past in preparation for embarking on a new, unfettered life. Southern Nguni initiates race down to the river to jump in and wash off the white clay which may have covered their bodies for seven or eight months.

Towards the end of the initiation period the Pedi initiates have a stone cairn built for them of granite flakes which they themselves have prepared by heating and cooling a rock. These conical cairns, a metre in height, bear a remarkable resemblance, though on a much smaller scale. to the tower in the Great Enclosure at Zimbabwe.

Initiation lodges are wreathed in mystery, rich with symbolism, archaic rites and recitations whose meanings have long been lost. But the most important and obvious symbolism rests in the concept of the death of an irresponsible child, who is a part of and dependent upon the maternal in society, followed by the birth of a man, the guardian of the strong moral and legal codes of his society. This process is broadly depicted in his removal from society, during which time he changes into the new person, shedding the feminine aspect of himself in the circumcision operation.

Outside their initiation lodge Transkei youths wind themselves in palm-leaf dancing skirts. The headdress varies according to the initiation school. Today this dancing dress has all but vanished.

PAGE 128 Swazi girls of marriageable age are called to attend a special puberty ceremony with celebration and dancing, held at the royal homestead. Dress is skimpy, comprising a skirt of bead-fringed cloth, a cloth torso band decorated with wool pompoms or tassels, and wool streamers on hip and head. Each district selects a uniform of special colours and all girls carry small dancing shields, and a large knife or decorated staff. After the ceremony these items are cared for by the older women of the family. Feathers adorn the hair in traditional Swazi manner. Red feathers of the loerie bird are worn only by girls from important families.

The importance of the initiates' withdrawal from society was brought home to me by the following experience. On one occasion, my mother and I were invited to visit a certain initiation lodge in the Transvaal. Unaware at the time that she was transgressing, my mother took several photographs of the initiates and their lodge. Very soon she was confronted by the master of the lodge. Not only was he angry; he was afraid. His charges at this stage of their lives were highly vulnerable to any form of witchcraft. I still remember his broken English and his loud, tense tone. One sentence has stuck in my mind: 'They will bring you trouble'.

As it transpired, he was quite correct. Three days later, more than 300 kilometres away, while we slept in an hotel, thieves broke into our van. A scene of chaos greeted us the following morning. Only one item was missing — the camera, with the offending film!

Some north-eastern Sotho, including the Pedi, Mmamabolo, Letswalo, and Matlala, as well as (historically) the Tswana, hold another lodge after the circumcision school. Among the Pedi the time gap between the two lodges is two years, during which the youths generally continue in their youthful way of life. The second lodge is similar to the first, though far less strict. The major function of such a lodge is to emphasise and consolidate the *esprit de corps* of the regiments formed in the first school.

WOMEN

Puberty Rites

The first menses of a girl may be marked by puberty rites observed immediately or some time afterwards either by her alone, or in a small group. Many tribes (including some Tsonga, the Pedi, the Lobedu and Southern Nguni) seclude the girl in a hut for the duration of her first menstrual period. A Lobedu girl must be secluded not only for her own first menses but for those of several other girls as well. The treatment of a Nguni girl at puberty bears some similarity to that meted out to her brother. Marwick has described the procedure for a Swazi girl:

> When a girl has her first menstrual discharge she goes to her mother and tells her that 'she has seen a thing such as she has never in her life seen before'. Her mother will ask to be shown, and when she realises what has occurred she will get some *imfe* seed (*ematimba imfe*) and a plant called *maguqu* and grind them together. She also takes water from sour porridge (*emanti encwancwa*), and cooks thick porridge which she gives to the child to eat. This is said to make the girl strong and is known as *ukwelashwa* or *ukuginiswa*. This is all done in private and the mother tells only her husband and her mother-in-law.
>
> The girl remains isolated in a hut (*ukufukama*) while the discharge lasts. From now on she is respected as a full-grown girl. It may be two or more years yet before she chooses a lover.
>
> While the mother is treating the girl she will instruct her as to how she should behave in future when she has her monthly courses. She warns her too not to allow any man to have connexion with her at such a time, otherwise she would do him harm, causing him a sickness called *lufu lwendlu* or *lugola* — a form of consumption affecting the man's chest and

Barbara Tyrrell.

A Transvaal Ndebele girl in ceremonial dress, prepared for her initiation. Girls may leave employment in the towns to don this dress and be initiated and, in contrast with the past, the bulky bead bracelets and bands may be removed. The beadwork and mirrors hanging down her back are to please the ancestors, who are carried on the shoulders of the living. The beaded ceremonial axe is an antique, preserved from historical times.

giving him an extraordinary craving for meat. This disease, it is said, can also be communicated to a man by a woman who has recently had a miscarriage. Among the other observances which a girl is taught during this time is to avoid shaking hands with any male and not to go in front of the *sibaya* (*enkundleni*) [cattle kraal], otherwise the cattle will abort; nor should she go among cattle for the same reason; nor should she eat *amasi* (sour milk) or drink fresh milk. The menses (*lihluli*) she is taught carefully to conceal, since they are a potent ingredient for bewitching people. A wizard would take them and dry them up in the sun and then grind them to a powder and put them into beer which was being drunk by a woman. Anyone having sexual intercourse with the woman would immediately die.

The menses of baboons are used in the same way; they are regarded as being equally potent because of the care which a female baboon takes to conceal them, and because of the general similarity between these animals and human beings.[3]

Traditionally, a Zulu maiden who finds she has reached maturity runs away into the bush or forest. Girls of other tribes, too, use an indirect method to inform their parents of the event. Like the Swazi, Zulu and other Nguni girls follow the procedure of seclusion behind a mat in the hut and observe the taboo on *amasi*, which holds for the duration of every menstrual period thereafter. The girls have plenty of company: their female friends must stay with them, and the many male visitors must produce small gifts to be allowed to join the pretty girls gathered there. Every night of the seclusion period is marked by singing, fun and goings-on among the young bloods and beauties of the community, while the girl who is the focal point of the activity sits quietly behind her screen and keeps her counsel. A Bomvana girl, like the male initiates, has to use new words for a variety of items, and her manner of eating is also changed — as in the case of the South Sotho and Southern Nguni male initiates, she must eat meat from the end of a long stick. When she emerges to relieve herself, she must be surrounded by other girls and covered by her blanket, which is pulled over her bowed head in the manner of a bride showing respect.

The end of this seclusion is marked by a sacrifice and a beer-drink and dancing party to celebrate the girl's emergence as a woman. This is also the end of the taboo on drinking *amasi*. The beer-drink party, with its crop of marriageable young maidens, each doing her best to please, is naturally of interest both to the local young men and to their fathers, who are in search of a daughter-in-law worth her bride-price.

A girl's puberty rituals are an expensive affair. The father has to supply several sacrificial animals as well as a good deal of beer for the festivities; as a result these rites are often omitted. However, a girl who has not been initiated is never really regarded as a full woman — among the Thembu she is called the equivalent of 'uncircumcised boy'. The symbolism of rebirth is implicit in the shaving of the head and pubic hair at the beginning of the seclusion period, so that fresh may grow in its place. Initiation is also associated with fertility and health. An uninitiated woman who proves barren or suffers from ill-health when married, may well be put through the ceremony by her husband.

Initiation Schools: the Domba

Of the large initiation schools for girls, the *domba* of the Venda (originally attended by both sexes but now only girls) is the most renowned. So firmly is the central feature of this school — the python dance — associated with the popular image of the African that at least one film producer, with more concern for dramatic impact than accuracy, has included it in a film on South Africa's most familiar tribe, the Zulu. Indeed, anyone who has witnessed the rhythm of the *domba* drums and the sinuous line of maidens writhing to the insinuating, urgent beat, has found the python dance unforgettable.

The *domba* school is not held annually or even regularly, but only when a particular chief's daughter is ready for initiation, or when he has had a good harvest. This latter factor is important as the initiates are unproductive for a long period and many girls attend from the districts of neighbouring chiefs. All must be fed and housed. The ideal duration of the school appears to be nine months or even more, but this is often reduced to about three months.

Before the beginning of the *domba* proper or entry into the school, the initiates must undergo certain rites. For the first of these, they are awakened in the small hours of the morning and led to the *khoro*, or courtyard, of their village, where the school is being held. Here the girls must remove all their clothes except their *shedu*, or strip of cloth, passing between the legs. and forming an apron front and back. They must then lie flat on the earth on their stomachs and eat porridge which has been placed in front of the house. At sunrise they dance the python dance for the first time, still clad in the *shedu*, which is their dancing attire from now on. They then dance every morning and night until the end of the school. At night the scene of dancing is lit by the red heart and leaping dark shadows of the sacred fire of the *domba* around which the 'python' — and, indeed, the whole school — revolves; for the fire must burn for the duration of the school.

The rhythms, beaten out on an orchestra of sacred drums, are fascinatingly complex, driven by a powerful urgency. The graceful *domba* is demanding and by the end of the initiation period the girls are shapely and amazingly uniform in physique.

The second of the introductory rites of the *domba* takes place on the second night of the school. While the first rites introduced the python dance, the second sets the tone of the school, establishing it as a place for learning the responsibilities of adulthood. The girls are made to sit down in the *khoro* in a long line, with their legs extended at right angles and then taught, among other things, the signs of pregnancy and the secrets of childbirth and motherhood.

In addition, they are told of a mythical chief Thovela and his wife, progenitors of the Venda — a tale abounding with love affairs, murders and divination by priest-diviners, told with the purpose of demonstrating the futility of committing adultery. It also cultivates respect for the divinatory powers of priest-diviners.

This frequently repeated story is the first of several parables and symbolic objects disclosed to the initiates. Sexual intercourse is demonstrated to the initiates by a couple under a rug or skin. Today this is often an older couple paid by the chief, but in the past the man used to be the chief's son and the woman one of the initiates. The unfortunate woman, often simple-minded or the child of a man of no account, was sometimes impregnated in this way. It is said that, after demonstrating to the other initiates the nine-month course of pregnancy and birth, she was traditionally fed to the crocodiles of the sacred Lake Fundudzi.

A further feature of the school is the learning of the secret passwords and formulae, and beatings as punishment for forgetting these. As in all initiation schools, discipline is tough and beatings frequent. The girls undergo the greatest ordeal of all in the concluding rites of the school. For the entire final

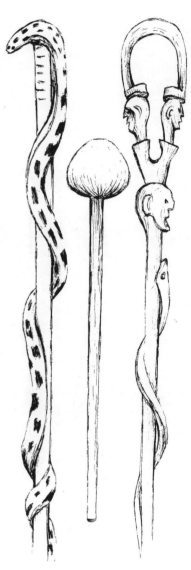

From left to right. A Pedi stick traditionally carries a snake. The typical Zulu throwing stick — short with a large knob. The three-headed stick carried by the teacher at a Venda initiation school depicts the python, an important Venda fertility symbol. [Arthur Smit coll.]

night, and on pain of a severe beating, the girls are kept either dancing or 'resting' with their arms vertically above their heads. With the advent of morning, their buttocks are rubbed with a skin irritant which causes extreme pain. They run to the river to wash, and then their hair is shaved (symbolic of shedding the past) and their bodies smeared with red ochre. After this comes a psychological ordeal — all the girls must be examined for virginity. Those who are found to be virgins are carried home by their mothers and applauded by all, while those who (by rather uncertain examination) are not, are beaten and derided by all present. After a short period of seclusion at home, the initiate emerges into society, a full-blooded, marriageable woman, who is expected to find a husband before the next *domba* school is held.

Initiation in Lesotho

The initiation of girls in Lesotho bears a rough similarity to the rites for males. While in the school, the girls — usually about ten in number — are called *bale*. The school starts with the new moon, when the girls run down to the river and are met by their women teachers, one of whom is dressed as a large snake — the *motonyane*. In the river they are bathed to wash away their girlhood and allow the woman within to emerge. In addition, the labia minora may be split or the hymen broken, and marks are made on the body. The nature and location of these marks depend on the clan of the girl.

For the first few days of the school, the girls are covered in black ash 'paint' but later daub themselves with white clay, as do the male initiates. The dress consists of a sheepskin apron, plaited grass ropes about the mid-riff, a grass veil concealing the face, and white clay beads adorning the torso. Attired in this way, the girls may be seen roaming about the countryside in groups in similar fashion to the male initiates of Transkei.

The girls' hut may or may not be set apart from the village; seclusion does not seem important, though identities must be hidden. At the school the initiates learn the traditions and taboos of the tribes, such as respectful observances towards men, the taboo on eggs and on sour milk during menstrual periods, and commonsense tips, such as avoiding eating meat that has crossed a river.

Pedi Initiation Rites

The Pedi have a so-called *byale* school for girls which is larger than that of the South Sotho. It is tribally organised and attendance is compulsory, unlike initiation in Lesotho, which is regarded as desirable mainly for status or fertility. An equivalent of the South Sotho girls' operation is performed on these Pedi girls who are afterwards called *bale*. Mönnig describes this operation:

> At a secluded place a rite is performed which is obviously similar in intent to the circumcision of the boys. The girls are told that an operation is to be performed on them. A knife is sharpened in their presence and they are then taken, one by one, made to lie down, and covered with a blanket. The knife is then pressed between their legs. Although they are not injured at all, the girls cry with fright when feeling the cold metal. As each girl is subsequently led away from those who are still waiting, the women who perform the 'operation' emerge from the blanket with their hands reddened with plant juices. Those girls still waiting their turn, thinking

A *bale* initiate in Lesotho. The beaded mask, strips of whitened clay beads on the torso, the heavy thong of plaited grass worn around the waist, and sheepskin apron and skirt are vital features of her dress. Her personal forked stick must never lie down lest it lose its power, so that, when initiates are not carrying their sticks, they stack them in a pyramid. A dog is usually a feature of the *bale* initiation school.

that the hands of the women are covered in blood, must obviously be terrorized. Although they do not undergo the pain that boys do when circumcised, the fright and bewilderment of the girls must be equal to that of the boys.[4]

After a month of seclusion, the girls wash themselves ritually, to emerge as new beings. For nine months they live at home, sleeping in groups. During this period they must be covered from neck to ankles in grass mats, and be extremely retiring. They may not speak to men. After this they go through another period of seclusion, followed by a ritual bathe, and their hair is shaved the second time. Like the men, they are then formed into a regiment and, covered in red ochre, go home to a warm reception and various gifts.

CONCLUSION

Puberty rites, usually an individual affair, are a recognition, acceptance and affirmation of the biological maturity of the individual. Initiation rites are, even more important, a recognition of the new adulthood of an individual and of his or her acceptance as a mature man or woman into society.

In Western society the young person faces an uncomfortable growing-up time. The passage from childhood to maturity often entails a protracted series of encounters between older and younger generations, with the younger fighting for a recognition not easily accorded them by the older. By contrast, initiations in African society are easier on the different age-groups, providing a clear set of rules dictating behaviour towards one another. The prospective initiate is removed from society to undergo experiences which separate him or her from society at large, as previously perceived. However, this procedure effectively binds the initiate into a specific social group and it is as a member of this group that he or she is not only welcomed back into society, but given an acceptable mode of self-expression and participation.

PAGE 137 This Ndebele girl wears her coming-of-age costume. Beaded hoops wound around a grass core, the rectangular beaded apron, goatskin back skirt and saddle of beadwork are highly decorative. Modern bead hoops are thicker than in the past and are decorated with plastic strips and gilt panel pins. Only leg and neck hoops are built onto the body, whereas in the past all hoops could be removed only by cutting. Here a bright beret takes the place of traditional headbands of beads.

This girls kneels respectfully to drink her beer. Prior to the dance and festivities, when she wears the finery for the first time, there is a seclusion period, during which she decorates her parental home with colourful murals and also prepares beadwork. Puberty rites and ceremonies of initiation into adulthood are important features of traditional life in most areas.

Barbara Tyrrell

Barbara Tyrrell

COURTSHIP AND MARRIAGE

INFORMAL COURTSHIP

COURTSHIP for the young African starts early, and romantic interludes frequently occur before puberty. Puberty, however, marks the start of courtship in earnest, and youngsters are traditionally warned at this time of the dangers of pregnancy. By the time a boy is fourteen he is a real 'young buck', sporting the latest of whatever the local or traditional dress may be. Prominent on his person, too, will be various pieces of beadwork, often containing love messages which have been presented to him by his girlfriend. In Transkei he may be seen wearing a highly decorated gourd *isidla* or penis-cover; in Natal the semi-Westernised boys can be seen marching along to visit their girls, shirts unfastened at the cuffs and hanging out, handkerchiefs knotted about their trousers below the knee, barefoot and with a bead 'love letter' around their necks. When the girls visit the local village, they will be gaily adorned in beadwork and bright clothes, and frequently wearing a colourful bead hat copied from some Western style.

When their children reach puberty, some of the northern peoples, notably the Venda, Lobedu and Pedi, allow them to build and live in miniature villages. The huts are constructed at the end of harvest time and are, as far as possible, imitations in miniature of their parents' full-sized homes. A 'chief' or 'headman' will be elected and each diminutive hut will be inhabited by a little 'man' and his 'wife'. She will cook for him, preparing mealie-meal and vegetables exactly as she has learned from her mother, and he will go off hunting during the day, returning in the evening with his catch, usually a bird, a rabbit or a fieldmouse. This mock homestead is a preparation for adulthood and a time for a great deal of contact between the sexes.

PAGE 138   In traditional communities, marriageable age is usually achieved by completion of the initiation rites and announced by the type of dress that is worn. This girl of the Ntwana people in the eastern Transvaal advertises her marriageable status by wearing a bright feather. Her neck, arm and leg ornaments are still those of girlhood. The evenly twisted and skilfully uniform circles of grass are made onto her person and remain there until the betrothal period when they are replaced by beaded grass hoops. With marriage she will don a cotton smock and change her hairstyle, as illustrated by the background drawing.

There are also different games which constitute early forms of courtship. Venda boys and girls form lines facing one another. A boy must step forward and point out the girl of his choice. She may either accept or reject him. Should she take the latter course, she must then choose another boy with whom to pair off.

The principal occasion for get-togethers of the Nguni youth used to be the dances at the girls' puberty ceremonies. Today, however, the various groups hold their courting dances in disused huts and even quarries. These are happy occasions of courting and intrigue, notable for the energy and elegance of the dancing. Usually held on a Saturday night, the dancing continues until dawn. Youths overcome by fatigue from these sessions can sometimes be seen curled up fast asleep beside the road on Sunday mornings.

The Nguni youth may court the girl of his choice for some time before achieving success. He will lie in wait for her in order to accost her on her way to hoe the field or to catch the timber company's lorry to work in the plantations for the day, or on her way to collect water. Whatever his ploy, he will receive the cold shoulder — a hard gaze and a cutting remark will be his only reward. She will try to avoid him. He may enlist the aid of various accomplices to keep him informed of her customary movements so that he can accost her. Herdboys, for a fee, are good at this and often play girl and boy off against one another, keeping emotions high and reaping good profits.

When and if the girl eventually decides to accept her ardent pursuer, she informs the older girls of her homestead that she has a soft spot for him, whereupon they visit his home with the happy news. He must then pay a return visit to learn the day on which he will be allowed to visit her formally.

The maidens of the loved one's homestead must now prepare for the party to celebrate this informal 'betrothal'. The local trading store owner will be confronted by a furtive group of girls at the window long after the store is closed and everyone gone home.

'Please do not speak of this,' they are sure to say as they are admitted to the evening dimness of the shop's interior. Their purchase will conform to an exact pattern: a specific amount of white calico, some beads, sugar and sweets and, perhaps, a whistle. As silently as they arrived they will depart, repeating their plea, leaving the trader trying to figure out who is being matched with whom.

When the boy and his friends arrive for the betrothal party, they are greeted with beer, food and lovely maidens — all the necessities for the party. The calico bought was for the making of the betrothal flag, which flies high above the boy's homestead for perhaps a week before being lowered. The sugar and sweets are highly formal gifts from the girl to show her acceptance of the man as a lover. The beads will have been worked into a personal 'love letter' which the man will wear round his neck. Several gifts of money are handed to the girl by the happy suitor, the amounts varying from area to area, but often quite large.

This betrothal is a fairly loose arrangement — in fact a boy may be betrothed to several girls at the same time. A real lady's man who has flown the flag of several maidens is termed a *soga* — an enviable reputation. The unfortunate youth who does not quite make it with the fair sex is the *shimane* and he is open to the mockery of society. In one respect, however, he is lucky: his betrothed friend may find himself deserted by his girlfriend, who is under no obligation to return the sum of money he has given her as part of the arrangement.

Intra-crural Intercourse

The betrothal sets the scene for the accepted form of love-making between sweethearts — intra-crural intercourse, that is, external intercourse without penetration. This practice, common in traditional society, has the tacit support of the community. Ethnocentric missionaries have roundly condemned this practice with the result, it is said, that it has been replaced by full intercourse. A Zulu youth once told me how disgusted he was by the downward trend of his people's morals: only the previous Sunday, he had met a girl and taken her off to a sugar-cane field for *ukusoma* (intra-crural intercourse) only to find that she was eager for the real thing. It need hardly be noted that his disgust was not matched by his response.

Pregnancy may, however, result from intra-crural intercourse, and this may be induced deliberately by a much-condemned form of magic employed by the boy. This form of bewitchment is known as 'pregnancy caused by a shadow'.

Love Spells

Love potions and spells are as many as they are powerful. In Nguni territory, one of the most powerful is the *fufunyana* spell which a man will cast on a girl or woman. This spell is quite irresistible and causes the girl to fall deeply in love with her bewitcher. In addition, while the spell is upon her, she has frequent fits. These are known as *ukugayiza* and are most impressive for the sheer, uncontrolled abandon of the victim and the volume of her hysterical screams. Such is the power of the *fufunyana* spell that it is extremely

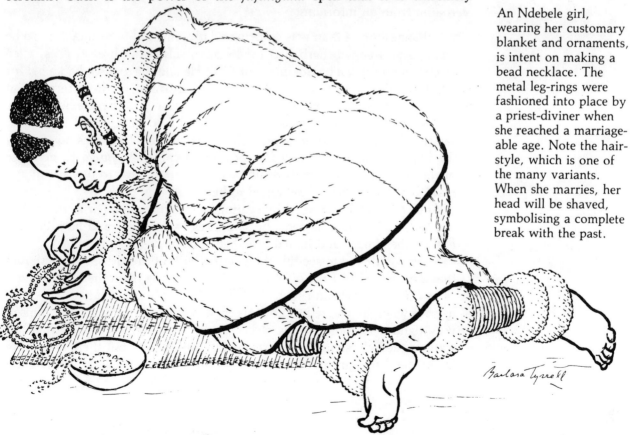

An Ndebele girl, wearing her customary blanket and ornaments, is intent on making a bead necklace. The metal leg-rings were fashioned into place by a priest-diviner when she reached a marriageable age. Note the hairstyle, which is one of the many variants. When she marries, her head will be shaved, symbolising a complete break with the past.

difficult, if not impossible, to remove. According to the Mpondo, the only sure way to get rid of it is for the afflicted maiden to sleep with the man concerned.

A young woman I know, unmarried and living near Richmond, suffered for years from the *fufunyana* spell, which took the form of frequent falling down and rigidity. Despite all efforts, the spell could not be removed. Even with the cooperation of her supposed enchanter, the spell remained and as a result of its effect she had to give up her studies at school. The medical diagnosis of her malady was epilepsy. Whether this was true or not, her problems eventually vanished with her marriage to another man.

It is arguable that the *fufunyana* spell is in fact far more dangerous to men than it is to their supposed victims, the young women. A girl finding herself infatuated with a man may accuse him of bewitching her and subconsciously (or consciously) produce symptoms to substantiate her claim. One Zulu man found himself in the chief's court at Mtunzini, on a charge of having bewitched a girl with the *fufunyana* spell. The unfortunate man was happily married (monogamously), and a good man who would not stoop to sorcery. Such is the strength of traditional belief in this spell, however, that each time he opened his mouth to protest his innocence the chief increased the fine.

A technique for casting this spell has been described to me by a knowledgeable informant. Meat is taken and left at a graveyard, where ants crawl all over it. After some time this meat, covered with ants, is taken and ground with specially prepared medicines. The hopeful lover must then sprinkle this concoction on the path or road when he sees his desired girl coming and call to her, ensuring that she crosses the road in coming to him. (The possibility that she will refuse to answer his call is not raised!)

The stories in circulation which deal with the effects and side-effects of love potions are many and colourful. Here is a typical example, quoted verbatim from an informant:

In Johannesburg a man was courting a lady. She did not fancy him so he went to an *nyanga* (herbalist) for help, to soften her breast. (Yes, even today that muti can be obtained for £20.) He and the *nyanga* had a bet for £20 that the *nyanga* would not be successful and in the afternoon at knock-off time he went to the *nyanga*'s home for the medicine. The *nyanga* gave him the medicine to blow and told him to call her name, saying, 'I want you to be here in my house tonight'. He was advised by the *nyanga* that when she came he should call the *nyanga* to give her medicine because her mind would be confused. He was to buy bread and make tea for her before he talked to her.

And so it all happaned. While eating he called the *nyanga* — the day of the bet — and when he came he said, 'Yes — you see!' and he called the *induna* (headman) and he paid the bet in front of the *induna*.

Several gathered to see this thing and after that the girl stayed with him that day. He said, 'Take off your clothes and hang them there.' She did it — so they lay down and switched off the light. He touched her and kissed her but when he wanted to go further he felt a cold thing around himself very tightly. He jumped out of bed and it was still there. He could not walk to the light switch. He screamed, 'I am dying!', but there were only himself and the girl and he walked on his knees to the light: no girl, no snake, no dresses. Nothing. He shouted all night, telling them that she had become a snake. 'This bloody *nyanga* has deceived me, taken my £20 and given a *silwane* (creature).

Induna witnesses were called the next day and went to the *nyanga* but he said, 'You have seen the girl. I found her eating bread and tea. What do you want of me? If you have quarrelled with your girlfriend, you are not going to get your money back.' The man wanted to go to the magistrate's office but there were witnesses of the event, so he failed. This man lives in a compound in Johannesburg.

COURTSHIP AND THE CHOICE OF A SPOUSE

Love or attachment between people may or may not lead to marriage. The Zulu youth of the last century often had a good deal of freedom in choosing and marrying his heart's desire and this is still the case today. The young people of many other tribes had far less freedom in this respect; parentally arranged marriages were the norm. So different is the African conception of matrimony from that of Western man that this was considered no great hardship.

A young man might inform his father that he felt it was time to marry and ask the latter to find him a bride. The parents, especially among the Nguni, would take pains to look for a good and compatible spouse for their son or daughter. In choosing a wife the standing of her family was investigated. Their financial position was considered relatively unimportant, but their social reputation was critical, as was freedom from the taint of witchcraft. A Nguni family whose homestead has known the presence of such unpleasant magical creatures as *impundulu*, *thikoloshe* or *ichanti* was and is best avoided in the search for an in-law.

Today few marriages are arranged in the traditional way partly due to the influence of Christian and Western concepts emphasising marriage as the union of two individuals. Church marriages are on the increase.

The change is also partly due to the fact that young men are able to work in towns, where they can earn enough money for the bride-price, which makes them independent of the goodwill of their elders. Despite the stigma attached to elopement, many — perhaps most — modern couples choose this as a way of getting married. A loose parallel may be drawn between this and the socially unacceptable yet common practice of 'living together' in Western society. The latter arrangement is becoming the norm in urban areas and is in fact often preferred by girls.

That many girls should prefer elopement is understandable, for under traditional law the father has complete ownership and custody of the children. Short of divorce, he can get away with almost anything without trouble from his wife, who has no claim or redress. In the past the parents of a girl might have resorted to physical torture to make her marry a man she did not like, but this form of coercion would lead to open revolt today. Schapera recorded a rather amusing but scathing little song sung by an unwilling Tswana bride-to-be:

I heard it said that I was engaged,
and one afternoon when I was at home,
as I was sitting I saw a fool coming;

he came dragging his coat on the ground,
and his trousers were made of khaki;
I said to him, 'Fool, whence do you come?'
And he replied, 'I am your fiancé.'
I gave the dog a chair, and his tail hung down.[1]

A principal difference between Nguni and Venda customs on the one hand, and Sotho/Tswana and Shangana-Tsonga customs on the other can be found in the way they choose a bride. The Nguni practise strict exogamy — a man's bride may never be of the same clan as any of his four grandparents. In this respect, the Swazi, who allow marriage into the family of a man's mother, are an exception. Sotho groups, on the other hand, allow marriage between first cousins where the cousins have different clan-names. This union is preferred by the Venda, whose rule of exogamy, like that of the Swazi, excludes marriage only to somebody with the same clan-name. A major advantage of endogamy or cross-cousin marriage is that the ties between two descent groups are strengthened and the *lobola* cattle are retained as the property of a group of near-relatives.

Bride-Price or *Lobola*

In the past, the reaction of Europeans to the system of 'buying' a bride with cattle was one of self-righteous indignation mixed with a healthy disgust and amazement at this negation of the humanity of the fair sex and their treatment as mere trade goods and cattle equivalents. Only now are they beginning to realise to what extent the traditional African concept of the individual in society differs from their own.

The individual in traditional society is primarily aware of himself as a part of his group, and his membership of this group provides him with an identity. The group regards him in the same light — it is in his blending with the whole that he exists and is of significance. The more members — workers — there are in a group, the richer the group, and the better able it is to exploit the environment. In a subsistence community these attitudes are logical and to be expected. Therefore, in exchange for the bride — a social and economic asset — her family must receive some compensation from the husband's family. Traditionally, this is the 'bride-price' — a concrete sign of good faith, commonly known to whites by the Zulu term *lobola*. The acceptance of the *lobola* cattle by the bride's father sets the seal on the marriage. In the bride's future life the cattle serve to guarantee that she is well treated. If she is treated badly she may return to her father with no reciprocal return of cattle, should the court decide that the fault lies with her husband. It is the transfer of the *lobola* cattle that legalises the membership of the children in the husband's clan and, as *lobola* cattle are often given to a bride's brother to be used in the payment of his *lobola*, the custom establishes a stabilising network of links in society.

African women have no objection to the system and in fact welcome the protection it grants them. A woman for whom a good price was paid is proud of her *lobola* value, while those who were obtained cheaply are shy and embarrassed when asked about their *lobola*. Monica Hunter (Professor Monica Wilson), writing of the Mpondo, says that when women wished to compliment her, they would say that she was worth a good bride-price. Traditionally, *lobola* was not a purely economic transaction. In the past, when times were difficult, a Pedi father could not withhold his daughter just because her suitor was hard up — she could be married for three stones. In addition, if a suitor had no cattle or money, he could promise his first daughter to his wife's family, or pay off his *lobola* over a number of years.

Also shedding light on the true nature of *lobola* are the observations of Vilakazi concerning the Zulu of the Valley of a Thousand Hills near Pieter-maritzburg. Nowadays, when the expenses of the trousseau and entertain-ment provided by the bride's parents are balanced against the *lobola* they receive, it actually costs them money to marry off a daughter. Vilakazi inquired of one old man to this area whether he was buying a wife when he paid *lobola*. 'He looked up mischievously and said, "Of course, Somtseu [Sir Theophilus Shepstone, an administrator who set *lobola* at a strict eleven head of cattle] told us to buy our wives!".'[2]

A standard price of ten head of cattle is still maintained. Occasionally, when the husband wishes to impress, or if his bride is a woman of standing, more cattle are involved. At present cattle sell for more than R100 a head. For a farm labourer earning as little as R20 a month (plus food and accom-modation), marriage can present a financial nightmare.

With the growing emphasis on individualism and the accumulation of material wealth, a father of attractive girls may attempt to extort exorbitant *lobola* prices, whereas in days gone by he would have asked an amount that the groom's family could easily afford to pay. Unscrupulous fathers and their equally wayward daughters have been known to make good profits from *lobola*. A girl is promised in marriage to a man working some distance away and the man will then start sending *lobola* cattle to his future father-in-law. Little does he know that the love of his life has in similar fashion captured the hearts and cattle of several other men. Eventually the day of reckoning comes, and the cheated suitors get their cattle back — but the girl's father has had free milk over a fairly long period and has very likely claimed several calves as well.

THE NATURE OF MARRIAGE

To the traditional African the purpose of life is the perpetuation and increase of the group. A person who does not marry and procreate is failing in his duty to the group. Initiation signifies the beginning of adulthood, but this status is accepted and confirmed only with marriage, which is therefore also an important rite of passage in a person's life.

African marriage is not the holy matrimony between two individuals tha. this union represents in Western society. It is a socio-economic transfer of a woman from one family to another, and her integration into the new group. The nature of traditional marriage does not exclude the possibility of woman-to-woman 'marriage': if a woman, especially a woman of rank, finds herself with enough cattle for *lobola*, she may take a 'wife' who will perform many menial tasks for her. This 'wife' is impregnated by her 'husband's' husband and the children of such a union find themselves in the unusual position of calling a woman 'father'!

Biological fatherhood is not important; it is the membership of children in a lineage by virtue of their mother's bride-price which is the critical factor. Should a woman elope with a man and no *lobola* be paid by him or his father, a senior member of her lineage can, at a later date, reclaim her and her children. This way of thought accords with the ancient Jewish 'law of the levirate', that is, the Hebrew custom of compulsory marriage with a childless brother's widow. In the event of a husband's death or impotence (sterility in a man is not recognised — it is always the fault of the woman) his relative, usually a younger brother, impregnates the wife. The children from this union are regarded as being descended from the husband himself, however. Similarly, in the traditional setting a woman's marriage is not considered complete until she has borne a child, particularly a male child. Should she die before such an event or prove sterile, the groom's family is entitled to demand a replacement, usually a sister, for whom little or no *lobola* is paid.

MARRIAGE CEREMONIES

The details of marriage ceremonies vary significantly in nature and length from tribe to tribe. In those tribes, notably the Sotho, where a daughter may have been promised in marriage before or at birth, or if *lobola* payment is slow, the marriage ceremony and negotiations may be drawn out over many years. In other instances, the entire ceremony may take place within a period of days. Most tribes have different marriage procedures depending on the circumstances, and nowadays church weddings are becoming more and more popular.

The traditional marriage — which today accounts for the minority of unions — is an arranged marriage. On the initiative of either the prospective groom or of his father, the groom's family approaches that of the girl and *lobola* negotiations begin ceremonially, according to strictly laid-down protocol (as described below). Other popular ways of initiating proceedings are by 'kidnapping' the girl or by her running away from home. These actions are carried out with the full knowledge of both boy and girl and they are usually resorted to in order to precipitate events if his or her parents are not well disposed towards the marriage.

PAGE 147   A bride of the Natal Midlands presents herself at the local magistrate's office, together with her groom, to register her marriage. For this important occasion she wears her built-up hairstyle of beadwork. The eyeveil, of beads or of beaded cloth, is all important, denoting, as it does, respect 'with the eyes' for her husband's parents.

Today the groom usually wears his best European-style dress for this occasion, but he may be fortunate in possessing a traditional set of animal skins and will then use these. The leopard-skin cape proclaims that this man is of an important family.

PAGES 148-9   This tree, common in Zululand, is a species of 'kaffirboom', or coral tree. The homestead has its small cattle kraal and modest number of huts, unlike the larger, extended family settlements which comprise a large number of huts arranged around the cattle kraal. The modern hut has low mud walls, differing from the traditional grass hut, which could be uprooted and moved. Even today one may occasionally see a whole hut travelling aboard a lorry, and writers from the earlier decades of this century speak of grass huts being carried — apparently walking of their own volition — across the veld.

The white flag on a tall pole indicates a recent engagement in the family.

Barbara Tyrrell

Barbara Tyrrell

Natal Nguni

Among the Nguni marriage procedures vary. A girl may run away to the home of a man without his invitation — very embarrassing for him, considering that a refusal to accept her hand may be taken as an insult by both the girl and her parents. If refused, she must be accompanied by a fine to heal her pride. Nevertheless, she might deem it beneath her dignity to return home single and continue arriving at the homes of prospective husbands in the hope of getting wed. Among some Zulu clans the presumptuous lass may find herself presented with a pot of water, to 'wash away the shame' at being refused.

At the other end of the scale, a man and his companions may forcibly kidnap a girl who is not willing and then, possession being nine-tenths of the law, open negotiations with her people. Even if the girl or her parents approve, many tribes regard it as unseemly that she should go willingly, and if tradition is observed she is dragged away, receiving minor abrasions as she is taken to her new home.

Nguni lovers who wish to marry must first observe the informal betrothal already described. For an arranged marriage, the young man must first approach his father indirectly, either through his mother or his uncles. Similarly, the father uses a go-between to approach the people of his prospective daughter-in-law. The go-between then visits the girl's father using a lengthy, delicate approach which tells the man only that someone from that homestead wants one of his daughters. He finds out the rest by calling his daughters to him and questioning them. The group consciousness of these people is such that not the girl herself, but one of her older companions, does the talking.

Lobola Payments

The first visit of the ambassadors, who are relatives from the prospective groom's homestead, is followed by another, which marks the start of *lobola* negotiations. The ambassadors, as a matter of course, plead the poverty of their master, while the girl's father behaves offensively and demands high payments. On the next visit, the ambassadors bring with them some of the bridal cattle and are once again received with abuse. This time, however, it is the entire establishment who turn out to abuse them verbally, by belittling the cattle, and even by physically assaulting the emissaries, who may do nothing but plead their poverty and accept the insults. Their forbearance is rewarded with the slaughter of a goat or an ox — the first ceremony involving both families.

PAGE 150   Umbrellas and sunshades frequently assume special significance in traditional society. Not only do they protect against sun and rain, but they take on an additional mysterious quality when covering the head of a woman who pays ritual respect to her husband's family.

The background line drawing shows a bride of the Ndebele covering herself up with umbrella and gala blanket on approaching the home of her groom, led there by a young niece. The square cloth pinned to the back of her blanket also denotes respect.

This bridesmaid wears the rectangular beaded apron which denotes that she is of marriageable age. She is a girl of thirty years ago and wears the many narrow hoops of the time.

The full *lobola* is not given on this first visit; only the first of several instalments. In addition to the bridal cattle, another beast is given to the girl's mother for her part in protecting the virginity of the girl. The bride's people reciprocate with gifts, and the two-way flow marks the gradual growing together of the two groups over an extended period. The presents from the bride's people are mostly pots of beer, which may be brought from her home for a variety of reasons, such as sickness in the groom's home or his return from the city.

The Marriage

The payment of the last *lobola* beast traditionally marks the beginning of preparations for the marriage celebrations. In practice, however, many marriages are completed with a portion of the *lobola* still owing. The bride and her parents must collect presents for their in-laws, her father must prepare the *isidwabe* or married woman's leather skirt, the parties of both bride and groom practise songs for the great day, and the groom's ambassadors are sent back home to order the brewing of beer for the festivities.

The bride's leave-taking is an emotional affair, marked by much tearfulness and singing of the family group's song or 'anthem'.

The blessing of the ancestral spirits is needed. Before the bride leaves her home, she visits various relatives who may slaughter a goat for her, sprinkling her with the gall, which the ancestors like to lick. This is prior to her anointment with the gall from the cattle of her husband's clan when she arrives there (see below).

The Zulu wedding ceremony proper is similar to those of other Natal clans. The first wedding — European or otherwise — I ever attended, was one between members of two clans in the Richmond district of Natal. It remains the most exciting wedding I remember. The wedding format outlined below is the same as that followed in this area and similar to ceremonies throughout Natal and kwaZulu.

Though Bhaca costume is the standard traditional dress in the Richmond area, the wedding ceremonial and the associated dress are typically Zulu. The wedding proper begins when the bride and her bridal party, made up of youngsters from home, arrive at the groom's home before sunrise on the appointed day. The bride does not go into the homestead, but settles beside a nearby stream with a few friends. The main party enter the homestead and proceed up the right-hand side of the yard to the 'chief wife's' hut (see p. 162). Their arrival has been eagerly awaited and is greeted with great joy and the ululations of women happy to welcome a new member — and worker — to their group. Outside the main hut, the bridal party are asked if they have 'money to enter the homestead' and an amount, usually about a Rand, is promised and later paid by the bride's father. After being shown to the hut set aside for them for the duration of the celebrations, the bridal party, singing happily, walk down the left-hand side of the homestead and out of the gate to where the bride waits.

Here the bridal party stay, refreshed by pots of beer sent from the homestead, until noon, when the men — including the bride's father — and the senior women arrive. Like the younger members of their homestead, they are

153

This Ndebele bride is an example of the importance accorded formal observances of respect in traditional life. She is completely covered by her blanket, which is also pinned at the front, her head is covered and she stands in a slightly bowed position with her eyes downcast, all showing respect for her husband and new in-laws.

Barbara Tyrrell.

shown to a hut previously set aside for them. Having been regaled with beer, they are directed to the spot where the younger members of the bridal party are seated. Here the two parties relax, drink beer and eat the meat of the goat sent to them from the homestead during the morning.

Early in the afternoon the bridal party (including both the younger and the older parties) are summoned by the groom's party and go immediately to the dancing area near the huts. The bride remains concealed beneath an umbrella and among the other girls at the rear of her party. Once at the dancing area the bridal party dance for a while in front of the groom's party, the young people taking the front ranks.

The time has now arrived for the speech by the bride's father. He stands before the people and addresses his new in-laws, both those in the flesh and their ancestors. His speech is along the following lines:

'We come to you people of this home and ask for friendship. Here: I give you my child. Treat her as you would your own daughter. She is a good girl. She is healthy. The only sicknesses she has are . . .' (he enumerates any ailments she might have). He then outlines various aspects of the marriage, such as the number of *lobola* cattle paid and how many are still owing, before imploring the ancestors that the union be fruitful and that his daughter soon become pregnant.

He ends his speech by staging a dramatic fight with an imaginary opponent (a performance common in the culture and known as *ukugiya*). This marks the emergence of the bride, who, along with her companions, dances from the rear of her party to stand in the front, facing her husband and his party. She is resplendent — her skin shining with fat, her body bedecked in beadwork and coloured cloths, and she is wearing for the first time the leather skirt of womanhood. Her eyes are hidden by a beaded veil of cloth, a token of her respect for her father-in-law. For her the entire marriage, especially the first few years, will be marked by respectful observances toward her in-laws.

In her right hand she carries a short spear or a knife. This is a symbol of her virginity (even in modern times, when all know this to be an empty symbol in most cases) and, as she dances, she brandishes it meaningfully. (I still recall that first bride I saw as a child, sweating with exertion and excitement, advancing on her husband, a meek-looking fellow. Ignorant as I was at that tender age of the symbolism involved, I promptly developed a healthy respect for the married state.)

The dancing of the bridal party is followed by a display by the groom and his young male friends, who retire to don their finery and then dance before the bridal party, who are now seated. Every effort goes into this dancing, as there is intense rivalry between the parties of the bride and groom.

After the dances, which mark the formal union of man and wife, a beer-drink follows, lasting deep into the night. Care must be taken that the different parties be kept separate as fights often break out. The loss of a member on the one hand, and the transfer of cattle on the other, give rise to strong feelings of competition and antagonism, which, particularly during the wedding dances or beer party, can flare up and cause a full-scale fight. One wedding I attended near Richmond was full of tension and restraint — a few weeks previously, at another wedding involving these two lineages, violence had broken out, resulting in several injuries and a death.

The morning of the second day is marked by two sacrifices before sunrise — one of an animal belonging to the groom's family, and the other of one of the *lobola* beasts. This is essentially a religious integration of the bride into her new family — her introduction to their ancestors — and the whole procedure is enacted in the ancestors' haunt, the cattle kraal. The gall of both animals (which the ancestors lick) is sprinkled on the bride, in this manner introducing both her and her ancestors to the shades of her husband's family.

The beasts are stabbed to death and the first blow should be fatal, as all subsequent stab wounds must be covered by money from the groom's people. Needless to say, an expert is chosen for the job of dispatching the cattle. Fines must also be paid if the stomach is cut while the beast is being skinned, for this must be pierced by the girl to symbolise her coming sexual union with her husband. A related tradition, which has nearly died out, is the placing of a string of white beads round the first stab wound in these animals as a symbol of the bride's virginity.

With the religious and social ceremonies of the union completed, the bride and her party dance to express their pleasure at the successful completion of the wedding. Then the bride's father distributes gifts to the various people in the bride's new home. These gifts — mirrors, blankets, basins — are always proudly displayed by all concerned. An inevitable part of the trousseau is a large wooden box, painted with red varnish and sparkling with mirrors, the like of which can be seen in most African shops in Natal.

While the dancing and the distribution of gifts are in progress, the meat of the sacrificial beasts has been cooking in preparation for the wedding feast that afternoon. This is a party which continues far into the night, with the local youths taking the opportunity of visiting the hut of the bridal party to court and observe these 'foreign' girls. Still among them is the bride, who has yet to consummate her marriage.

On the morning of the third day the bride and her party arise early. Like her counterparts in wedding ceremonies to the south, she shows her mettle by gathering wood and water for the home. These tasks are completed by midday, and her bridal party then return to their home, officially ending the wedding ceremonies. Only that evening — the third day after her arrival at her husband's home — may the new bride sleep in his hut.

Though the marriage has taken place, the bride has yet to be fully integrated into the life and 'body' of her new family. The rites of integration, usually involving a sacrifice, are performed over the next few weeks or days. The new bride is allowed to eat meat and *amasi* (sour milk) in her new home. The latter is important from the bride's point of view as *amasi* is a staple food; for her husband's people it is significant because an outsider may under no circumstances eat the products of cattle as these are closely linked to the lineage ancestors.

Nowadays wedding festivities start on Saturday so that all may attend. The legal system has created the need for a policeman or offical to be present to officiate at the wedding and obtain the consent of the bride and groom. In addition, the marriage must be registered with the local magistrate. This is done on Tuesday, the day after the festivities close. This is always a colourful day in Natal villages, especially in the vicinity of the local magistrate's court, as the young brides make a bright spectacle, dressed in their ceremonial regalia.

Southern Nguni

Cape Nguni ceremonies are similar in outline to those described above. When *lobola* negotiations are over, the bride-to-be will set off from her home after the sacrifice of a beast. She is accompanied by a small party. The leave-taking, as with the Zulu girl, is a sad occasion and the bride will cry — especially if she is unaware of the identity of her future husband and his family. At the groom's home, her party is housed in a hut and they present his family with part of the meat from the animal killed before her departure from her childhood home. This, together with the sharing of meat from a sacrifice performed the next morning, effectively links the two families together.

After a period varying from a few days to two or three weeks of seclusion, the bridal party emerge from their hut for the wedding celebrations proper. These include the sacrifice of an animal or animals and the display of bride and bridesmaids in their wedding garb in the cattle kraal. This is an important occasion and many men will be present, seeking good-looking daughters-in-law among these girls. On this day the bride performs her domestic duties for the first time before an audience of local women, who comment on her performance as she cleans a hut or, in a veiled procession with her bridesmaids, fetches water from the river. (The order of things can be somewhat different if there are delays in the payment of *lobola*. I witnessed the 'wedding' of a Thembu couple who had lived as man and wife and produced several children in the time it had taken the husband to collect sufficient cattle to 'pay' for his wife.)

The day after the wedding there is usually some speech-making and the bride's trousseau, which often exceeds R100 in value, is examined. Singing, drinking and dancing usually continue for some days, after which the bride's party return without the bride.

Sotho

Among the Sotho and other inland tribes marriage is centred to a greater extent on the bride's home, and she may remain there until the birth of her first child. This event marks her true entry into the ranks of her husband's clan.

When agreement has been reached with his son, a Pedi father will first visit the girl's parents to see which way the wind blows. All indications being favourable, he will initiate formal negotiations. A mediator sent to the girl's parents asks for a 'gourd of water' or a 'little dog'. The girl's father knows what this signifies. If he agrees, and the groom's people are able to pay an acceptable *lobola*, he will send the mediator away with the words, 'Go in peace, I will inform her people'.

Both families must come to an agreement separately before they once again confer via the mediator. A successful negotiation is then sealed by the gift of a beast or blankets from the groom's people. After this agreement there is a time-lapse, the length of which depends on how long it takes the suitor and his family to accumulate sufficient cattle or money for *lobola*. The father and the groom call a meeting of close relatives, each of whom pledges something towards the *lobola*. The size of the payment is not decided by the bride's people but the amount paid is usually as high as possible, because it is a matter of family honour on the part of the groom's people.

The cattle are delivered to the bride's home. The coming delivery is announced to the world by running up white flags on top of long poles. After the cattle have arrived, the young men who brought them and have witnessed the transaction are closeted in a hut with beer, meat and, most important, a selection of the young maidens of the home. The wedding feast is a merry, day-long affair of meat and beer and a ceremony called *leeto*, held later in the afternoon, when the groom and bride, arrayed in their finery, are symbolically shown their roles in life. A woman may hold a pumpkin in front of the bride and show her a broom, while the groom is imbued with the virtues of courage by a man who makes stabbing motions with an assegai. After this the bride goes — reluctantly — to the groom's home where she presents to her new mother-in-law a portion of the meat from the beast killed for the wedding celebrations. The mother-in-law's acceptance of this meat is symbolic of her acceptance of the new bride (who then returns to her own home until the birth of her first child).

In Lesotho the wedding feast is held on the day the *lobola* cattle arrive at the bride's kraal. Like the Pedi, the womenfolk of the bride's kraal playfully attempt to prevent the cattle being driven into the kraal — an action symbolic of their reluctance to let the bride go. The feast really gets under way only once the bride's father has accepted the *lobola* cattle — with which he pretends to be highly dissatisfied. A beast is sacrificed and skinned by both families, the bride's people being responsible for the left side and the groom's for the right. It is said that the family who are first to complete their task will emerge the dominant one in future relations.

The day after the sacrifice, the two families mingle, when the groom's mother and other female relatives share the intestines of the sacrificial animal with the women of the bride's home.

Venda

A Venda marriage is somewhat different from those of other groups. On the completion of negotiations, the prospective but seemingly unwilling bride is enticed with presents all the way to the groom's home, where she must stay for two to three months on probation. Before she will agree to start working in what will probably be her new home, she must be presented with an additional gift. Until she receives this gift, she behaves in an extremely disrespectful manner, sitting with her legs straight out in front instead of tucking them under her. (The South Sotho bride also behaves in this manner until her father officially accepts the *lobola* cattle, making her a wife.) When and if finally satisfied, the groom's people allow man and wife to be joined in a ceremony which places greater emphasis on the personal aspects of a marriage than is the case with other groups in South Africa. The ceremony has been described by Stayt:

The medicine-man gives them a clay dish and tells them both to urinate in it, first the man and then the girl. Then he mixes drugs and water with the urine. He makes small incisions in the knees, hips, abdomens (just below the umbilicus), and necks of them both and rubs from the male into the female and vice versa. He then gives them some of the mixture to drink. After the conclusion of the ceremony the two are husband and wife.[3]

I have given only an outline of the ceremonies which serve to link husband to wife, or rather, to link two family groups by the transfer of a woman from one to the other, as well as establishing an ongoing relationship between both the living and the dead of the two groups. This relationship is characterised by the exchange of what Professor Krige has called 'institutionalised gifts', the largest of which, the *lobola*, is both preceded and followed by others, all serving to cement the relationship between the two family groups.

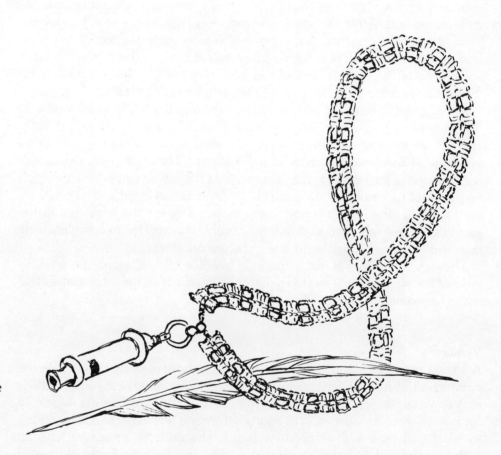

A whistle and a feather, both of which adorn the person of a fashionable young Bhaca man on a courting mission.

PAGE 159 Early traditional dress has been replaced by bright cloths supplied by the trading store. The manner and style in which these are worn have assumed a meaning and become associated with ethnic identity. Head cloths, by their colour and way of tying, may reveal not only the home area of the wearer but also her social status.

Head cloths are splendidly worn by the married women of Sekhukhuneland in the Eastern Transvaal. Shoulder covering is also important to the married woman, for it protects the child's eyes from flies which carry eye diseases in remote areas.

Barbara Tyrrell.

Barbara Tyrrell

MARRIED LIFE AND THE HOME

TRADITIONALLY the new bride left her home to live with her husband's family. Today the young couple often set up home on their own, away from the groom's parents. This change is mainly due to the fact that the young man earns his own *lobola* today and can be independent of his father's cattle and household.

Polygynous marriage is the norm in traditional society. However, polygyny is becoming less common, though Mönning has noted that among the Pedi most men have a second wife by the time they reach middle age.[1] However, those men who are wealthy enough to afford many wives are often also sufficiently Westernised not to want a polygynous household. The only people who still maintain large polygynous homes are chiefs and other noble personages who are able to afford it. In times past, chiefs could have up to a hundred or more wives, and Moshweshwe is reputed to have asked a young woman who her husband was (with a view to getting her for himself) — only to discover that he himself was the lucky man!

While the husband is undoubtedly the central figure of a traditional homestead, the structure and routine activities of such a homestead are determined by the status and chores of his wives. For this reason I will deal first with the wives' role in the home.

RANKING OF WIVES

A wife who is the member of a polygynous household holds a definite rank and is a pivotal individual in a social subunit or 'house', comprising herself and her children as well as their hut, possessions and the fields allocated to them. Most inland peoples appoint a 'great' or 'chief' wife, who is the mother of the heir. In the case of a commoner this woman is usually the first wife,

---

PAGE 160 Wood gathering is traditionally women's work and the size of a load carried on the head can be astonishing to Western eyes. This girl in her finery is one of a group that traditionally accompanies a new Bhaca bride on her first wood-gathering mission as a married woman. The wood has ceremonial significance.

This girl, by her beadwork apron, hip draperies and other beadwork, announces herself to be single but ripe for marriage. The deeply reddened cloth with the teased-out fringe is worn only at this stage of her life.

A carved blanket board, which is suspended horizontally from the hut roof or wall so that blankets may be draped over it. The design on this one shows the layout of the huts in a typical homestead. Behind the cattle kraal (bottom, centre) is the hut of the Great Wife. To its right is the hut of the left-hand wife, while that of the right-hand wife is on the left. The smaller huts are for poultry, grain storage and possibly beer brewing. A wealthy man may have his own private hut behind that of the Great Wife and, if he has many dependents, huts for them. Note the typical domestic activities. [Arthur Smit coll.]

while a king's great wife is usually chosen later in life, some time after his accession to the throne. Other wives are ranked in order of marriage or, in the case of the Tswana, in order of betrothal. The various Nguni people (with the noteworthy exception of the Swazi and Bhaca, who follow the procedures as outlined above) have a more complex system for the classification of wives in a polygynous home. This involves the division of a household into as many as three 'houses'. Most important of these is the Great House, the house of the Great Wife, mother of the heir. Affiliated to this are the 'right'- and 'left'-hand houses. (With the decrease in the size of settlements, the left-hand house, especially, has fallen away in many areas.) The layout of homesteads is based on the various houses. The traditional ideal for a Zulu homestead is illustrated above.

THE WIFE AND HER WORK

Under traditional law, the woman is always a minor and in most issues the husband considers her his responsibility. Her ownership of property is restricted. A wife's 'house' in the homestead has its own utensils; whatever the members (she and her retainers) may have earned by their own efforts — through the sale of pots and baskets, for example — belongs to her. A female diviner may have a considerable income and claim this as her own. (Near Illovo in Natal, I visited a man whose wife is a renowned diviner — with three bank accounts — and witnessed there, on occasion, discreet but nonetheless fierce little scuffles for possession of a client's payment!) A wife also owns the grain she grows on the land allocated to her by her husband. But this does not imply full ownership, as it is conditional on her membership of the family group. In a polygynous home each wife manages the economics and grain of her own 'house' and, unless petty bickering intervenes, the co-wives of a woman who has run out of grain will help out. A man will also allocate cattle to each house: these are for the use of that particular wife and her children as members of the homestead, but are not owned by them. A wife's ownership of property in relation to her husband is similar to his ownership of land in relation to his king and state — a form of conditional usufruct protected by traditional law rather than absolute possession.

The position in which a woman finds herself when married contrasts markedly with her single status. The union brings with it greater changes in her life than in that of her husband, especially if he already has a wife or wives. In a society of small groups and tightly controlled, well-defined family relationships, the new bride finds herself (at least in Nguni territory, where exogamy is the norm) a stranger in the home and on the bottom rung of the social ladder. The attitude required of her towards most other adults in her new home may be summed up in one word: respect — and with it all the associated avoidances and servility. Above all, she must show respect towards her father-in-law. As he was probably the person who paid the cattle (particularly in the past), she might find herself addressing him as 'husband'. She may not look into his eyes when speaking to him but must keep her gaze demurely downcast. In many areas this is emphasised by the bride's having to wear an eye-veil of cloth, hair or beads, depending on the tribe. In Transkei, a headcloth may be worn low over the eyes. These observances of respect, which tend to disappear with the passage of time and the wife's increasing status, are to be expected in a society noted for rigid social categories and clearly defined relationships. Even the matter of seating in a hut is not left to the individual: different areas are reserved for males and females. Woe betide the young wife who smears (with dung) the men's side of the floor! This task may be performed only by her mother-in-law. In an orthodox home, the young wife may not even cross the magic line to chase a dog stealing meat, but must content herself with aiming projectiles at it from the women's side.

Perhaps the most significant person in the life of a new wife (who belongs not only to her husband but also to his family) is her mother-in-law. Western women who chafe against the domineering mother-in-law would do well to consider what a traditional mother can demand of her son's wife. After having spent a large portion of her life as general work-horse, the mother-in-law is only too glad to welcome another pair of arms, young and strong, to work for her. The older woman may even leave most of the work to the new wife and have this woman wait on her as well. In polygynous homes, the older wives will find a great deal of the work burden shifted from their shoulders by the appearance of a new wife. Indeed, far from resenting her, many an overworked woman welcomes a new co-wife. Mönnig has noted that a Pedi woman may ask her husband to take a second wife to help her.

What constitutes this burden of work? It is the duty of the woman to collect firewood, carry water, do almost all the agricultural work, collect herbs, clean, decorate and maintain the huts, cook all the food, make beer, and care for the children. In addition to these chores, she may also have to make mats and pots. A woman is the basic cog in the mechanism of traditional society, responsible for keeping the whole culture alive.

During the planting and growing seasons, when weeds are rampant, as well as the harvesting season, the housewife is busy in the fields for most of the day. When the crops are harvested the maize must be decobbed and stored. Later, when maize is to be eaten in its most popular form, stiff porridge, the grains must be pounded and ground to flour. The northern and eastern Sotho and the Venda pound their maize with a large wooden pestle and mortar to produce meal, while the Nguni and other tribes to the south use a grindstone. Today these grindstones, worn into hollow rock basins by continual rubbing, have become redundant with the availability of commercial meal. Many of them now feature prominently in Natal gardens as

In Lesotho, colourful blankets have replaced the skin kaross as traditional garments. The design on the blanket commemorates V-day at the end of the Second World War. Note the typical apron of this woman and the fact that the blanket is pinned to the centre of the chest; a man pins his blanket on the left shoulder.

Barbara Tyrrell

extremely functional and attractive birdbaths! The preparation of this maize meal is a time-consuming process; one batch can represent as much as six hours of stamping. According to Stayt, the orthodox Venda housewife must arise at one or two o'clock in the morning to begin her work. He wrote:

> Staying near a chief's village it is difficult to obtain much sleep, as the ground shakes with the continual thudding of the stamps, which can be heard coming from all directions throughout the greater part of the night. [2]

This process must be repeated two to four times a week in order to feed the family. The cooking of porridge from the flour is a task lasting several hours. Also time-consuming is the collection of wild herbs for garnishing. The waterhole which has to be visited twice daily may be two kilometres or more distant. Those who live near a main thoroughfare may have to visit the waterhole even more frequently, as passers-by are entitled to 'drop in' to slake their thirst. Hospitality is an essential feature of traditional society and it is obligatory to put up a traveller or stranger — even if he is a personal enemy.

In addition to these duties there is the daily washing of utensils. In the past, before the advent of matches, the housewife went to great lengths to preserve her fire to avoid having to fetch coals elsewhere. The wood for the fire must be gathered several times a week — a task which can involve hours of collecting, and a round trip of perhaps fifteen kilometres or more, the second half with a massive pile of wood on the head.

Children must be fed and cared for. Here, fortunately, the busy housewife has helping hands. Her older daughters, if she has any, as well as the old women of the homestead, assist in the care of children. For the first part of its life, the child in the traditional home is not under a strict regime of feeding and nappy-changing and does not pose the same problem as its European counterpart.

Although the woman has a heavy and monotonous workload, she does not suffer from the same nervous tension that haunts the Western woman who not only cares for her family but possibly also holds down a job. The African woman and her society have their own version of the Spanish *mañana* philosophy or its Afrikaans equivalent, *'môre is nog 'n dag'*. Should she not feel inclined to hoe the maize field down by the stream today, she

A Zulu wooden pillow. An important function of such a pillow is said to be to prevent insects from crawling into the sleeper's ears and, for a woman, to lift her head-dress off the ground. This pillow belongs to a mother: she is depicted on the left; her hut at the centre; and a tree to symbolise her role as provider. [Arthur Smit coll.]

A young Zulu woman in the Msinga district grinding corn on a well-worn stone, a practice now made obsolete by the advent of commercial mills. Note the string skirt, a derivative of the early fibre skirt, and the plaited hair which she is growing in preparation for the high, red-ochred head-dress of the married woman. Her bracelets are of metal wire, coiled around hair from the tail of a horse.

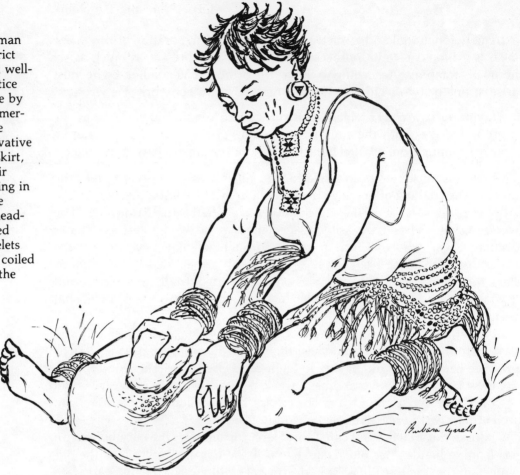

will not do so. The weeds are certainly getting out of hand, but, after all, they can't grow that much overnight. This is not to say that she shirks her work: she cannot afford to. A slovenly woman's attitude is reflected in the untidiness and lack of cleanliness of her home; after a lazy planting and growing season, she may have to borrow grain from others. This makes her despised and unpopular. Another reason to take the day off could be a beer-drink or ritual sacrifice; she generally requires her husband's permission to attend, but as he often goes himself, he will probably be willing.

THE HUSBAND

So different is a man's life today from what it was in historical times that the two life-styles must be treated separately.

Traditional Duties

In contrast to his wife, who was a real work-horse, the husband did comparatively little work in and around the home. A survivor from the *Stavenisse*, wrecked on the Wild Coast in 1686, wrote:

> They are generally kind, compassionate, and hospitable, but lazy in their nature; for the women perform all the hard work, as digging, delving, threshing, and making the huts, besides cooking and dressing the victuals, whilst the man do nothing but milk the cows and make the kraals.[3]

If a man had grown-up sons to herd his cattle, his domestic tasks were few. He woke up in the morning at dawn, not because he had to but simply because he liked it that way. His wife would already have been up for some time, possibly several hours, going about the chores of the house, one of which was to bring her husband water for his ablutions. The remainder of the day would see him possibly looking after the cattle or chatting with a few friends outside the huts (of a Nguni homestead) or in his own or a friend's courtyard (if he was a Pedi or Tswana). There may have been an interesting case on over at the local headman's court and he may have spent some time there, perhaps arguing a friend's case with characteristic eloquence. Sundown would see him home again for supper and an early night after a pleasant chat around the fire. (The young people would enjoy themselves until a much later hour.)

Abundant time and commitment to one's tasks are evident in this early Xhosa pipe. [From Shaw, 1938, Plate 93.]

His services to the community also extended to hut-building, hunting, the clearing of bush for new fields, carving, some basket-weaving, and the curing of hides. He may have been an ironsmith. Recently I examined a saw made from old pipe and sheet metal that was as good as and cheaper than commercial models. The maker, a gardener, had apparently set himself up as the local metalworker in his township. Today this skill can also be applied to the manufacture of firearms, or their modification. For instance air rifles are obtained and adapted to accept a .22 rimfire cartridge — highly illegal but apparently effective.

The men were far from being drones, however. They were the protectors of society. This protection extended not only to defence (and attack) — involving both formal military service and the protection of the homestead and its cattle — but to the morals and traditional fabric of society. The men were — and remain — the custodians of the law, and the repositories of traditions and customs. It was the old greybeards who gave depth — and still do — to society, re-telling the legends and sagas of the past which enriched the meaning of an individual's life, with its temptations and tears and emotion, in terms of the group's life. Without such an anchor lodged on moral bedrock, a culture is lost, and a people without a culture with which to identify are also without stability, purpose or significance. This stability took a very concrete form in the law-courts, where every man could plead a case or give evidence, and in the chief's council, which advised and controlled the leader.

Contemporary Realities

Aspects of the old masculine role remain. When a couple walk along a road or path today, the man still walks in front, unencumbered but for a stick or two, while his wife trails flat-footed behind, burdened down with anything from live chickens to a cardboard box of groceries, a sack of meal, or even, twenty years ago, a wind-up record player — sometimes playing!

The man is not simply being lazy. First, it would be beneath his masculine dignity to demean himself by carting goods — the work of women. Second, he walks in front, sticks in hand, because no self-respecting traditionalist will venture out of his home on a journey unarmed lest he be attacked by either human or animal; his duty is to protect his womenfolk from danger. With the advent of European rule, which put an end to petty raiding and warfare, the man has lost much of his importance as a protector.

White rule has also terminated his 'call-ups' to the royal village to serve in the army which — especially among the more militant tribes such as the Zulu, Pedi and Swazi — occupied much of his time, particularly during his youth.

Military duty has now been replaced by economic necessity and every man, at one time or another — usually most of the time — finds himself working in the city, far from his home and family. At times so high a proportion of men are away at work that women even find themselves looking after those hallowed objects, the lineage cattle. The traditionalist migrant labourer has his roots in his home soil, however, and seldom gets caught up in the cities where he works, in the way Western man is and expects others to be.

This is not surprising when one considers, first, the profound difference between his traditional African home environment and the exploitative, rushed life of a Western commercial centre and, second, the blinding and stifling stereotype view that Westerners have of the migrant labourer. Professor H.S. Alverson has shown how the black industrial worker is in a double bind: expected on the one hand to manifest initiative and ambition (in an unfamiliar and restrictive work environment) and, on the other, to be docile and submissive — to fill the common stereotype. Alverson summed up the African's solution; 'One of the African's secrets of survival in South Africa is to keep the White man as ignorant of him as possible.'[4] Underlying the overt life of industrial South Africa, there is an invisible social framework held together by meanings and aspirations that simply could not make sense to Westerners who deal with the bland image which every black labourer learns to project.

The gulf separating traditional thought and Western economic thought is wide even for a farm worker, and is well illustrated by the following statement made by an informant from the Natal Midlands:

It happened at my parents' farm [i.e. the European-owned farm on which they worked]. One man would come late to do his sugar-cane weeding

---

PAGE 169   Colourful blankets in Lesotho have replaced the traditional shoulder capes of animal skin. A man's blanket is pinned on his right shoulder so that his right arm is free to use either a stick or a riding crop. A woman pins hers on her breast, her hands tucked underneath, her burden on her head.

This man wearing his rain hat of woven grass, watches the passing scene, while the woman, wearing the apron and skirt of marriage, passes by demurely.

Hat-making is the handicraft of males — a skill learned in boyhood days when herding cattle in the hills.

PAGE 170   A new Ndebele bride attends a social function dressed in all the bead finery that she prepared during her betrothal period. Ornaments and bead patterns vary according to district. The blanket was part of the traditional dress for many years, but is now almost unobtainable. Both beadwork and blanket lore have been replaced by plastics and cheaper forms of decoration. A married woman's apron, once entirely beaded, may now be a hotch-potch of pieces of plastic, but is worn with the same degree of pride as of old.

Beside the bride is a girl of marriageable age, who wears a beaded rectangular apron of stiff canvas to announce her status. The beaded hoops with a grass core are built around neck and legs and, though bulky, are not as heavy as they appear to be.

Barbara Tyrrell

Barbara Tyrrell

Barbara Tyrrell

task but went at it faster than any. Everyone complained, saying that he had an *imikhovu* (zombie familiar) invisible and working by day (because the witch gave him medicine to make it invisible).

Imikhovu would work one half of the field, starting at the opposite end. They, the other workers, cried bitterly because the man was being helped by an *imikhovu* and the farmer said the man must go.

These things (zombie familiars) are made to help with work, even loading. Helping load, they would be hungry. You could hear them cry in the hut, 'We are hungry. Father, we are tired.' People heard them.

The man was chased away. He lost his job.

It is apparent that the roles of man and woman in African society are broadly the same as in most others: the woman is the stable influence, representing the strong, steady, conservative-though-malleable energy of life, which maintains the culture; the man was and is the protector of both the physical well-being of society and the laws which give it form and direction. He is also the innovator who introduces change into the old pattern and revitalises society.

This Mpondo man demonstrates one of the imaginative uses of a mundane article such as the safety-pin. The facial scarification associated with the ancestors and finely plaited hair are typical.

THE HOMESTEAD

While the homestead, as an aspect of the material culture, belongs later on in the text, it is so strongly linked to the nature of the family or group who inhabit it, that I will discuss it here, separate from a description of traditional huts.

Nguni Homesteads

The Nguni do not organise their separate homestead units into towns but build them scattered about on the hill and lands where their herds roam. Each homestead is known as an *umzi*. As the trend among the Nguni is for a young couple to set up home at some distance from the groom's father, dozens of groups of huts dot the countryside. In the past, when a man had

---

PAGE 171 A decorative and practical method of straightening and lengthening hair is by binding it in tufts with strands of grass. This girl, influenced by both the Tsonga and Swazi traditions, is wearing the beads, cloths and bangles of her courting days.

The line drawing depicts a Tsonga boy on a courting mission, as shown by the small courting shield, the courting feathers in his hair, the cross-over bead bands and other beadwork. The bead ornaments have been made for him by the girl of his choice.

In all areas courting is marked by colourful dress and an elaborate trafficking in messages, gifts and tokens that accompanies the arranging of trysts. Age-group friends are ritually involved in these transactions, as are parents and relatives.

PAGE 172 These Bhaca women from southern Natal dance their way across the hills to a party at a friend's homestead. They approach in single file as a sign that they come in peace. They wear the gala dress that was common some twenty years ago when beads were plentiful.

Today married status is still indicated by lengthened, red-ochred hair, although now sometimes augmented with twists of wool or string. The style of dress is relatively unchanged, but the beadwork on the clothes is missing. Goatskin skirts are still correct and essential wear for married women of the tribe, and goats are plentiful both for feasting and for sacrifice.

many wives, his sons would set up home with their new brides in a part of their mother's 'house'. These homesteads, housing several families, could almost be called villages. A modern example is the homestead of the Swazi queen mother, which (ignoring the brick house of the queen mother herself) is said to be the largest traditional village in the southern hemisphere.

Homesteads are built around the 'chapel' or sacred centre of the ancestral religion — the cattle kraal. This traditionally round, now sometimes square, enclosure may range in diameter from five metres to (in the case of the Swazi royal kraal) 60 metres. The huts may encircle the kraal or, more commonly, form a semicircle which, as the traditionalist prefers his home to be on an east-facing slope, is above and to the west of the cattle kraal. Around the encircling huts there may be a second enclosure of thorn bushes which serves to keep out both unwanted animals and humans.

The Great Hut, home of the Great Wife, is centrally placed opposite the entrance of the homestead. This hut is the most important in the homestead, and is held in great respects by all junior wives, who may not enter it. Along with the cattle kraal it is the religious focal point of the homestead — the 'chapel'. In it are kept the sacred objects such as sacrificial spears, the horns of their victims, or special parts of their innards loved by the shades; all these items are either tied to the rafters or stuck in the thatch. The *umsamo* (Zulu) or 'altar' at the rear of the Great Hut is the most important *umsamo* in the homestead. The position of the huts of the other houses in a Zulu homestead is shown on page 162.

Apart from the huts belonging to wives and their houses, there are several other huts: those used for storage of the harvest; those of unrelated 'hangers-on'; those of the young boys and the young girls; and, in the case of a wealthy nobleman, his private hut located near the Great Hut. In the absence of such a hut, the homestead head spends his time in the huts of his wife or wives. Few commoners are rich enough to obtain all these wives and huts and nowadays even those who are well off are often Westernised and have largely discarded the traditional ways.

Sotho/Tswana Homesteads

The size and layout of Sotho settlements vary to a much greater extent from place to place than do those of the Nguni. In some areas, especially the Lesotho highlands, and among certain clans, such as the Tlôkwa, the settlements are small, limited to one family with perhaps a few unrelated or distantly related people attached.

In other areas the separate homestead units may be clustered in large villages and towns. There are villages in Lesotho housing as many as 500 families. The towns of Botswana are the extreme example, and may house the entire tribe. Serowe, for example, with a five-figure population, is the home of the Ngwato. Such towns are the contemporary versions of the early stone towns of this part of the world.

As among the Nguni, the Sotho and Tswana wives are placed, according to rank, in a roughly horseshoe-shaped homestead. Each wife's main hut (where the cooking is done), together with the sleeping and storage huts, forms a unit which may or may not be surrounded by a reed palisade or mud wall. The Pedi call the front or public part of the enclosure the *lelapa*, a term common to various Sotho/Tswana tribes. A woman's house or unit in a homestead is often referred to as her *lelapa* and the huts which constitute her unit all face on to the *lelapa*. The courtyard of a Lobedu woman is located between her sleeping hut and her living hut. These hut pairs (cooking and sleeping huts) form two large concentric semicircles around the *khoro*, or meeting-place, and may, in the household of a wealthy man, completely encircle it.

Venda Homesteads

Like the Lobedu to whom they are related, the Venda have homesteads comprising a *khoro* flanked by a double semicircle of hut pairs, each pair consisting of a living and a cooking hut which together enclose a private courtyard.

In historic times the Venda were well aware that their strength lay in the bushy crags of their native Soutpansberg mountains and they constructed their villages accordingly. These villages were usually grouped around a chief's residence. They were large, surrounded by a solid stone wall, and often perched perilously on some precipitous hillside beneath a towering cliff. I have visited a village of about twenty huts, situated on so steep a slope that the *khoro* had to be placed some distance below, astride a broad saddle on a ridge. In keeping with the modern trend, today's homesteads are smaller, often consisting only of a man, his wife and their children, and located on the plains. This system is much appreciated by the women, who no longer have to walk long, steep kilometres to keep their homes supplied with water.

OLD AGE AND DEATH

OLD AGE

MANY Europeans move into old age amid protestations and desperate but vain attempts to cling to the myth that life is youth. To the African, old age brings with it not only freedom from much of the daily routine, but status and the respect of society. The aged are not considered a burden for whom old-age homes must be sought; they play an important role in the life of the community.

The old men have the responsibility of upholding the laws and customs of their people. It is the wise old grandfather whose words will carry weight in a family quarrel — provided, of course, he has earned his position by fitting conduct. Should such a quarrel not be resolved within the family circle and be taken to the traditional court, it will receive the attention of the greybeards. The old men (and women) have the important task of passing on the traditional histories to the younger people. One of the greatest evils brought about by Shaka's wars (see p. 30) was that the people who suffered most were the aged — the repositories of the priceless unwritten history of the people who constitute some four-fifths of the population of modern Southern Africa.

A woman gains more status and relief from duties with age than her husband and brothers. Throughout the first part of her life she is haunted by the ritual impurity stemming from her sexual functions, and by the need to practise respect avoidances in speech and behaviour. But after the menopause and with increasing numbers of her descendants, she has fulfilled her traditional role and can get away with all sorts of things unheard of for a younger woman: she may bare herself from the waist up if she finds the sun hot in the fields; she may walk with impunity into that most hallowed of all places, the cattle kraal; she may even enter a council and air her views.

If the husband of an older woman is dead, she is technically a dependent of her son. In practice, she is an important person in her son's life and may largely organise his daily routine. The greatest power she wields is over her daughter-in-law, whom she may rule with a rod of iron. To the children, grandmother is a special person, as is grandfather. As children grow up, their relationship with their parents become more formal, but the elderly can afford to relax and enjoy the youngsters. There is usually a warm and special relationship between the old and young of a homestead. The children gather round the old women in the evenings to hear the old tribal tales. They are cared for by them when their mothers are away at the trading store, or in the fields, or collecting wood.

DEATH

And God said to the Chameleon: 'I have a message which you must take to mankind. Go and tell them this: tell them that human beings are to live forever.'

Chameleon rolled his eyes in solemn acknowledgement and set off. But he could only jerk along; and he was not overly interested in any case. He tarried frequently by the way and rolled his strange eyes at the iridescent bellies of the bluebottle flies, hoping one would come within reach of his deadly tongue. He had not gone far when God changed His mind. He called Lizard (or a millipede or hare, according to different versions): 'Lizard,' He said, 'I have a job for you. You are to take a message to mankind. You must tell them that their fate is death. Death, do you hear? Death.' Lizard wagged his lithe tail and was gone on his mission.

It was not long before Lizard passed Chameleon, who had stopped for a while in the hot midday sun. He was amusing himself by idly trying to match his skin to the hot red brown of the dusty path.

And so it was that Lizard, with his terrible tidings, arrived first and was accepted as God's messenger. Who would, who could, believe the belated glad tidings of Chameleon? Death was in the world — as much a part of man as his toes and fingers. No, more so: a man may live without those appendages, but not without death.

As effective as the serpent and fig-leaf epic, the story of the lizard and the chameleon is widely told among the tribes. All Southern African tribes agree on another aspect of death: that there are two kinds — death caused by the appearance of Time's scythe in due season; and the death by accident or disease of a younger person, with few or no descendants to perpetuate his or her memory. This catastrophe is so foreign to the traditionalist's view of a benevolent universe that he can only conclude that such a fate is sent by the one creature that knows evil — a witch. Berglund writes:

> A timely death is in the Zulu language expressed by terms such as *ukugoduka*, *ukudlula*, *ukuhamba* and *ukuqubeka*, which all give notions of a passing on, a continuation. An untimely death is described as *ukufa*, *ukubhubha*, and *ukugqibuka*, which imply a breaking off of life.[1]

Euthanasia

Euthanasia is surely as old as man himself. Old people who were sick and unable to fend for themselves, could look forward to a little help in entering the world of the ancestors. A Swazi or Zulu patriarch for whom life had become an intolerable burden and who was himself a burden to his people, might indicate his feelings and be laid out across the entrance to the cattle kraal just before the cattle were driven in for the evening. During the Spartan days of the great Zulu kings, an old man who was too decrepit to appear when summoned into the royal presence or to his regiment, soon found himself 'sent home' by a group of warriors who visited his earthly home. An old woman, beyond caring for herself, might be taken far from home and left

Mfengu woman and homestead scene, Ciskei. Sitting in the woman's position with legs tucked beneath her and to one side, she wears the white apron of marriage, but her red-ochred face reveals that she is not yet a mother. Around her waist she wears a tobacco pouch to stock her typically short Mfengu pipe. Note the amputated top phalanx of the little finger of the left hand: a custom associated with propitiation of the ancestors common among the Southern Nguni, especially in certain clans.

in a deep donga. A Venda, if old, sick and nearly unconscious, might have, as his last earthly memory, the smell of a burning python skin held under his nose to asphyxiate him and facilitate his passing.

Funeral Rites

The disposal of the corpse after death depends not only on the tribe but also on the status of the deceased. An infant or stillborn baby will be buried with little or no fuss; only the silent heartache of its parents will follow it into the spirit realm. Young people who have not yet attained the dignity of full adulthood will be buried with some ceremony, while the aged and important are given a royal send-off with the appropriate mourning observances to follow. Among the Nguni, the strong patriarchal attitude is evident in the far greater concern expressed at a man's funeral than at that of a woman. Sotho tribes show their respect for important women (and fear of them as ancestors) by suitably elaborate burial ceremonies.

The actual burial rites are not complicated. The Zulu accompany the deceased to the graveside in a procession, the men leading and the women behind with hands folded on their breasts. South Sotho mourners each

throw in a handful of earth, and even traditionalists will ask a priest to say a few words over the grave. Thembu mourners also throw earth into the grave before it is filled. In historic times in Lesotho an ox was slaughtered and had to be eaten before sunrise. Just before dawn the whole village would gather, each person holding a little chyme taken from the dead animal in his or her hand. As the sun appeared, each would throw this chyme into the grave with the words, 'Sleep in peace for us'. Most tribes mark death and burial by loud and prolonged ceremonial wailing at various points. For example, Zulu women wail as soon as a death has occurred and then again after the interment.

When Shaka's mother, Nandi, died, the wailing continued for many days — an emotional spectacular that involved the killing of thousands who did not show sufficient grief. A woman does not have to be grief-stricken to wail; it is the formal method of condolence and showing respect. Only the Lobedu and South Sotho do not indulge in this.

Implications of Death

To the traditionalist, death has two main attributes which must be taken into account in rituals for the dead. First, dying is an important step in the life of the deceased as it is synonymous with birth into the ancestral world, a passage that requires the performance of certain rites. Second, death brings with it a contagious, black aura that infects all it touches. Removing and dealing with this form of ritual impurity is the prime motivation behind many of the rites.

Ritual Impurity

The corpse, as a ritually impure object, contaminates its environment and is interred as soon as possible, even on the day of death. So powerful is this impurity that in the past among the Nguni, a dying man was taken out to die in the veld lest he taint the hut. If he died in the hut, it would be pulled down or burned. When the head of a family died the entire homestead was moved.

All associated with the death are believed to be heavily contaminated by ritual impurity. This state demands the practice of certain avoidances: the impure among many tribes will abstain from work in the fields on the day of death (an abstention also in force after hail); there is a taboo on the eating of sour milk for three days to a week (a taboo associated with most forms of ritual impurity); and a ban on sex. The gravediggers and those handling the body should be stark naked (today they often wear a loincloth), so that their clothes do not become ritually impure. If a close male relative is not available to bury a Mpondo, then a beast must be given to an outsider who will undertake the task and, in exchange for the payment, expose himself to the impurity. After the funeral there must follow the ritual cleansing of all people — family and others — and of objects (spades, picks and so on) connected with the corpse and burial. The Nguni achieve this by using strengthening 'black' medicines and possibly, by killing a goat to 'wash the hands'. A person who does not take these precautions to purify himself endangers not only himself, but all those with whom he comes into contact.

Another protection against the ritual impurity or aura of death is provided by the widely practised 'inversions' of conduct and speech. Sentences or phrases will be worded in reverse (a practice not confined to traditionalists).

Berglund provides a photograph of the minister of a Christian sect with his clerical collar reversed for a funeral.[2] Many Nguni and South Sotho do not remove a corpse via the door but make a hole in the back of the hut for its removal; Bomvana use a hole made on the men's side of the hut for a man and on the women's side for a woman; Zulu take the added precaution of entering the death hut in reverse, so that all footprints face outwards, thus compelling the contagion of death to leave. The end of the period of abstention may be marked, among the Nguni, by a second sacrifice about a month after death. A South Sotho family, if sufficiently wealthy, may sacrifice a sheep for each member a week or so after the burial of an important man.

The Grave

The traditional grave is peculiar, by European standards. Oval in shape and one to two metres deep, its most notable feature is the niche, up to two metres long, cut in the side at the base. Into this niche the corpse is placed. A Pedi grave, however, does not have a niche. Older Mpondo people informed Monica Hunter (Professor Monica Wilson) that although niche graves are now in use, there was a time in living memory when a grave was merely a shallow hole. Graves with a niche are common in Africa, however, and some West Africans dig a side tunnel up to ten metres long at the bottom of their graves.

The proper burial posture of the corpse is with the knees up, as if squatting. This is also the birth position, and symbolises birth into the spirit world. Should *rigor mortis* set in before the corpse is arranged, the tendons at the knees and elbows must be cut in order to bend these limbs. This may be done anyway, as it forestalls any witch who may wish to use the deceased as a zombie familiar. Additional protection against witches is obtained by using quantities of stone to fill the grave and by frequent nightly inspections of it after the burial.

The deceased, squatting in his or her niche, faces a specific direction. Most Nguni dead buried outside the homestead area, are turned towards it. The head of the homestead, buried in or beside the cattle kraal, faces the chief hut. The Sotho and inland tribes do not show this desire to include the deceased in the beloved family circle; instead they manifest a nostalgia for the ancestral home, and their corpses face either east or north-east. Nguni who die violently or from an inexplicable illness, are turned away from the homestead lest they contaminate it.

A dead man does not depart without his possessions or unclothed. An important Venda, for whom a black ox has been killed, will have the skin as a shroud (a custom encountered throughout Africa). Personal possessions buried include snuffboxes, spoons, milking-thongs, pipes and so forth, as well as weapons. It is said by some people that these articles are needed by the deceased in the next world, but others say that the objects are useless to their owners after death and are buried simply because they are ritually contaminated. No knives are buried in the grave, and the head of a man's spear

PAGE 181   An Ndebele mother threads beads onto a rectangular medallion of strong card covered with black cloth. The metal rings on her arms and legs indicate her married status. The beadwork rings have a grass core and are made on the body.

Barbara Tyrrell

is removed or the shaft broken, because sharp objects or weapons may be used against the family, not only by the living but by those in the land of the shades. Before the advent of the European, when iron was still extremely scarce in much of the Nguni territory, this exclusion of metal objects from the grave had obvious practical advantages.

Various foodstuffs are also placed in the traditional grave: sometimes pumpkins, but always grain, especially sorghum, the traditional cereal. The purpose of this is not to provide the person with seed or food for the world of shades (which is poorly conceptualised anyway); rather is it based on the concept of reciprocity — in giving, there is hope that the deceased will in turn exert himself to ensure good crops for his living relatives.

Western ideas and religions have wrought great changes in all aspects of traditional life, and this influence extends to the individual's last resting-place. The traditional squatting posture and type of grave have been largely superseded by Western-style graves and, if money is sufficient, coffins, and even a hearse. Today the usual Western-style grave may well have a recess on one side to take the coffin. Western society has brought with it funeral insurance too. Catering as it does for a people to whom a decent burial is important, it is a thriving business.

The Grave Site
The grave site is an index of the social status of the deceased. Among all the tribes the cattle kraal is the burial site of honour. The head of the homestead in Nguni territory is usually buried at the entrance to the cattle kraal. This is also done for the important deceased of the Sotho tribes. Among the Sotho the term 'important people' embraces certain women, notably the wife or wives of the head of the homestead. Among most tribes people of lesser importance are buried some distance from the homestead. The Pedi bury lesser individuals in the 'private courtyard' behind the hut. The Pedi grave site is chosen by a spouse or a closely related woman, while the Venda rely on the priest-diviner to indicate the actual site.

In the past, burial was not the only method of disposing of a corpse. During the reign of Shaka the corpse was sometimes dragged out and left to scavengers. This was also done among the Southern Nguni at an early date (as reported by early shipwreck victims), but later only the bodies of those who died at war were treated in this way. The South Sotho, on the other hand, took pains to bury their men killed in battle lest enemy priest-diviners and war doctors used their remains against the tribe or clan. Nguni who have died violently should not be buried in the homestead, as they taint it by their fate. Among some tribes the corpse of a person struck by lightning must be buried near a river in cool soil as this unfortunate accident renders the victim

---

PAGE 182   Twenty years ago beads were plentiful and beadwork was of the highest order. This Bhaca married woman wears a full complement of ornaments typical of someone of her status. Hair, for marriage, was and still is red ochred under its sausage-like, beaded knob of firmly stuffed cloth. In early marriage the ochred hair is worn covering the eyes, betokening respect for the groom's parents. It may be parted only after the birth of the first child and then only by permission and with ceremony. During the Second World War beads were in short supply and wool ornaments were devised. The woven grass head pins show the style of earlier days.

ritually 'hot', and therefore a target for lightning. Similarly, the corpse of a drowned man must be buried near a river because that river, if cheated, will claim another victim.

Mourning

Mourning entails a ban on many activities and on all celebrations and conviviality. The period of mourning depends on the status of the deceased and the mourner's relationship to him or her. The official mourning period of a woman for her husband is up to a year. A baby is not officially mourned at all, as it was not yet a true person. The mourning period of a man for his wife is measurable in days, a reflection of the relative attitudes towards the sexes; and the death of the head of the homestead is mourned by the entire family group for a month or more.

Ceremonial mourning not only facilitates the expression of grief but is a catalyst for the transition — rebirth — of the community as a whole. The new community that has emerged without the physical presence of the deceased must carry on. Overtly it is the rite of passage marking the transition to death of the deceased. However, it can be likened to the initiation ceremony which marked the birth of an adult, who then had to confirm his new status as a group member by marrying and joining the living genealogical line: the newly deceased has attained a new status but has not yet been fully reintegrated into the ongoing life and meaning of the group. This reintegration is of vital importance, both for the deceased and for his descendants.

Women of different tribes traditionally mourn the deceased in a variety of ways — by shaving the head, for instance. This Bhaca woman has honoured her people's tradition by washing the red ochre from her hair and plaiting it.

THE BIRTH OF AN ANCESTOR

D EATH, as the individual's most personal and isolating experience, must be followed by reintegration into the group. The power of death, which wrests the individual from society and represents, through him, an alien threat to that society, must be tamed; the deceased must be incorporated into the solid body of the community as an ancestor.

The 'bringing-back' ceremony to reincorporate the individual into the group is one of the most important in traditional life. Through it death, the basic enigma of and threat to human existence, is conquered and manipulated to produce its social opposite: the ancestors, the social explanation of life to man, the meaning of society, its moral code and muscle.

The time separating an individual's death from his bringing-back ceremony varies. The Thembu, among others, hold an *izila* ceremony some weeks or months after death to affirm and establish contact between the recently deceased and the living. The inclusion of the shade into the ranks of the lineage ancestors is achieved by the sacrifice of a goat or beast which 'brings back' the shade. This rite is performed about a year after death. A shade causing trouble by sending sickness or appearing in dreams and demanding to be 'brought back' will be granted its wish with all possible haste. A young priest-diviner I knew had been dead for four years before her people could collect enough money to provide the sacrificial animals for her bringing-back ceremony; as a priest-diviner, her particular ceremony entailed the sacrifice of four cattle, costing R400 or more. In her area R20 to R30 a month (plus food and lodging) was the average wage paid a farm labourer.

A 'BRINGING-BACK' RITUAL

To try to capture the significance of this ceremony I shall use just one example: the bringing back of a woman which involved two sacrifices (a goat and a cow) and spanned a period from Thursday, 13 October to Sunday, 16 October 1977. For the sake of those involved in these rites, I have used fictitious names and specify the locality only loosely. It is near Pietermaritzburg, Natal.

The example I have chosen comprised two clusters of rituals, designed to repatriate the shade in two different senses. Two years prior to the perform-ance of these rituals, the head of the household, whom I shall call Mbovana Shange, had lost his mother, who had been buried about 100 kilometres away near the Umzimkulu Valley. On two occasions following her death he had sacrificed a white fowl to her and the family shades to 'make them happy', and thereby ensure good fortune for the household. All this time however she had been separated from the family in two distinct senses. On the one hand she had endured geographical separation from her son, due to the distance of her grave from his home. This situation was remedied by the 'opening of the road' ritual, which commenced with the goat sacrifice. The cow sacrifice, on the other hand, was part of a ritual designed to 'bring back' the old lady in the sense of ending her social alienation by reincorporating her into the lineage as an ancestor.

The shade of this woman had made her wishes quite clear by appearing to the family members in dreams. Shange's wife, Nogwazi, had been particularly affected. Her mother-in-law had often approached her while she slept. On many of these occasions she had carried in her arms a baby which she told Nogwazi was a symbol of good fortune. These benign dreams, all indicating the desire to be integrated into the family, could, however, have been followed by ill-fortune had they not been heeded.

The series of rituals began with the brewing of beer three days before the first sacrifice. Like many other peri-urban people, the Shange family could not grow sufficient maize or *mabele* (sorghum) in their township garden, and these ingredients had to be bought. The beer made in this way retains the quality of 'coolness' which is so pleasant to the ancestors. Like all beer, it was brewed in the 'place of the ancestors', the *umsamo*, and by Thursday, the time of the first sacrifice, the *umsamo* was cluttered with a wooden barrel and a large three-legged pot, which together contained about 250 litres of beer. In addition there was a small clay pot of beer brewed as a special offering to the ancestors.

Like many of the homesteads in the township, that of the Shange family did not consist of round huts. There were only two oblong huts — the kitchen, about three metres square, and the main hut, which consisted of two rooms, each about the same size as the kitchen hut. The room with the door to the outside was the general congregation room with the *umsamo*, while the inner room was Shange's bedroom, with an iron bed in one corner, a rickety table and some shelves. The room was very untidy, with clothing everywhere. On the table was a carton of commercially brewed African beer (which is largely divorced from any association with the ancestral spirits).

When I and my two companions arrived on the Thursday night to witness the goat sacrifice, we were made comfortable on a bench against the wall opposite the *umsamo*. As we walked up to the hut, we noticed the sacrificial goat tethered by the pathway. It was a young female with a white coat broken by pale brown patches. We had not been seated long before the animal appeared at the door, securely held by a young boy, one of Shange's sons. The opening of the road rites had begun.

Desirable at 'opening of the road' rituals is the presence of a priest-diviner. Shange was fortunate to have a priest-diviner sister-in-law, who agreed to officiate for the entire period, including the second or 'bringing back' rites performed to achieve social integration of the shade. Among the first of her

Nguni priest-diviner plays the drum of the diviner, an instrument based on the base drum of European military bands. Note the various decorative items, including bladders, feathers and skins, taken from sacrificial animals.

Barbara Tyrrell.

functions was the preparation of *ubulawu* medicine for the goat sacrifice. *Ubulawu* is a class of 'white medicines' which are attractive to the shades. Most priest-diviners in the area are equipped with a three-pronged 'spirit stick' about half a metre long. The diviner put her spirit stick into the *ubulawu* medicine, which was in a clay pot, and twirled it between her palms. After a minute, the mixture was frothing, with white foam running down the sides of the pot and on to the floor. It is said that only a good-natured person is able to make *ubulawu* froth well. The foam on that pot amply confirmed our opinion of the priest-diviner.

While this was in progress, the goat was turned towards the *umsamo*, firmly held by two of Shange's sons. Shange addressed the ancestors:

'Keep us all from illness. Everybody. Everybody. Even our grandchildren. Give light and have everyone join here today. Kanyisile [a son who had died in babyhood], be present also.'

At one stage the goat knelt and was hastily pulled to its feet. It is unlucky for the goat to kneel on such occasions, for kneeling is a position of weakness. It should stand, thereby strengthening the entire procedure.

A child laughed and was immediately reprimanded: 'Don't laugh, child; they are going to kill it.'

When the *ubulawu* was sufficiently whisked, the goat's head was forced into it and it was seen to take a small drink, which is a good omen indicating acceptance by the ancestors. A small child, dispatched earlier to the kitchen to fetch coals, returned with these on a piece of corrugated iron, which she placed on the hearth in the centre of the hut. The priest-diviner then put the sweet-smelling *imphepho* herb (*Helichrysum odoratissimum*) on the coals and burned this, producing a sweet and fragrant smoke, that is said to clear the head for the spirits, and to make one strong. The goat's head was held in the smoke so that it was forced to breathe it. Unburned *imphepho* was then passed over the goat from its nose along its back to the tail, under the tail and between the hind legs. The goat was now ready for sacrifice to the ancestors and was moved to where it would be killed.

'Bring it close to the food [beer],' the priest-diviner instructed and the two young boys complied. They then gripped the fore and hind legs, and picked the goat up so that it was suspended upside down.

Shange emerged from his room with a spear — the sacrificial spear of the lineage, used on all such occasions. When not in use it was stored under his bed. It was very blunt and he had to make several attempts before he succeeded in piercing the goat's hide. This lineage always stabs the goat just below the sternum, pressing the spear upwards into the thorax.

The last of the evening light had fled and the interior of the hut was dark but for the glow of the coals and a tiny paraffin lamp. The desperate yelling of the goat filled the shadows but found no response in the impassive faces of those present. As it convulsed in pain, the goat's huge shadow jumped and loomed on the wall, but the audience, in the spell of communion with their dead, appeared oblivious to its suffering.

Shange turned to some children sitting against the wall close to the spot where the goat was being killed and said, 'The space is small, will you move over a little'.

Apart from the order, the only sound was the agonised crying every time Shange moved the assegai buried deep inside the goat's thorax.

Traditionally, it is good when the goat cries a great deal, for the sound is pleasant to the ears of the ancestors, being regarded as not only an attractant but also as an indication of their presence. Shange's lineage (and many others) are notable for the prolonged agony endured by their sacrificial animals. But there is no awareness that cruelty is involved — the cries of the doomed animal, which can continue for up to half an hour, are simply part of the ritual.

On this occasion the goat died in about fifteen minutes. Throughout this period the goat was repeatedly stretched to enlarge the gall bladder, an important item in any sacrifice to the ancestors. In addition, Shange slapped the goat repeatedly with his flat hand, each time eliciting a scream of agony. This slapping is deemed necessary because during his life a man receives many medicines from priest-diviners which build up a certain bitterness in his flesh. This is transmitted to the goat when he stabs it, but by slapping it, he retracts the bitterness into himself and thereby ensures that the meat will be good to eat.

The goat's cries were now weak, and the people in the hut were again chatting happily. At last, manoeuvring the assegai in the goat's chest, Shange said in response to a particularly desperate cry, 'That's right in the "battery" [heart]'.

This comment was greeted with much laughter and ribald comment. The priest-diviner (who happened to be Shange's sister-in-law) chuckled, 'Oh small father [brother-in-law], how funny you are'.

There followed general amusement and remarks on the theme of the goat's 'battery', comparing the animal to an FM radio with a flat battery. Meanwhile the cries grew rapidly weaker. At this stage my white companion buried her face in her hands, which made for more hilarity and laughter.

At length the crying ceased.

'Stretch it even more!' Shange ordered the two holding the goat, and they complied. A baby cried and someone laughed. The baby's mother commented that it was afriad of the goat's death cries. Another woman, referring to the gravity of such a communion with the ancestors, said, 'Little boy, don't you know this is a wonderful thing you have witnessed?'

Shange pressed his finger on to the goat's eye and, finding no reaction, pronounced it dead.

As usual, the goat was immediately skinned and dismembered on the spot, in an atmosphere of relaxed bonhomie doubtless brought on by the success of the sacrifice and the inferred presence of the ancestors. Most Africans have a thorough knowledge of the internal organs of animals and how to butcher them. A knife was called for and Shange and his brother (who had travelled from Cathcart in the eastern Cape to attend) set to work, carefully opening the carcass. Not a drop of blood or fluid was spilled — had this happened the affected area of the floor would have had to be smeared immediately with fresh dung to foil a witch bent on stealing the (dried) fluid. As it was, the entire floor was smeared the next day from the centre outwards to drive out any evil influences. Mixed with the dung used to smear it was a special medicine which would put to sleep any witch who entered bent on evil.

Various internal organs played a role in the ritual. The *mhlehlwa* or mesentery was removed immediately the animal was opened up and hung from the wall above the *umsamo* to attract the ancestors. The *incekwa* or third stomach beloved of the spirits, was hung above the *umsamo* so that they could gather and lick it. In addition, the *incekwa* plays an important role in subsequent phases of the 'bringing-back', as will be seen.

The gall bladder, enlarged by stretching, was removed and kept. Two nights later the gall was sprinkled on the joints of the right-hand side of the bodies of all the members of the family. In the spirit realm, all things are reversed — black is white and white is black, darkness is light and vice versa. The bitterness of gall is, accordingly, sweet. This sprinkling on the joints attracts the ancestors and their blessings to the family. The reason for the choice of the right-hand side is that this is the strong or positive side and therefore associated specifically with the shades.

Scene in the *umsamo*, the place of the spirits, in a hut during a 'bringing-back' ceremony in the Natal Midlands. On the floor is the beer brewed for the ceremonial bring-back of the ancestor. Hanging, from left to right, are the thong used to lead the sacrificial animals, the sprig of buffalo thorn, *Ziziphus mucronata*, which lured the ancestor back to the home, two gall bladders drying, the mesentery drying for medicinal use, and the third stomach of a goat which the ancestors are attracted to lick and so make acquaintance with the new member of their company.

Following the ceremony of the sprinkling of the shades, the bladder was blown up to be worn by Shange for one week before it, too, was transferred to the *umsamo*.

An interesting aspect of the dismemberment was causing the goat to 'smile'. A smile on the face of the sacrificial animal endows the entire operation with 'light' and happiness. To my Western eyes, however, the smile of that goat hardly achieved its object: the severed head, bloody in the dim orange glow of the lantern, was held up and the mouth cut open along the jawline almost to the ears so that the long rows of teeth glistened, red-flecked white in a ghoulish grin.

During the dismembering the intestine was removed and, without washing, cut into three-centimetre squares which were salted and eaten raw by the men. (The reason for not washing off the raw excreta is the belief that this will result in the 'invasion of the hut by an army'.) Certainly, this belief (as I found when I accepted a piece) makes for a strong taste! When I had finally chewed and swallowed the intestine, I was reassured, 'Now you can be sure no wife will dominate you!'

Another part of the goat eaten that evening was the pieces of skin along the sternum, together with some attached flesh, which was not removed with the rest of the hide. This portion was cut up, cooked and eaten, as it is dangerous for a stranger even to see it lest he have evil intentions and bewitch the family.

The rest of the meat was eaten the following day by family members. The large stomach, together with its contents, was hidden away to await the sacrifice of the cow. The bones, too, were put aside for later. The hide, however, was removed carefully to preserve for sale to defray expenses. In the past, the skins of sacrificial animals were sewn into a cloak which was always worn by the person performing the sacrifice.

During the dismemberment process, the company chatted as they would at any other time: about the neighbours, the 'modern woman' and so on. Beer was passed around. It was good, as Nogwazi's beer always was, and elicited comment. Every adult present had to partake of this beer, as it was the 'beer of the ancestors'. Usually, when attending a sacrifice, one is presented with a portion of the liver of the goat, cooked on the coals, but that evening was an exception and the drinking of beer was our part of the communion.

While the company chatted, the priest-diviner was yawning and exclaiming ever more frequently and loudly. At length there emanated from her corner a low whistle, twittering urgently across the scale. The ancestral spirits had arrived to speak!

The response in the room was immediate. Conversation ceased. A chair was fetched and placed so that the priest-diviner could sit with her back to the assembly, facing the corner nearest the *umsamo*. The stage was set. Everyone waited — not long, as it turned out — for the ancestors to speak. Here is a transcript of what followed:

PRIEST-DIVINER (*translating the whistling of the spirits*): We, *the ancestors*, are very happy to see you all here.
COMPANY: *Makhosi!* [*Chiefs* — a praise-term for the ancestors.]
Whistling

PRIEST-DIVINER:	We are very happy to see *everybody* in this home here.
Whistling	
PRIEST-DIVINER:	The people of Shange are also very thankful and give praise in their happiness.
Whistling	
PRIEST-DIVINER:	We never tire of this [sacrifices]. We are happy.
COMPANY:	*Makhosi!*
Whistling	
PRIEST-DIVINER:	Indeed, my children, never be weary of doing these generous works.
COMPANY:	*Makhosi!*
Whistling	
PRIEST-DIVINER:	We give praise.
COMPANY:	*Makhosi!*
NOGWAZI:	Indeed, *ngoma*, we convey our gratitude and happiness to the ancestors.
Whistling	
PRIEST-DIVINER:	We say goodbye. And indeed my children, don't be tired of doing these works.
COMPANY:	*Makhosi!*
Whistling	
PRIEST-DIVINER:	We are going.
COMPANY:	*Makhosi!* [followed by one voice above the rest:] We thank you Great Spirits.

There followed a collective sigh of contentment. The ancestors were placated, they were happy, they were well-disposed towards the living. Chatter burst forth and the room took on a really festive atmosphere which the priest-diviner enhanced with one more message: 'The *makhosi* say they are very happy to see these white people and have sent special thanks for their attendance.'

Eventually, at about 10 o'clock, we left. Everyone was eagerly awaiting the return of the meat which had been taken to the kitchen hut to be cooked, and the festivities continued until midnight.

The purpose of this sacrifice was to gather the lineage ancestors in preparation for the actual 'bringing-back' of the shade of Shange's mother. This was to take place the following day.

The old lady had died while living with her brother some 80 kilometres away. We were to supply the transport and the following day (Friday) at eight o'clock, as promised, Shange and his brother arrived at our house. The journey took us along a bumpy dirt road which wound ever deeper into the broken and beautiful country near the Umzimkulu River. At length, after we had taken several side roads, the track vanished and we had to walk.

As this was the 'work of men', I alone accompanied the two brothers to the grave. The path wound deep into a spacious valley. Groups of women looked up from their labours in the tiny maize fields.

'Where are you from?' they asked. We told them.

'Where are you going?' they continued, 'What are you doing?'

'We are doing work.'

'Oh.' They knew exactly what was meant by this reply.

We passed an old man. When he heard the nature of the mission, he nodded his grey head and smiled sagely.

'Thank you, thank you, my children,' he said, 'Thank you, thank you. You do well. Thank you.'

The homestead where the mother's grave was to be found lay at the bottom of the valley beside the river. I was completely enchanted by the quiet beauty of the place. This peace was reflected in the eyes and manner of the people. The dead woman's brother greeted us quietly yet warmly. Then, without further ado, he led us to the grave, a mound under a clump of bushes 30 metres below the homestead's three huts.

Shange's younger brother had been carrying a small suitcase of the sort often used by schoolchildren for their lunch. This he opened. Inside were a knife, a sprig from the small tree known as buffalo thorn, *Ziziphus mucronata*, and the *incekwa* (third stomach) of the goat wrapped in newspaper.

Shange took the sprig and placed it carefully on the grave. He then took the newspaper bundle and handed it to his brother, who unwrapped the *incekwa*, pouring some of its green contents into Shange's cupped hands and the rest on the sprig where it lay on the grave. Shange then took the *incekwa* from his brother and laid it on top of the sprig. He squatted down before the grave and looked up at his uncle who stood nearby.

'What do I say?' he enquired softly.

Speaking also in subdued tones, the old man told him, and he repeated the words with slight variations:

'Here: we have brought you your food, old lady' he said, addressing the shade of his mother, 'Come with us and enter into your children.'

He then stood up, took the sprig and the *incekwa* in his right hand and walked up the hillside, accompanied by his brother. He was bent over, dragging the *incekwa* and sprig along the ground and never looking back. Even when, some 10 metres along the path, he took 30 cents from his pocket and handed it to his brother, telling him to take it to the old man as tobacco money, he remained bent over and did not look back.

When Shange's brother, carrying the suitcase, caught up with us about a kilometre from the homestead, we stopped. Shange wrapped the *incekwa* in newspaper before replacing it in the suitcase. The sprig, however, he carried all the way to the car.

On the way up to the car, Shange walked with some determination, not stopping even when his brother dropped behind to relieve himself and to cut bark from a tree beside the path, with a knife which was also produced from the suitcase. This bark was to be mixed with water to make medicine for vomiting. Ritual vomiting plays a significant role in many ceremonies, and acts as a form of purification. In this case all family members vomited every morning for a week, using medicine made from this bark.

Back at the car, we stood chatting for a while and the atmosphere was so normal that when Shange said casually as he climbed into the car, 'Come on old lady, let's get in,' I was momentarily confused. So totally and undramatically did he accept the unseen presence of his mother as a fellow traveller that I had all but forgotten the purpose of our journey.

The trip back, accompanied by the invisible ancestor, was uneventful. When we reached Shange's home, the brothers alighted together with suitcase and deceased mother. Shange, still carrying the sprig, asked his wife where he should 'place his mother'.

'Put her by the *umsamo* where the meat of the cow will be.' Shange obeyed the instruction without comment. The road had been opened.

The next day (Saturday) the sacrifice of the cow was to take place — the second, most important of the two groups of rites. This sacrifice marked the actual integration of the old lady's shade into the family circle and home. Often, especially where the deceased is interred near the home, this sacrifice is the only one performed; the preliminary sacrifice and the journey to 'fetch the spirit' fall away.

Shange had had difficulty obtaining a cow but eventually bought a Friesland from a local dairy farmer. Knowing the reason for the purchase, however, the farmer had refused to sell it alive. Thus, when the wagon bearing the sacrificial animal arrived at the homestead, its cargo lay dead in a pool of blood.

Had the normal course of events been followed, the sacrifice would have been carried out in the family cattle kraal (or in front of the huts where this structure would have been located). Before killing the cow by severing its spinal column, the shades, especially Shange's mother, would have been addressed, praised and exhorted to reside with and care for the living.

In general the shade of a woman or a child is not considered as important as that of a man and a goat is sacrificed for their 'bringing back', as is the case with an unimportant man. In fact, the previous 'bringing back' of this lineage, which we had attended, had been to reintegrate the shade of a two-year-old child 'Kanyisile', in response to the child's requests in Shange's wife's dreams. On this occasion, while the goat was being killed and while, his voice low and impassioned against a background of the goat's failing cries, Shange appealed to his child to return, he had had alongside him in the flesh, holding the tiny paraffin lamp, his mother. She, too, had applied gall of the sacrificial goat to his arms and feet in order to attract and unite the ancestors about his person. Now she, in her turn, demanded the status of a real but unseen family member or ancestor to be present when the family gathered.

When the carcass had been offloaded with much wheezing and shouting by the assembled men, they set to work dismembering it. Roughly the same internal organs as the goat's are of ritual significance. The *incekwa* was taken indoors to be hung, not above the *umsamo* but in Shange's bedroom, where it was meant to attract his mother's shade. The *mhlehwa* was removed and hung alongside that of the goat above the *umsamo*. It was large, a good omen, duly noted by the onlookers. The main stomach of the cow was slit open and emptied beside the carcass and the goat stomach retrieved from its hiding place and emptied over this.

All this was done under the watchful and professional eye of the attendant priest-diviner. During the initial stages of the skinning she had been occupied in the preparation of about four litres of medicines which she stirred in a tub, using the ritual spear. She then poured this carefully on to the mixed stomach contents, while Shange's wife worked the pile with her hands. When the contents of the two stomachs had been thoroughly mixed, the last of the medicine was poured on to the pile and the priest-diviner stabbed it repeatedly with the spear, which she finally left standing in the centre.

The purpose of this procedure was to forestall any witch or person of malintent who might steal this sensitive substance for use in witchcraft against the family. Should any person have attempted this after the treatment, they would have been stabbed (in the gut) by the spear, as were the stomach contents. The principal role of the priest-diviner in the series of rituals was to serve as protector against any possibility of witchcraft at a time when the lineage was often vulnerable to this form of attack. In addition she was the general orchestrator of the proceedings and the communicator with the ancestors.

Secure in the knowledge that Shange's mother was safely 'one with the family', with the prospect of much meat and beer, the mood of the gathering was happy. Shange's wife, adorned in bright scarves in honour of her mother-in-law, was particularly talkative and full of laughter: 'Today I'm a woman in my own yard. She can see for herself that she's come home today,' she exclaimed happily, emphasising the importance of the mother-in-law/daughter relationship in a traditional marriage.

The prospect of meat, beer and a party attracted a great many acquaintances from the surrounding area. By sundown, when the beast was completely dismembered, twenty or thirty men sat around the fire chatting happily, eyeing the stacked meat and calling for beer.

Before any meat could be consumed, however, the 'old people' or ancestors had to be fed. Shange's wife cut strips of meat and took them into the hut, where they were placed on a small pile of glowing coals in Shange's bedroom. While they were roasting, she said: 'This is the food I have prepared for you, oh maid of Mswane [the old lady's maiden name]. We are happy to have you home and this is your food.'

The priest-diviner looked on from the door (she could not enter the room because her relationship to Shange demanded this respectful observance).

'Burn the meat well,' she instructed Shange's wife, who continued with her appeal to the ancestral world as follows: 'Eat, all you lovely spirits, even my children Boneni and Kanyisile. Turn around and look at me. Even those who have gone before. Let them come back, for I know where they are. Bring them all back to me.'

The priest-diviner interjected again, 'Is the meat all in one pile? Spread it a little so that it will burn quickly.'

By now the men were gathered at the doorway complaining that they wanted to start cooking their meat. The priest-diviner ignored them at first and then said to Shange's wife, 'Tell me when that meat is well burnt and I will bring the *imphepho*.'

A little later she added, 'As soon as all the meat is burnt, the men at the door can eat; as soon as the old ones are eating, then the men may eat as well.'

All had to eat of the meat as it was the meat of the ancestors. We were no exception and one of the men turned to me saying, 'Today you are growing up, for you shall have your pieces of meat of the ancestors too.' In addition to tasty strips of roast meat, we were given some liver which, by virtue of its strong associations with the ancestors, would 'give good courage on any journey or undertaking in life'.

The meat of a sacrificial beast is divided according to a strict set of rules. One portion of special significance is the right shoulder, which is kept overnight in the *umsamo* as an offering to the ancestors. The right side of any animal or man is the 'strong' side and therefore fit to be offered to the ancestors.

When the beer and talk flowed merrily and the meat of the men sizzled over the coals under the first pale stars of the night, we left the Shange family and their guests. The celebrations continued well into the night, and the next day (Sunday) guests kept arriving in a stream that petered out only on the third day (Monday), by which time the meat, beer and Shange's wife's energies had come to an end.

The rites associated with butchering the cow were not the last, however. The regular morning vomiting, already mentioned, continued until the following weekend. In addition, the goat's bones and some of the cow's, as sources of medicines for witchcraft, had to be eliminated. This was done the following week by burning them according to a special ritual. They were burned until white, then a piece of goat mesentery was placed on them and allowed to burn away, before sprinkling *imphepho* on them to invoke the presence and strength of the ancestors. After another short period of burning, when the bones were again white, beer was once more sprinkled over them. This beer was taken from a pot specially set aside for the ancestors and stored in Shange's room (along with the bones of the goat). All the bones were then incinerated and those bones which would not burn were securely hidden by Shange's wife, to forestall any witch who might use them for medicine.

The end of the ritual marked the departure of the priest-diviner. Before leaving on Monday, she took official leave of the lineage ancestors: 'Big spirits of Mthethwe [Shange's wife's family], together with the Shange spirits,' she said, 'I am leaving you well at home now. May fortune be with you.'

The cost of this whole proceeding is indicative of its significance to these people. The rituals required several bus and taxi rides, which cost a total of R23; the presiding priest-diviner charged a mere R7 for her services, including medicines; the beer ingredients cost R10, the goat R28 and the cow a handsome R140 — making a grand total of R208! Shange is indeed lucky that he receives R100 a month for his job on a farm — relatively good pay. Other farm labourers, earning as little as R20 a month plus rations and housing (by no means uncommon) would have been severely taxed — and are, for such a 'bringing-back' is not a luxury, but a necessity.

The cost in this case was actually R348, as between drawing the money and reaching the farmer who was to sell him the cow, Shange lost R140 from his open shirt pocket and had to draw the sum again. This unfortunate loss was apparently part of a pattern in their lives at this time. In the words of Shange's wife, 'He would take money to go to the store and then look in his purse and there would be nothing left', or 'I was numb in the head (and therefore lost money), yet I'd had nothing to drink.'

Before the 'bringing-back', it had been decided that all this trouble demanded a remedy. A 'Sioni' (Zionist) had been consulted and had, for a fee of R6, agreed to perform the necessary rites to placate the ancestors. Shange had had to buy four chickens whose sacrifice on the appointed evening had initiated a prolonged series of rituals connected with the ancestors.

Shange's mother was now one of those ancestors, a part of the living lineage providing meaning and significance in an otherwise alien and lonely world. Today, when the Shanges supplicate the ancestors, she is one of those waiting to help or to discipline not only the presently living but those yet to be born — for as long as her name is remembered.

A priest-diviner switches the ancestors on her shoulders. The white beads in the switch protect against evil.

LIVESTOCK

CATTLE

SEVERAL livestock types, including goats, sheep, horses, pigs and poultry, feature in traditional society, but it is around cattle — called 'wet-nosed gods' by the South Sotho — that traditional society revolves. Cattle are the pride and visible wealth of a man. They provide the means whereby a man may obtain brides for himself and his sons; with cattle he pays fines and bribes to the chief; sour milk (*amasi*) forms an important part of his diet. Perhaps the most significant feature of the cattle culture is that these animals are closely linked to the all-important ancestors and for this reason are the preferred sacrificial animals. Little wonder then that in traditional society a man would devote much of his spare time to composing praise poems about his favourite ox, while a neighbour would spend substantial sums of money procuring medicine to make himself invisible for the purpose of stealing cattle.

Early African Cattle

Cattle are old associates of African man. The first cattle of the African continent were probably the straight-backed, longhorned members of the widely distributed urus group. These African cattle were distributed over North Africa — a fact attested to by many rock engravings — some eighty centuries ago. That ancient hearth of civilisation, the Nile Valley, is regarded as the most likely area of their domestication, which would make them Africa's only indigenous cattle.

For many thousands of years these 'Hamitic longhorns' reigned supreme. Then, about four and a half millennia ago, the pharaohs of Egypt started

Cave painting in northern Nigeria, depicting a humpless longhorn cow, one of the ancestors of the sanga bovine type adopted by the Bantu-speaking people. [After Epstein.]

PAGE 199   This Nguni priest-diviner's drum consists simply of a metal drum with ends removed and animal skin stretched over the openings.

Although the young apprentice priest-diviner on her way to a consultation is in charge of the drum and is chief drummer in her 'school', other apprentices of the school, as well as the head priest-diviner, may all take turns at playing. It is usually taken along when the priest-diviner is on a 'call': visiting the sick, diagnosing and treating ill-luck or attending a ceremony.

This young woman is in her second stage of training, as shown by her hair, which is long, with white beads threaded on certain strands. The white (or red) ochre body paint, characteristic of the initial stage, has been ritually removed.

Barbara Tyrrell

capturing cattle of a new type in Syria and Persia. These were the European shorthorn or *Brachyceros* cattle, which became the dominant Egyptian breed for a century after the Hyksos invasion of 1700 B.C..

Egyptian longhorn ox from the 5th dynasty. [Drawn from a photograph in Epstein, p. 222.]

During the same period, yet another breed was making its appearance on African soil. From the eastern margins of the Great Salt Desert of Iran, a longhorned, humped breed of cattle filtered down to the sultry heat of the Indus Valley. From here these zebu cattle (*Bos indicus*) reached Africa, some imported as war-spoils into Egypt from the north, others via the Horn of Africa.

Perhaps it was these zubu that were adopted by the Khoikhoi in the dim past and driven south by them. Today the descendants of the Khoikhoi cattle are renowned as the hardy Afrikander and (excluding recent stud imports) are the only pure zebu on the continent. Pure *Brachyceros* are today found mainly in West and North Africa. The original Hamitic longhorns are all but extinct in their native continent, but have survived outside it. Early longhorns carried north across the Straits of Gibraltar are the ancestors of various Portuguese and Spanish breeds. With the discovery of the New World, these Iberian cattle were taken there and thrived to become the famous 'longhorn steers' of Texas and the cowboy classics.

Sanga Cattle

It is the 'Hamitic longhorn'–zebu cross that came to occupy a position of great importance in Africa as the traditional cattle of the Bantu-speakers. The descendants of this bovine cross are the sanga cattle, named from the Ethiopian word for bull, and, despite the zebu-derived hump they share, they are the most varied bovine type on the continent.[1]

The original stock were probably driven west and south in two migrations, with the westward one leaving sanga cattle on the shores of Lake Chad. The southward migration has spread sanga cattle in a long belt from Ethiopia to South Africa. They were presumably carried south to the Great

---

PAGE 200   A pregnant woman of the Ngwane tribe, Natal Drakensberg, wears a modern version of the buckskin apron of former times. It is believed that by wearing the skin of so beautiful and strong a creature, these qualities will be transferred to the developing foetus. Conversely, in the hands of a witch, a spear or stick pointed in the direction of a pregnant woman may well cause abortion or, if towards a young wife, result in her sterility. A representative of the ancestors, the priest-diviner (background) is responsible for protecting society from evil, whatever its source.

Lakes region by Cushites of Mediterranean stock, from whom the Bantu-speakers adopted them before setting off down the tsetse-fly-free corridor which roughly follows the Great Rift Valley.

Sanga cattle have been replaced in Kenya by the shorthorn zebu — a subtype derived from the crossing of zebu with *Brachyceros* in India — owing to the extinction of the traditional cattle in Kenya by the rinderpest epidemic at the end of the last century.

Among the most impressive cattle are those sanga with horns of large basal circumference. Outstanding in this respect are the Ankole cattle of Ruanda, which may carry horns more than a metre long, and with a capacity of about twenty litres. Certain Watusi cattle, a type of Ankole, can have horns over two metres long, which may seriously hamper their head movements.

A sanga skull and horns from Botswana, which can reach a span of over 2.5 metres.

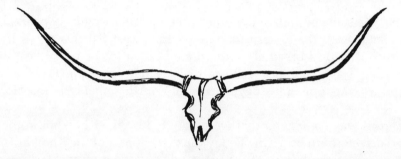

Rock painting in western Natal of an early sanga.

Southern Sanga Breeds

Southern sanga cattle, on the other hand, have horns of a smaller diameter. These vary in length from moderately long (Zulu) to the massive weapons of Setswana cattle, which can measure over two and a half metres from tip to tip. The southern sanga are divided into several groups: the Setswana group, subdivided into a number of breeds, occupy large areas of the central arid regions of the subcontinent; the Barotse cattle of Zambia and Botswana; the Ngwato cattle of Matabeleland (Zimbabwe); the Batawana cattle of Lake Ngami; the Makalanga of Francistown/Plumtree; and the Damara cattle of Botswana and South West Africa/Namibia. The Setswana type is the traditional beast of the Sotho people of the Transvaal, the Shona subtype being the beast found in Lesotho.

Wherever the Nguni have settled — to the east, along the coastal belt from the Save River (Mozambique) southwards to the Great Fish River — the Nguni group of sanga was the traditional beast. There are several breeds, including the Landim in Mozambique and the Swazi, Zulu and Pedi breeds. All Nguni cattle are characterised by moderately long horns, small size, square face and fairly prominent hump. In colour they vary: the typical Pedi beast is black with a white belly, while a common colour for Zulu cattle is white with black points. There are the famous *nyoni-ai-pumuli* or 'the-bird-does-not-rest' cattle, the royal beast of the nineteenth-century Zulu monarch, Cetshwayo. There are two possible origins for their name: one is that it derives from the long march southwards when their Zulu owners did not stop long in any place; the other that it dervies from the fact that none of these animals 'rested' long in its owner's herd before being confiscated by the king! During the warring days of the Zulu nation, every regiment was associated with a particular herd (of similarly marked animals), which supplied the hides for all its shields; these identified them in the same way that shoulder flashes do in a modern army.

After taking some pains to follow the history of the traditional cattle of the Bantu-speaking people, it must be said that these have all but vanished as pure breeds, owing to indiscriminate crossing with European imports. This has resulted in the indifferent scrub cattle that account for the majority of African-owned stock today. One of the characteristics of Bantu-speakers' cattle — also seldom seen today — was the zebu-derived hump. Indeed, the clay oxen moulded by youngsters still retain this hump — an interesting example of the durability of man's cultural memory.

Cattle and the Economy

In the past cattle supplied meat and hides, but were seldom slaughtered exclusively for this purpose. Economically, and perhaps emotionally, the Nguni were closer to and more dependent on their cattle than were their inland neighbours, who were (and still are) more accomplished agriculturalists. This is exemplified by the attitude towards cow's milk: the men from most inland tribes do not drink milk, which is considered the food of women and children, but among the Nguni milk is one of the staple foods — despite the fact that their cattle yield very little, two to three litres a day being considered normal.

Milk is rarely consumed fresh but almost always left to go sour. The different groups traditionally use different types of vessels for fermenting milk. Most Nguni use a gourd with a large hole for pouring in the milk and removing the curds, and a small hole in the base, plugged with a maize-cob, for draining off the whey. The early Zulu fermenting vessel was a skin bag, later phased out by Shaka after a visit to the Mthethwa people who used gourds. The South Sotho still use bags to transport and store their milk.

The carefully carved Zulu milking pail is a sacred object by virtue of its association with the lineage cattle, and may not be removed from the homestead.

Dung is an important by-product of cattle husbandry and has many applications, ranging from its use as a hard, mildly antiseptic floor-covering to its utilisation by the Tswana woman who wishes to delay the onset of menstruation after childbirth in order to avoid becoming pregnant again too soon. According to Schapera, she will seek out an acquaintance whose menstruation usually resumes late after childbirth and have this fortunate woman smear a cross of cow dung on her back in the belief that this will transfer that woman's tendency to herself. With food in short supply over much of the interior of Southern Africa, dung is collected and dried for making fires — an essential feature of the domestic scene, especially during the bitter winter nights of bleak and mountainous central Lesotho.

The Cattle Culture

The traditionalist's close ties with and astute observation of his cattle have led to the development of a vast and intricate cattle lore. The Zulu, for example, have more than a hundred terms for different types of cattle. The Mpondo have at least fifty-seven terms for the different markings and five for horn shapes, while the Pedi distinguish sixteen types of cattle on the basis of coat colours. Each animal has a name; all males in the homestead know it by this name and can recognise it on sight.

In former days, one of the more important objects in the life of a man was his favourite ox, and the ornamentation of this beast (among the Nguni,

South Sotho and Khoikhoi) was a favourite pastime. Such ornamentation included slitting of the dewlap to produce a variety of shapes and protuberances. In addition, the horns were manoeuvred into an assortment of magnificent shapes by scraping and wetting, and a popular practice was to treat horns so that they hung loosely in their sockets and could be moved. The Southern Nguni and South Sotho learned from the Khoikhoi the art of ox-riding. Riderless ox-racing was also a popular and spectacular sport for these people. Soga has left us the following description of a nineteenth-century ox-race:

> In cattle races there is nothing to correspond with the lining up of horses at the starting point. This is impossible with groups of cattle that may number as many as a hundred head, and of all ages and sex, for each picked racing ox is accompanied by its home herd. Nor is any special signal given to start the race. When one of the contestants is ready he starts his own cattle, and his opponents have to take that as a signal that the race has begun. All the groups of racing cattle must, however, be somewhere in the neighbourhood of the starting point.
>
> Dunga's cattle were placed above the Mzonga bush at the Shixini, while Ngcabiya's were below it, and had to go through it so as to get to the ridge along which the race was to be run. While still below the bush the sounds of Dunga's men urging on their cattle with shouts and whistling reached the ears of Ngcabiya's men. They were thus taken at a disadvantage. These tactics, however, are not considered blameworthy, as everyone takes what chances come to him, and does not complain if another gets the better of him. Notions of fairness don't come in where winning at any price is the main object in view.
>
> Ngcabiya's people responded at once and set their cattle in motion, but the bush had first to be negotiated, so as to get to the ridge above.
>
> Racing cattle are as keen and knowing perhaps as horses, and it needs little urging to get them to do their best. They also have an uncanny knowledge of their principal opponent.
>
> Immediately the shouts and whistling (*ama-kwelo*) began Ngcabiya's racer, '*Bungc' one-ndaba*' (escape with news), jumped into the Mzonga bush and took the path at speed, and followed it till he emerged on the ridge above. Here he got the scent of Dunga's cattle which were already some distance ahead. Alongside of him were a hornless (*in-qukuva*) cow, and her son a red ox left-handed (*i-nxele*), that is with one horn growing downwards and the other upwards. The rest were a little way behind, pushing their way through the bush. Lowering his head to the trail of Dunga's cattle '*Bungc' one-ndaba*' let himself out, his two mates close beside him. At the head of the Mnqinda rivulet these three caught up with Dunga's cattle. Some of Ngcabiya's footrunners had kept up with the three, and shouted to their opposition in derision, 'Go on,' they cried, 'whack your rubbish up, Ngcabiya's ox is here, the blood of men is going to flow today . . .'
>
> Ngcabiya's three racers ahead of their companions, drew level with Dunga's herd. The red ox ranged himself alongside '*Nokotsoyi*', Dunga's special racer, and on whom the issue of the race hung, and giving him a dig with his upright horn turned '*Nokotsoyi*' out of the herd. Following him

up he pushed him toward the Mnqinda rivulet where he gored *'Nokotsoyi'* to death. Who dares affirm that animals cannot reason? The idea of a foul never entered into the mental make up of Xosa racing men. Instead, the red ox's action was regarded as indicating a high standard of intelligence. He knew *'Nokotsoyi'* was his companion's chief opponent and took measures to prevent him winning the race.

When the racers reached elu-Gwadu stream Ngcabiya's racer had taken the lead of the two herds. This and the fact that Dunga's 'hope' had been killed by the red ox so infuriated Dunga's men that they attacked Ngcabiya's party, and blood flowed.[2]

Shades of Roman chariot-racing! The central role of cattle in the culture is also evident in the rapport between the herdsman and his animals and the control he has over them. Most early European explorers were struck by this. Alberti, who encountered the Xhosa in the early nineteenth century, remarked, 'No well-trained dog follows the command conveyed to him by a whistle more promptly than happens in the case of the cattle of those Kaffirs'.[3] General Cathcart was confronted with this obedience when, in 1884, he confiscated a large herd of South Sotho cattle, only to have them stampede through their guard during the night in answer to the whistles of their owners. Today, South Sotho herdboys may lead their herds with the melodies of their flute-like pipes.

The Swazi had much the same kind of control over their cattle. During a war, cattle could be led to a safe place by herdboys, who blew commands on a kudu-horn trumpet. Marwick was told that such was a herdboy's control over his cattle that no stranger (particularly one with clothes on!) could approach the herd for fear of being trampled to death.[4]

Stayt, staying among the Venda, encountered a little herdboy who appeared to have an almost supernatural rapport with his charges.[5] At milking time the calves were kept in a pen while their mothers were milked. When each mother had been milked the boy would whistle and softly call the name of the calf. Inevitably, the correct calf would immediately leave the group and trot over to its mother.

This scene is not limited to the Venda, to the past or just to cattle. Mönnig relates a story illustrating the peculiar control of a black man over animals.[6] Researchers at Onderstepoort Veterinary Research Centre were having difficulty in holding still a particular antelope in order to take blood smears, when a black man offered to help. Scepticism turned to incredulity when the unnamed black walked into the antelope's enclosure and spoke to it in a loud voice before being followed by the animal into the stable, where it lay down for him 'completely pacified' while blood smears were taken. This procedure was repeated daily for a considerable time and witnessed by the nonplussed scientists.

Perhaps the most enduring link between a man and his cattle is the religious association. While a traditionalist is proud of his cattle and conscious of their material value, he regards them in a much more profound way than Western man does his particular status symbols. It is not only a desire for personal wealth that causes many Africans to long for cattle of their own. The meaning of cattle lies deep in their hearts and is entwined with the roots of traditional history, society and religion. A man's cattle are

This carefully fashioned pipe clearly shows the maker's love of cattle. [From Shaw, 1938, Plate 94.]

not his alone; they are the communal property of his lineage, of the living and the dead, and belong to him only as the 'sacred trust' of his lineage ancestors. A man's cattle are holy objects and with them he has a very special, mystic link, for it is through them that he has perhaps his most meaningful communion with the ancestors. It is not surprising that when the need arises in certain rituals, townspeople may cordon off an area which is then designated as a cattle kraal. This area may even be retained permanently, despite the absence of any cattle in the town, and be reserved as the place where men can sit and talk.

That a close rapport with and love for cattle exist is beyond dispute, although the form this love takes may appear very strange to Western eyes. To speak of a traditional love of cattle and then to describe a ceremony that I watched (or tried to before turning away), during which a cow was skinned alive in Thembu territory, seems a gross contradiction. Similarly, it seems impossible to reconcile this union of man and beast with cruelly conducted sacrifices in honour of the ancestors.

Yet there is a union. When watching sacrifices — and hating the suffering inflicted on the animal — there were deep parts of myself that seemed to understand the ritual, and even respond against my will. But it could not be denied that the animal's agony was terrible. Only since listening to Dr Vera Burhman, a Jungian analyst, describing and explaining her own feelings on such an occasion in terms of archetypes — deep psychic forms that filter up from our inner beings to structure conscious existence — have I come close to an understanding of the power and relevance of the sacrifice. Western man has all but lost contact with this legacy of the past, the seething life of the unconscious. But the traditionalist still experiences this profoundly. It is in this deep realm that he and the animal have their communion, and act out the ancient and barely rational play of the sacrifice.

The characteristic sanga hump, now lost because of interbreeding with European cattle, is still evident in this drawing taken from an early photograph of a Nguni bull.

Sacred Cattle

Though all cattle are in a very real sense sacred, certain animals or herds may be selected as the principal links with the ancestors. Venda and Lemba lineages that can afford to, keep a sacred black bull as the embodiment of the ancestors. When it becomes old it is killed and the ancestors exhorted to enter another, younger bull, preferably descended from its predecessor. Similarly, Mpondo lineages have an ancestor's beast, recognisable by its uncut brush. The Bomvana keep two herds of cattle for sacrificial purposes, with illustrious and somewhat fanciful histories. Those kept by the Tshezi group are descendants of the single beast of the Mqadi (the 'cattle-of-the-medicines') herd which survived the ravages of rinderpest at the end of the last century.

Fabulous stories are told of these Mqadi cattle. They could detect mal-intent in the heart of any would-be assassin, disguised or not, and would attack such a person without hesitation. Today the cattle are still highly respected and protected. The sour milk (*amasi*) from the Bolowane, the other sacred herd of the Bomvana, may be drunk only by young children and women past childbearing age (i.e. persons free of ritual impurity) as a protection for the cattle. Only men may eat their meat.

GOATS

The original African goats are fairly big; adults weigh 30 to 40 kilograms. Both sexes are horned. The coat can vary but is usually white and brown with medium-length hair. In males the hair on the upper limbs and neck is long; in females, the entire body has a covering of long hair. Characteristic, too, is the 'beard' on the chin; the origin of the Afrikaans term *bokbaardjie* (*bok* — goat; *baardjie* — little beard) applied to a small beard on the chin. Most people who have travelled in the frequently overgrazed black-farmed areas, have seen herds of these large animals standing on their hind legs to browse in the trees. They even climb thorn-trees in order to reach the last of the green in a stricken landscape.

The Dutch East India Company landed Dutch and Indian goats at the Cape and these crossed with the Bantu type owned by the local Khoikhoi, resulting in the sturdy, widely distributed 'Boer goat'.

Goats are particularly important to the Nguni, and are gaining in importance owing to two factors: first, overgrazing has led to the deterioration of pastures, many of which are now adequate only for goats; second, goats are considerably cheaper than cattle and are thus more commonly used as sacrificial animals. Their death cry is, it is said, attractive to the ancestral spirits and hence indicative of their presence. Having watched a number of

A goatskin is pegged out to dry. This and other tasks associated with livestock care are traditionally the responsibility of men.

goat sacrifices, I cannot see a goat without hearing in my imagination the pitiful wail and thinking of its probable fate.

SHEEP

Wild sheep are not indigenous to Africa and the domestic sheep of the continent are therefore 'imports'. The early Bantu-speakers' sheep were of the hairy, long-tailed type, but these were replaced (save for relatively small areas in Angola, Zimbabwe and, formerly, the western parts of South Africa) by a more useful animal, the fat-tailed sheep. The value of these sheep on the hot African continent to a people unskilled in the art of weaving lay not in their wool; to the Bantu-speakers the great feature of the fat-tailed sheep was the ready source of fat in its tail, useful to a nomadic people unable to keep pigs. Like the sanga cattle, the original sheep strains are losing their identity through cross-breeding with later European imports.

PIGS

Pigs, found in all Bantu-speaking areas today, are a relatively recent introduction. Pork is not popular and many people refuse to eat it. Most notable in this respect are the Lemba or 'Black Jews', who abhor pork. These animals are becoming popular, however, notably in Transkei, where their omnivorous habits are useful in the absence of toilets.

POULTRY

The domestic fowl, the only original traditional poultry, has been long known in Africa, as is evident from the universal distribution of the word *kuku* for fowl. Before the advent of the European, several groups of local Bantu-speakers owned fowls. The Pedi are reputed to have kept a tailless variety. The Natal Nguni (the Lala) and Mpondo had domestic fowls before the arrival of the white man, and the fowls of the Xhosa, reported by the

PAGE 209   The traditional Swazi youth had to spend much time on his appearance. His hair was his special concern: it had to be lengthened, straightened and teased out into an orderly mop. Washing and tending to it was done at the waterfall, which served the useful purpose of disentangling the strands. A mirror set in a wooden hand-carved frame was — and still is today on ceremonial occasions — a vital accessory when hair was combed and feathers placed. These had to be placed with the utmost care with regard to angle and position. Bright cloths were worn across the shoulders and on the hips. This young man is engaged, as shown by the tuft of horsehair threaded with beads suspended from his waist.

PAGES 210-11   As the creature whose legendary sloth ensured that his message, the promise of eternal life, arrived on earth after the lizard's tidings of inevitable death, the chameleon is feared and hated by traditional communities throughout Southern Africa.

In the background a corpse is carried off for burial. All those associated with the funeral, especially with the preparation of the body and the grave, become ritually impure and must be cleansed. In the past many tribes buried their dead not lying down as illustrated but in the squatting position.

Barbara Tyrrell

nineteenth-century chronicler Alberti, were of a small, combless variety. The Zulu, on the other hand, kept no poultry and were apparently amazed by those brought by Europeans.

Groups that kept domestic fowls did not lay great store by them and seldom ate them. The Mpondo valued them only for their feathers. Traditionalists believe that one should not eat eggs as they make one lascivious. A highly valued breed in Natal today is one with brushed-forward feathers, which apparently came from China. Kept as protection against lightning, it is caught in the midst of a storm and taken inside the hut to protect the dwelling and its inmates.

In general, pigs, poultry and those animals which are not herded are the responsibility of women. Although people are often proud of their sheep and goats, this pride does not approach the reverence shown to cattle. I have yet to hear of a pig being offered to the ancestors, but fowls are common sacrificial animals. White birds are preferred as white is the colour of purity and pleases the ancestors. In all fowl sacrifices which I have witnessed, death was brought about by means of a safety pin in the brain; this is done to avoid blood, which is offensive to the ancestors.

One way of protecting the young bean plants in the background. In the foreground are medicinal herbs.

PAGE 212   The gourd and bow musical instrument is traditionally for the sole use of the unmarried girl in Zululand or Swaziland. The gourd sounding box is moved back and forth against and over the left breast to achieve a rounded rhythm, tinkled out by striking the taut wire of the bow with a reed. Two tones are achieved by striking either the upper or lower sections of the bow. This instrument provides popular musical accompaniment on a long walk.

This Swazi girl from the bushveld wears the red flower of the coral tree as a matter of personal taste. Her hair has been lengthened, straightened and bleached by the constant application of yellow household soap, smeared on and left to dry. In the past, this bleaching was achieved by other means, including the washing of hair in the oxygenated water at the foot of waterfalls. Colourful cloths, imported from the east, are worn by members of both sexes.

HORSES

Horses were a European import but were quickly adopted by many Bantu-speaking people. The South Sotho of Lesotho, inhabitants of a rugged country, are the most notable horsemen. The origin and evolution of their own breed of horse, the famous Basotho pony, is fascinating. Started in 1811 on the initiative of the then governor of the Cape Colony, Lord Charles Somerset, the next forty years saw the importation of many fine English thoroughbreds — a breed of high repute derived from Oriental stock. This resulted in the development of the well-known 'Cape horse'. Unfortunately, the quality of the breed was irrevocably ruined by the importation of many highly pedigreed but poor-quality animals during the latter half of the nineteenth century.

Before this happened, however, many of these fine horses, stolen, pillaged and bought from the European by various indigenous peoples, had turned up in Lesotho. The Basotho pony soon became a definite and prized breed, and the South Sotho notoriously daring and skilful riders. They were and remain indifferent horsemasters, however, for they leave the supply of food and shelter to nature in a mountainous, harsh country, and are cruelly demanding of their mounts.

Most ponies are bred in the remote plateaux of the Maluti and Drakensberg mountains where night temperatures may plummet below minus ten degrees in winter, a time of howling blizzards and swirling snow. A large herd of these semi-wild horses lives just behind the Drakensberg escarpment at Mweni where, at an altitude of over 3 000 metres, the Orange (Senqu) River has its source. I have seen these horses grazing with apparent unconcern right in the teeth of a vicious winter blow that had me shivering despite the heavy clothing I wore.

But the Basotho pony of today is not of the same famous breed whose name he bears. After reaching a peak in numbers and fame in about 1870, Basotho ponies were exported in large numbers, often being replaced by animals of inferior quality. The decline continued, until the purchase of 3 000 Basotho ponies by the British forces during the Second World War finally brought an end to the Basotho pony as a breed.

However, having watched these tough little horses carrying their quite merciless riders over treacherous paths, and the laden packhorses tramping the high, cold, trading trail that winds north from Mokhotlong and up along the escarpment, I feel justified in echoing the experts who, writing of the Basotho pony of the past, have called it the most hardy, plucky and sure-footed of any type or breed of horse, even more so than the well-known mountain mule.

MEDICINES FOR LIVESTOCK

As the most important possession of a clan, cattle are protected against whatever ills might befall them by a well-developed system of remedies and procedures. An owner has at his disposal a vast collection of medicines and rites to bring health to his herds, to protect them against such dangers as poisoning, ritually impure women and, above all, to ensure their fertility. However, while a man appreciates well-bred, fat cattle, his prime concern is

with quantity, not quality, and in order to increase their numbers he is all too ready to sacrifice the condition of his herds and his lands.

Treatment by the smoke of medicinal fires, popular for crops, is also used to treat cattle. It is usually done as a general tonic and to protect the animals from harm. Bhaca treat their cows with hippopotamus fat in order to attract bulls (and all tribes have at least one remedy to treat impotence in the bull!)

Attempts by the authorities to protect black-owned cattle against tick-borne diseases, which include restriction of their movements and compulsory dipping, have not been well received. The restriction of movement, for instance, brought an end to the popular sport of cattle-racing in the south, and dipping was at first regarded as a rather underhand and diabolical way of irritating the black man by slowing the increase of his cattle. The traditionalist, of course, maintained that the European would never treat his own stock in the same stupid and obviously harmful way!

A typical scene outside a remote trading store in the mountains of central Lesotho: the loading of pack donkeys.

AGRICULTURE

THE traditional crops of Bantu-speaking people in Southern Africa include gourds, pumpkins, beans, cocoyams, groundnuts, sweet potatoes and, most important, grains — maize and two varieties of sorghum. The non-food crops are tobacco and Indian hemp. From the whites in Southern Africa, Africans have received new types of beans and groundnuts, as well as vegetables, notably potatoes.

Time has seen many changes in crops and agricultural methods. Some plants have been grown for generations; other 'traditional' crops such as maize and tobacco are comparatively recent acquisitions.

The story of agriculture on this planet goes back as far as 10 000 years when, in the 'fertile crescent' between the Tigris and Euphrates rivers, or in the Carpathian foothills, early man tentatively grew and protected the first proto-crop plants. About 5 000 B.C. this new art was introduced to the Late Stone Age herder/hunter-gatherers living along the Nile. By the Dynastic Period of Egypt, some 2 000 years later, the impact of agriculture on Africa was so great that the towns and villages were strung like closely threaded beads along the banks of the Nile and the population was large enough for about 100 000 people to be seasonally engaged in pyramid-building.

This early agriculture along the Nile was not without parallel to the south. In a broad band across Africa to the south of the Sahara and on the periphery of the Congo Basin rain forests, primitive agriculture or vegeculture was being practised by Late Stone Age people, possibly ancestral to the Bantu-speakers, as early as 2 000 B.C.

GRAIN CROPS

The hope for the survival of modern man lies in grain crops. To early man they were the key to effective settlement of the savannahs of sub-Saharan Africa. While the idea of cereal agriculture may have been imported from Egypt via the Sahara (which until about 2 000 B.C. was green and well watered), the Egyptian grains, emmer-wheat and barley, were not used in this new surge of agricultural development. Instead, the new agricultre of the sub-Saharan savannahs evolved from the domestication of two indigenous cereals — sorghum and elusine (finger millet). Professor Desmond Clark considers the Great Lakes region of Africa an important dispersal point for the spread of cereal production into southern and south-central Africa, dating back to the beginning of the present era.[1] This spread is believed to have been contemporaneous with that of Early Iron Age pottery from East Africa down the Great Rift Valley to Zimbabwe (where a local variant of this pottery culture is known as Gokomere) and South Africa. It is probable that these early potters and agriculturists were the first Bantu-speaking migrants to the south.

In South Africa, Portuguese sailors shipwrecked as long ago as the sixteenth century found the Nguni people along the coast cultivating three different grain crops which were probably varieties of sorghum.[2] The tribes of the interior also relied on sorghum as their agricultural mainstay. *Sorghum vulgare* or 'kaffir corn' is indeed recognised as the ancestral crop. It is sorghum that is thrown into the grave at a traditional burial in Lesotho, and as already mentioned, several tribes give newborn babies a mouthful of sorghum as their first food in order to introduce them to their people's ancient cereal.

Maize has replaced sorghum as the principal grain crop, used both for eating and for brewing. Though maize was brought to Southern Africa by the Bantu-speaking people, it is not indigenous to the continent, but came from the Americas in the ships of early Portuguese navigators.

The earlier and more southerly of the Sotho tribes had not come into contact with maize by 1822. When the Pedi received the new grain some ten years later, they rejected it after one season's trial. The early Southern Nguni (according to reports of shipwreck victims) were possibly cultivating maize in the seventeenth century but by the eighteenth century shipwrecked sailors were definitely reporting on the new grain in Nguni fields.

Agricultural Implements

The use of the word 'agriculture' in the present context may give the reader a false picture of the rather primitive nature of traditional grain growing. Prior to contact with the white man, the African used only two implements for cultivating the land: the digging stick and the hoe. The hoe was the more efficient and varied considerably in shape according to the tribe. It was most common among the interior peoples, who had freer access to iron and other metals. Hoes were of sufficient value to be used as substitutes at a fairly good rate of exchange when cattle were in short supply. Among the Nguni, where iron was virtually unobtainable, the standard agricultural implement was the 'digging stick', about a metre long and made of fire-hardened wood. The ends of this stick were flat-edged or pointed and in the middle it was weighted by a pierced stone. Many of these stones have been excavated throughout Southern Africa. Digging sticks were still being used in Pondoland and probably in other localities as late as the second half of the nineteenth century.

Methods of Cultivation

The traditional methods of cultivation varied from group to group. Among the Sotho tribes, the ground was hoed first and then scattered with seed. The Tsonga dug little holes, into which they placed two or three grains (a primitive version of modern 'drilling', an increasingly popular technique). The Nguni peoples, with their scant interest in agriculture, simply cast the

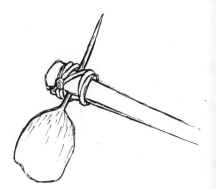

A traditional Tswana hoe. The design varied from group to group. [S.A. Museum, Cape Town.]

seed onto the ground, which was then dug over, grass, weeds and all. The Mpondo woman kept a store of seeds in her mouth, which she spat out on to her field as she hoed it. The increased availability of the iron hoe to the Nguni, first of African, then of European manufacture, led to their adoption of the more advanced agricultural practices of the Sotho.

The European plough has revolutionised traditional agriculture. Not only does much less effort produce much more food and beer, but the plough has also radically altered the roles of male and female in traditional life. Preparing the ground, traditionally the work of women, has been taken over by men, who are the handlers of the cattle that pull the ploughs. As ploughs are expensive, not everyone is able to own one, and this has resulted in the renting out of these implements, thus thrusting commercialism into the casual, slow-moving core of traditional life.

Fertilisation and irrigation were unknown, although Africans were well aware that the site of an old homestead provided fertile agricultural ground owing to the build-up of human and animal manure. The traditionalist is a keen observer and all the soil types in an area are sure to be recognised and named. There may be as many as seven types and these are differentiated according to their fertility and suitability for different crops.

Grain Storage
The traditional agriculturalist was and still is notoriously improvident. Although he stores grain for the year, little effort is made to build up a surplus against a bad season. The good season's bounty is enjoyed but little or nothing is put aside.

Storage containers for grain vary from group to group. On the whole the Nguni peoples of the coastal areas traditionally store their grain in bell-shaped pits about a metre across, usually located in the cattle kraal. However, this method of storage is becoming increasingly rare. Often a fire is lit in a newly dug pit to harden the walls, which may be lined with grass. The opening is closed with a stone and sealed with dung. Despite these measures damp creeps in and the grain spoils slightly — a fact which becomes obvious when the pit is opened! Despite the foul odour, some find such grain tasty, probably for the same perverse reasons that make gorgonzola cheese attractive to certain white people! A danger of this form of grain storage is that people — children especially — may be overcome by the fumes when the pit is opened, fall in and be asphyxiated.

Along with the Nguni, the other groups who use pits for storing grain are, strangely, the Venda and some Sotho of the north-eastern areas. The use of this storage method among the Venda is surprising, as they and the Nguni are geographically separated as well as substantially different in other respects. The Sotho tribes generally use large baskets for storing grain, each capable of holding some 1 500 kilograms. The Nguni ancestors of the Zulu also used such baskets to store their maize and can remember bringing them with them when they migrated from the west. Baskets similar to these are found near Lake Chad in North Africa (where the sanga cattle characteristic of southern Bantu cultures are found). The Reverend Leydevant, a missionary in Lesotho, has drawn attention to the similarities between these baskets and those used in ancient Egypt.

The Tswana in the west use large clay vessels for grain storage. These are usually slightly raised above the ground. Several groups add the ash of the burned, dry leaves of a particular aloe, which is supposed to preserve their grain. Researchers who thought the technique might prove useful found it totally ineffective.

OTHER CROPS

The other pre-European crops of the Bantu-speaking people — pumpkins, groundnuts and beans — have probably been their staples from the time of their first emergence as a linguistic subgroup.

High-yield crop plants suitable for tropical forest areas are not indigenous to Africa. The early proto-Bantu-speaking colonisers of the Congo basin had to rely on inferior crops. The plants which paved the way for the effective settlement of the great rain forests came from an unexpected source — south-east Asia, probably the jungles of southern Borneo. The people who brought them were the ancestors of the present-day inhabitants of Madagascar, who arrived early in the Christian era. Along with the outrigger canoe (East African coast) and the xylophone (most forest areas of Africa), they brought several types of yam and banana, which is a staple of the Central African Highlands. One of the yams, the cocoyam, is still grown by the Nguni people and known as the *idumbi.* This potato-like, long-maturing tuber is a delicacy to both blacks and whites. In Swaziland, the traditional *njugu* bean is the subject of a research and development programme aimed at exploiting its potential as an economic and rich source of protein for the future.

Still later introductions are various kinds of bean and groundnut, potatoes, and sweet potatoes. Casava, an exotic common to the north, is soon to be introduced in Transkei after a series of tests. The sweet potato was introduced into Africa by the Portuguese and was thriving there by the end of the seventeenth century. The Zulu had the sweet potato before the arrival of the European in Southern Africa and called it *umHlaze,* using the same word root as found to the north of Mombasa, whence it was brought south. They dropped this name in favour of the English 'potato' (pronouncing it *uBatata*).

THE STARS, THE SEASONS AND THE SKY

The traditionalist's way of life has not withdrawn and insulated him from the realities of survival in nature.

With the planting season over, summer, the growing season, means back-breaking labour for the women — hours, days, weeks out in the fields, hoeing weeds from before the break of day to past sundown. But this is always tempered by the easygoing attitude of the countryside — and a beer-drink down at a neighbour's homestead is a valid reason for neglecting the hoeing for an afternoon.

A popular method for getting work done is the institution of work parties. A woman will brew beer and invite her friends over to help work in the fields. Drinking and working will go hand in hand but the 'hostess' will try to restrain her guests/helpers until the work is done. Then all are free to join the party. However, should a neighbour who has not helped arrive for the party she is unlikely to be turned away. Unless, of course, she makes a habit of that sort of thing . . .

At harvest time the same system is used to gather mealies and shell them. In days of old, the only means of shelling was by hand. Today mechanical shellers are often used.

Traditionalists were well aware of the link between astronomical phenomena and the regular cycle of the seasons. Though in days gone by the chief initiated the planting season, he took his cue from the heavens. The Pleiades, that striking star cluster in the northern sky, well recognised by men the world over, played an important role in traditional society. To the women, its appearance above the eastern horizon in spring warned of arduous work to come, for it was known to all groups as 'the ploughing sign'.

In respect of this observation of the stars, the Bantu-speakers use sidereal time, but, like the Roman, they divide their year into 'moons'. These 'moons', largely superseded by the modern system, have been well documented. I list the moons of the Zulu, as recorded by Bryant,[3] by way of summarising the annual cycle of life and work in the fields:

(1) *uNcwaba*:   (the new grass moon) July — August.

(2) *uMandula*:   (the first-fields moon; from *ukuwandula*, to start cultivating) August — September.

(3) *uMfumfu*:   (the sprouting moon; from *ukuFumisa*, to bud or sprout) September — October.

(4) *uLwezi*:   (the frog-hopper moon; from *uLwezi*, frog hopper larvae) or else *uZibandela* (the overgrown-paths moon; from *ukuZiba*, to cover up, and *iNdlela*, path) October — November.

(5) *uMasingana*:   (the searching-about moon — when the women search the gardens for the new pumpkins; from *ukuSinga*, to look for) November — December.

(6) *uNtlolanja*:   (the dog-copulating moon; from *ukuHlola*, to inspect; *iNja*, dog) December — January.

(7) *uNdasa*:   (the food-abundance moon) January — February.

(8) *uMbasa*:   (the fire-kindling moon, signifying the approach of winter; from *ukuBasa*, to kindle a fire) February — March.

(9) *uNgula-zibuya*:   (the threshing-ground-preparing moon; from *ukwEngula*, to remove the surface scum or soil; and *isiBuya*, a threshing-ground) March — April.

(10) *uNtlaba*:   (the aloe-flowering moon; from *iNtlaba*, aloe plant) April — May.

PAGE 221 A young mother, her baby no more than a few days old, takes a break from hoeing the weeds in her maize field. Caring for the crops is woman's work, as is gathering the harvest, preparing and cooking it. The necklace worn by this young Xhosa woman is a health charm for her baby, and her head scarf, worn low over her eyes, shows that the child is her first-born. It is also a sign of respect for her husband's parents.

(11) *uLutdlana:*   (the little-dust moon; from *uluTuli,* dust); or else *uNtlangulana:* (the little-rubbish-sweeping moon; from *ukuquba,* to sweep off) May — June.

(12) *uNlangulana:*   (the big-dust moon; from *ukuQuba,* to raise dust) June — July.

(13) One of the great headaches of those Roman patriarchs who saw to the orderliness of the world was the intractability of the moon, which has between twelve and thirteen 29½-day cycles a year. The same problem presented itself to the Zulu elders, who spent many a long hour debating when and whether to insert the thirteenth moon. As a result, this errant moon has been nicknamed *uNdid'amaDoda* (the men-puzzling moon; from *ukuDida,* to perplex, *amaDoda,* men).

Other peoples struck the same problem: Stayt noted that the Venda call the contested moon 'men forget' or '*khangara vhana*'.

Though astronomical knowledge is not, strictly speaking, a strong feature in traditional society, the Pleiades and the moon are far from being the only heavenly bodies recognised. The Venda recognise *Makhadi,* the rhinoceros, which is formed by the sword and belt of Orion, and *Tuda,* the giraffe, formed from part of the Southern Cross and the Pointers. Orion's belt is also recognised by the Zulu, Xhosa and South Sotho, who call it *Impambano, amaRoza* and 'pig' respectively. The brightest star in the sky, Sirius, is noted by all groups. The Venda know it by two different names depending on whether it appears as a morning or evening star.

Sirius, incidentally, occupies a position of great importance in arcane religious societies the world over, including some in Africa, such as that of the Dogon of West Africa. To these people, Sirius is the origin of the gods or God. The Dogon have for centuries been aware of certain features of the Sirius system which were discovered by Western astronomers (using powerful telescopes) only early this century. How they came by this knowledge is a mystery. Venus, like Sirius, is recognised by probably all the tribes and is also known by two different names according to whether it appears as the evening or morning star. To the Zulu, Venus as the morning star is *iKhwezi,* and as evening star, *Khomomotsho.* The Xhosa name for the morning star is the same as that used by the Zulu, while Venus as the evening star is *U-cel' izapolo* (the one who asks for a little milk from the teat — i.e. the star which appears at the evening milking). The South Sotho call the evening star *Sefalabohoho* or 'crust scrapings', for that is all he gets for supper who arrives when Venus has already risen. Alternatively it is simply referred to as 'the one who asks for supper'. Venus at dawn is to the South Sotho what the

---

PAGE 222   Beer is poured respectfully in the kneeling position, the container a large calabash or dry gourd, the cup, a smaller dried gourd. Beaded cups are very characteristic of the Ndebele, a people known for their colourful beadwork. Until very recently, every woman of any consequence possessed a beaded gala blanket, the broad, bright stripes of which are the hallmark of Ndebele dress, but today, economic circumstances and the large sums of money commanded by these blankets have forced many to sell them.

Beaded head streamers are the prerogative of women whose sons have been through initiation school. However, the hold of tradition has been eroded and this younger woman wears her mother's streamers purely for decorative purposes.

English call it: 'morning star'. As a last example, I might mention Taurus Alpha. This star is not very popular with Venda women, for it is the first star they see on opening the hut door in the small hours of a winter's morning, and the sign that their day's domestic chores have begun.

RAIN AND FIELD MAGIC

Fertiliser may be something new to Africa and not often used, but the traditionalist has long recognised the value of magical medicines in ensuring good crops. Several groups — the Zulu, some other Nguni, the Pedi and Venda included — have or had an institutional system for the medication of the crops of the whole tribe. The Zulu chief would procure, among other items, exotic substances such as a lion's vomit, the body of a neighbouring tribesman and soil from the fertile fields of neighbouring tribes, in order to attract their fertility to his own land. From these substances, his 'doctors' would make a large ball of medicine which would then be distributed to every homestead for use in doctoring crops. Pedi and Venda chiefs distribute doctored seed for their subjects to mix with their own.

It is, of course, considered quite wrong for a man to doctor his own fields using privately obtained medicine without first informing his neighbours, for through his actions he is appropriating the fertility of their fields for his own. The Church frowns on any sort of magic, so the operation is usually carried out in secret. A group of neighbours may, however, agree to treat their fields simultaneously and this is considered legitimate (except by the Church!). Such fields are believed to be rather dangerous owing to the power of the medication used. A man unwise enough to urinate in one of these fields would soon have cause to regret his rashness as his private parts would become swollen and painful.

A popular method for ensuring good crops is the lighting of a medicinal fire to the windward of the field. A large variety of medicines are burned on these fires. These vary, according to the latest trend and from tribe to tribe, and can include exotics such as whale bones and elephant excreta. The South Sotho have a similar device for keeping cutworms at bay. They burn alternate layers of cutworms and leaves of the affected plants beside the fields. The fight against pests forms an important part of the agricultural activities and, apart from such (to the Westerner) obviously efficacious measures as watching fields and scaring birds, magical procedures such as the above cutworm remedy are in constant use. The spontaneous reaction of someone brought up in Western society might be to mock such magical remedies, but similar procedures were recommended by Rudolf Steiner, respected for his contributions in other fields, notably education.

Fields may also be doctored against two-legged predators, and a Mpondo stealing from a field might find himself with an unpleasant and persistent sore under his chin. Humans find themselves built into fertility remedies as well. Here an informant tells how:

> You need grains, new beans, mealies and pumpkins. These are all burned. You must then mix them with the medicines from the river. This burnt medicine is then licked by the chief and headmen. Sometimes the chief says to cut the foetus from a woman, or other parts. Also an old man's

hand. You put the grain in the hand and it will be buried in the chief's fields to make them flourish. The foetus is burned and used with other medicines for licking. They still do it but in secret. For this ritual they must have human things — any part, but the front part of a woman especially. These things must be taken from a living person who can be killed when it has been removed. X was doing it, making medicine.

Rainmaking Rites

Perhaps the greatest problem facing the South African farmer is the notorious capriciousness of the rainfall — which largely means its frequent absence! As this particularly affects the inland tribes, it is among these people that the delicate art of rainmaking is most developed and receives most attention. I have already mentioned the great Modjadji, rain queen of the Lobedu, who owes her throne and the security of her little nation to potent rainmaking rites, and who is reputedly able to control rainfall, directing or withholding it from neighbouring tribes depending on their attitudes. In the heyday of the rain queens of the Lobedu, the footpaths to their stronghold were well-used highways carrying a traffic of pilgrims come to beg for rain for their peoples' lands. Her grove of ancient cycads, secret place of the rain magic, was renowned and regarded with the deepest awe.

Most tribes have an institutional magician or rites to ensure good rainfall. In the western Tswana areas (the north-western Cape and eastern Botswana) where the rainfall is erratic or non-existent, the chief and his rainmakers are very important. Indeed, in traditional society, despite the influence of Christianity, the authority of the chief rests to a very large extent in his mystical power to generate rain, for rain is the life of the people; without it they will die. Schapera has described the rainmaking rituals of the Tswana admirably in his book *Rainmaking Rites of Tswana Tribes*, and here I rely heavily on his descriptions of rainmaking.

The Tswana tribes practise two types of rainbringing rites: those performed early in the season, forming part of the regular annual cycle, and those performed as emergency measures in the face of drought. With the coming of Christianity, in the latter part of the last century, the Tswana country came to be known as the 'missionary road', and converted and traditional chiefs alike were persuaded to replace their annual rainmaking rites with prayers in church. This was mostly done, but often supplemented on the side by traditional rites, which largely comprised the use of medication and exhortations. The reader is referred to Professor Schapera's work for a full description of these long and complex rituals. The exhortations themselves are often poetic, as can be seen from the following extract recorded by Schapera:

> I speak about rain;
> shoulderers of chiefship,
> clever carriers,
> those with the crying horns,
> I speak about rain,
> let the eland die,
> let there be downpour,
> let the clouds bubble up.[4]

Rituals performed in the event of drought, as opposed to routine measures, are also many and varied. Sacrifices may be performed and for these the sacrifical beast is invariably black, representing dark rain clouds. Any other colours on its coat are apt to cause lightning. The term 'black ox' among the Tswana need not be interpreted literally, for human sacrifice may be resorted to when drought threatens and the need is great. Not without foundation is the Kgatla saying: 'Corn doctored with an idiot's flesh yields abundantly'.

Human sacrifice to procure rain and to ensure the survival of the group was reportedly common among many of the tribes, who saw nothing wrong in this practice. The 'rain hunt' was also a common institution among the Sotho and Tswana: the men of the tribe would set off on a hunt on the orders of the chief and capture specific animals, which were then sacrificed.

Drought can be caused by ritual impurity/'heat' such as that generated by a foetus buried out of doors instead of in the cool of the hut. For the first (greater) part of the growing season, the chief and his rainmakers should refrain from sexual intercourse in order to avoid the ritual 'heat' associated with it or the pregnancy of a wife, also characterised by 'heat'.

There is the illuminating story of this century which involved a renowed rain queen and a European woman. Despite the queen's powers, drought had long reigned in the realm. On the eve of the brewing of powerful rain medicine in the hope of defeating the cursed drought, the great queen happened to give audience to a white woman. This woman, a dedicated Christian, expressed deep sympathy for the plight of the queen and her people. Not only this: she offered to pray for rain.

The aura of deep rain magic and fervent Christian supplication rising from two different homes reached the clouds. The rains came. The drought was broken. Not long after, to the white woman's great surprise and pleasure, there appeared at her door, without explanation or thanks, a valuable and ancient glass bead. Such beads are treasured and passed down from generation to generation through the ages: so cocooned in the cloak of the tribal past and sacred to the name of the ancestors are these beads that they are beyond price.

The European woman was thrilled and grateful to accept the gift. But, to my knowledge, oblivious of the deep dilemma that confronted the black rain queen: had it been her traditional medicines, or was it the power of this great foreign god? What if it were the latter?

To acknowledge this help and to make this great, foreign god in all his naked power benign in respect of her and her people, he had to be placated: the bead was delivered.

HERBS

I have described the work of the traditional wife in a later section and will not elaborate on cookery. A group of foods I have not mentioned are the wild herbs. Most tribes know a large number of edible varieties. Despite their seasonal nature, these foods, which are eaten as a side-dish or mixed with maize dishes, form an important part of the diet. Among several of the Nguni tribes traditional men scorn this source of vitamins, saying it is 'women's food' and therefore inferior.

BEER

Central to the culture since time immemorial are the brewing and consumption of traditional beer. People gather at beer-drinks, acquire prestige by holding them, and use beer to arrange or attract communal labour for their fields or for hut-building. Nowadays, many Christian converts are trying to replace beer with tea, but this latter insipid and foreign beverage cannot adequately replace beer in traditional life — or as a source of vitamins. In addition to the

Straining traditional beer using cylindrical grass strainers. Note the variety of containers and the pile of beer-soaked grain on the mat — which often goes not only to the crops but to the heads of the local poultry! Scenes such as this may be encountered even in a very Western-ised setting.

African Heritage

Beer is always placed on an eating mat as a token of respect for this beverage so strongly associated with the culture and the ancestors. This clay pot is 'asking for more' — it is empty, as indicated by the inverted grass cover. Nearby a drinking gourd rests in an enamel basin.

social function of beer, it is vitally important in religious practices and its meaning is inseparable from religious beliefs. That Nguni people brew their beer in the 'place of the ancestors' within the hut is no accident, and a small pot is always left in this holy place as an offering to the shades. A Sotho may empty the dregs of a calabash of beer on the ground, as an offering to the shades. It is poured on to graves, rubbed into incisions on a patient's body, or simply drunk as a sacrament. In short, beer enjoys significance far beyond that of being simply an alcoholic or nutritive beverage.

In the lowveld regions of the Transvaal, where the marula tree and the lala palm grow, the people make wines or ciders from the berries of the marula and the sap of the lala. The marula season is marked by a buoyant atmosphere of bubbly conviviality. The Phalaborwa people are especially dependent on the marula trees which grow in that agriculturally rather poor part of the country. Not only do they ferment liquor from the flesh of the marula fruit, but they also make meal by grinding the pips, and use the wood for carving and building. So valuable are these trees to the tribe that only male specimens may be chopped down and then only with the permission of the chief or headman. The Hananwa of the Blaauwberg, to the west, also make good use of the marula tree.

TOBACCO AND INDIAN HEMP

These two plants are exotics in Africa. Both were carried south by early migrants. Indian hemp was introduced to East Africa in the early part of the Christian era by Arabs whose dhows sailed the Sea of Zanj. It is known today by a whole range of African names, and acquired the popular name of 'dagga' from the word used by the Khoikhoi.

Tobacco, a New World crop, was introduced into Africa in the north-west and quickly spread across the length and breadth of the continent.

A traditional cow's-horn hemp pipe, used by sucking through the large end while holding water in the mouth. Before it became illegal, hemp smoking was the prerogative of the old men, who would blow bubbles through a hollow stick (usually straight) onto a smooth floor to create bubble armies with which they did battle. [Arthur Smit coll.]

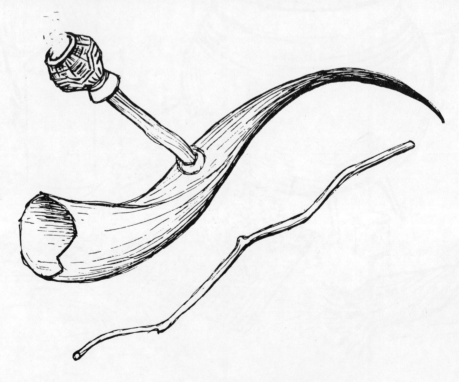

When the Arabs introduced hemp, they brought their way of smoking along with it: clay waterbowls or bubble pipes have been excavated at many sites in Southern Africa. Clay bubble pipes have lost their popularity, however, in favour of those made from gourds and particularly from horn. Of the several types of horn pipe seen, that with the bowl inserted on the stem near the thin end of the horn is the most common. The smoker, with a mouthful of water, inhales from the large open end of the horn. Should this be very large, he presses his cheeks against the opening to close it. In the past, hemp smoking was the prerogative of old men; the young were forbidden its pleasures. The elders would also play a game which was an integral part of the pleasure and ritual of hemp smoking. Crouched around in a circle each blew a bubbly mixture of smoke and water down a thin reed to produce lines of opalescent bubbles on the ground. These bubbles were the play armies of the old men. Part of the art of such sport was to talk and shout through a mouthful of water. A Zulu linguist of my acquaintance who, as a child, watched these old hemp smokers, can imitate to perfection the odd and excitable manner of speech which resulted from a head full of hemp and a mouth full of water!

I watched an old man's 'tobacco-fired' demonstration of bubble-smoking and the bubble game. But most of the time he was distracted for reasons other than hemp because the mere possession of a smoking horn, let alone the hemp with which it is associated, attracts the unwelcome attention of the police. When he left for home, the horn was well and truly concealed under his blanket.

Today tobacco pipes are basically copies of the European pipe, but are made from a variety of materials — clay, bone and, most popular, wood. These are often beautifully carved, with lead inlay and beadwork. Many 'traditional' pipes betray their origins by the 'spur' beneath the bowl, peculiar to earlier European models.

Pipe-smoking among the Southern Nguni has become an integral part of their culture and every traveller through Transkei is familiar with the elegant blanketed women and their long, wooden pipes. A closer inspection of these pipes will reveal one important difference from European pipes: each is fitted with a detachable mouthpiece. This is not for hygienic reasons in the Western sense, but for 'hygiene' of a quite different order. The pipe-bit, having been in the smoker's mouth, is in close contact with her and she is thus highly vulnerable to the evil influences that can be transmitted through it to her in accordance with the principles of sympathetic magic.

A township bubble pipe — an advance on keeping the water in one's mouth as the early marijuana smokers did. [S.A. Museum, Cape Town.]

A Xhosa pipe, obviously borrowing from a European counterpart. The small protuberance beneath the bowl is a feature typical of European origin found on African pipes of various styles. [After Shaw.]

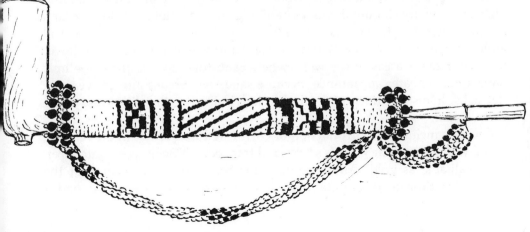

Beaded Xhosa pipe. The detachable mouthpiece is to avoid any contagion — magical rather than microbial — when the pipe is passed around. [Arthur Smit coll.]

HUTS

STRUCTURE AND MATERIALS

THOUGH the dwelling or 'huts' of the various groups share a circular plan, their style varies from district to district, and with the passage of time there have been changes in design. Basically, there are three types of hut: the 'beehive' or domed grass hut which used to be widely distributed in Nguni country until this century; the common wattle-and-daub or sod-walled hut with a thatched roof; and the stone-walled hut.

Today the traditional Nguni hut is vanishing. Rare examples are still to be found among the Swazi and Zulu (notably in northern Natal). This sturdy and weatherproof hut is constructed by using plaited grass rope to tie thatch on to a cleverly constructed hemispherical lattice of saplings. The dwelling displacing the beehive hut is the wattle-and-daub hut with a conical, thatched roof. This structure is closely identified with the African in the minds of most whites. Among the people to the north and north-east, the Pedi of Sekhukhuneland, the Lobedu and the lowveld tribes, the thatch often extends far beyond the walls, forming a verandah which is supported by a circle of uprights. The shaggy, untrimmed thatch and twisted support poles often used, make these huts, in their rich tropical settings, quaintly attractive. The plastering of the walls of the Lobedu sleeping huts, where no fires are made, used to reach right up to the roof, producing a very neat and pleasing interior.

Stone huts are found where wood is scarce, as in the bleak Lesotho highlands. In the mountainous eastern regions underlain by dolerite and basalt, rough blocks of this rock are juggled together to produce a wall which, while not particularly neat, is solid and weatherproof. In the lower but also treeless areas to the west, where sandstone occurs, the stone huts have a much neater appearance, because sandstone breaks into convenient, flat slabs. In historic times many Sotho clans built grass huts like those of the early Nguni.

Changes include the introduction of corrugated-iron roofs. In the remoter parts, where thatching grass is scarce and transport difficult, corrugated iron is as valuable as gold. Any mountain climber who has wondered at the absence of tin-roofed mountaineers' huts in the Drakensberg, has had a

Above: typical Mpondo huts. Note the succulent grown on the roof as magical protection against lightning.

secondhand appreciation of the South Sotho concept that theft from a non-family member is not a crime!

Those who abandon thatching for cold corrugated iron are not simply looking for a status symbol. The thatched roof of a cooking hut can harbour an almost unbelievable collection of cockcroaches. On casual inspection of such a hut, only one or two may be seen, perhaps none. However, if the owner chooses to clean out the thatch, he lights a smoky fire against the wall, close to the roof — and countless shiny cockcroaches scuttle out, blackening the wall. The local poultry, needless to say, thrive on such clean-outs!

The Sotho in many areas of the Orange Free State and Transvaal, as well as the Ndebele, no longer live in the traditional round huts of their early ancestors, but in patterned square huts. Attractive walled courtyards and original gateposts, all colourfully, patterned, are characteristic of Ndebele homes; finger-patterning in the plaster of the front of the houses and pastel designs are the hallmarks of the Sotho.

The floor of the hut is a well-swept, hard surface of cowdung or antheap soil. The housewife may smear her floor as often as once a week to preserve a good finish. In or near the middle of the floor, in a depression, is the hearth. This has no chimney and the smoke must simply find a way out through the thatch. When a fire is burning, especially a dung fire not yet drawing properly, a low pall of smoke fills the hut, burning the eyes and nose. The inhabitants appear not to mind this and they sit on the floor where the atmosphere is less dense.

A Zulu beehive hut.

MAGICAL PROTECTION

In addition to protection against the elements, the animal kingdom, and ill-intentioned humans, a man's home must fend off all forms of magical and supernatural attack. Woven into the walls and palisades of a traditional settlement is a clever and comprehensive set of magical defences. E.J. and J.D. Krige described the defences of a Lobedu homestead of the nineteen thirties:

> At the entrance you trip over a slate-coloured river-stone, jutting out a few inches above the ground. This is a charm laid when the village is built, to keep out witches; it makes them cool, causing them to forget their evil designs. It is part of a more comprehensive scheme for the protection of the village: the gate posts are of special wood (*khirale* or *modutu, Celtis kraussiana*) smeared with medicines on the day they were set up; round the circumference are medicated pegs (*diphoba*) of *khirale*, the whole being completed by a magic circle drawn by the sister or the father's sister, if she is still alive, who drags a 'doctored' branch of thorny *mukhaba* (*Ziziphus mucronata*) round the circumference. If this is not done by her before the doctor begins his work, it must be done subsequently, when the precaution of smearing the soles of her feet with medicines is taken lest by entering she 'opens up a way for witches'. The methods of various doctors are not the same. Sometimes a goat is killed and very often one finds at the entrance to a village a stick, 3-4 ft long, on which were the roots of *titigwani* lily (*Hypoxis villosa*) or pieces of skin of the goat that was killed. This 'medicine of the village', some of which is always kept by the owner, is important for curing certain illnesses caused by witches and may be eaten with the first-fruits. Every year the village needs to be 'awakened' (*hu dzosa mutse*) by the renewal of these protective medicines, a process which [the homestead head] carries out naked at the dead of night by sprinkling around the hedge certain medicine, an ingredient of which is river or sea sand. The river sand has the property of making the village appear as an expanse of water before the eyes of the sorcerer, who thereupon concludes that he has come to the wrong place. A village may have no visible hedge, but the invisible charmed enclosure is never absent.[1]

The means of magical protection described above are common to many tribes.

Medicated pegs are an essential part of the home's supernatural armoury among all tribes. Upon entering a Nguni hut, one cannot help but notice these pegs, which project slightly from the floor between the doorway and the hearth. These pegs and other forms of protection for a typical Natal Nguni house are best described by a priest-diviner:

> Each house must have four pegs next to the fireplace, two by the door, one on top, one in the yard, one in the cattle kraal, one in the goat house, one among the fowls, one by the gate or passage, and one by the big gate. At all the entrances make crosses with 'black medicine' [see p. 71] on the outside of the door and windows. This is also done for *thikoloshe* and *mamtsotsi* [the lightning bird]. This is called *ubutela*.

Before you enter your hut you must put a clay pot of water and a broom outside the gate. When he [the herbalist who is treating the homestead] comes he puts this *ntelezi* and *isitolom* [medicines] all mixed into water. All the houses must be opened before he comes. He does not talk to anybody. His suitcase is closed. He has his assistant with him and he can direct the assistant to do the work. The medicine is on the end of the pegs. Pegs are pointed. They must not be from a big tree, but should come from one with green leaves with pale undersides which shine in the sun. Then you must use *ntelezi* and boil *amakhubalo* medicines and use these next day all over the yard and in the huts. Then crosses must be made and the pegs medicated and put in. Then you must take a hoe to a higher place, dig a big hole and all vomit there for one day when the herbalist is there.

Put four new needles, north, south, east and west and a new razor blade used for incisions, and paper with blood on it, into a hole and burn them. *Ntelezi mpinda mshaye* is a tree with both male and female parts and grows long and round. When you cut it, it must be as thick as a slice of bread. Push the needle upwards in it and place it in the hole. The thorn of the *isinqawe* tree must be put in the middle facing down. Also put in black, white and red *amanyazangoma* [medicine for trapping those who kill people].

Next day take a bucket full of warm medicine and carry it to this hole. Each must drink and fill his stomach, and take the medicine which is then poured on lighted dry grass. Each blows this fire, jumps the fire and goes to the hole. They stand there and talk, each with a pinch of medicine on the tongue, and spit on the hole saying, 'Here I am, the one who wants me, I'm here.' No names are mentioned. The name is that of a witch and if he does things he will die by needles. Fire — they are on the safe side of it. They must put two fingers, or the feather of a fowl if you do not know, and vomit. Then they wash their hands and face with the medicine, all standing round the hole.

The herbalist tells them to walk straight home all covered in blankets, in single file, not looking back and when they go there, he sprays them with *ntelezi* on the broom. Then they take the broom, bucket and pot home, not looking back. The herbalist covers everything and follows. The *dengezi* [potsherd in which medicines are burned] must be on the fire. He puts medicine on it and all lick, smoke and eat raw *amakhubalo* medicine.

After all the work he must tell them two things. They must not fetch water at night, must not give out salt at night, must not allow neighbours to take live coals: these things work against the medicines. The herbalist is paid R40 for the whole job. This medication is done again after two years and if it is the same herbalist, he will not charge as much — they are his people now. They keep the *ntelezi* and have it close while it is thundering outside, even when the *ntelezi* is rotten and smelly.

In the old days an old man, the head, would take a stick for his hat and throw it outside. Even if they are away the family does this. Whenever it is thundering and you are travelling, with food especially, never enter these homesteads, you will be weakened if you have not had treatment. Lightning will get you. Women (even widows) may ask the herbalist to do this or go out naked and show their backsides to the lightning, rain or not, when it flashes.

Before building a hut, a Pedi will bury four medicated stones around the periphery of his projected homestead. The owner and the priest-diviner in attendance then start at the back of the hut site and walk around it in opposite directions, dragging medicated sticks, until they meet at the entrance. They have thus created a magic circle of protection. The two sticks are then tied to the ground across the entrance of the hut, so that all who enter it must step over them.

The Venda procedure for safeguarding a projected hut is similar: after selecting a site, the priest-diviner places a medicated stick at each of the four cardinal points and two more sticks across the entrance when the hut has been constructed so that anyone entering it must cross them. This idea of 'disarming' the visitor by forcing him or her to cross a magical article in the doorway is common. The Zulu bury a certain bulb and the Lobedu a stone under the homestead entrance. In Lesotho a collection of pegs treated with magic oils is to be found at the hut entrance.

In the Christian setting protective magic may be adapted slightly for use on traditional (and Western-style) dwellings. The local missionary — if he is of a suitable denomination and disposition — may be called on to bless the house or sprinkle holy water.

One need not even invoke protection in order to be given it. Our home in Richmond, Natal, was 'protected' by two blue flames, one on each gatepost, which burned (so it was said) every night, kindled apparently by priest-diviner friends, who were frequent visitors to the house.

BEADS AND BEADWORK

MAN has always been fascinated by the proverbial 'baubles, bangles and beads'. Glass beads are uncovered in sites of great antiquity. In Africa natural objects have been whittled, bored and strung together as beads seemingly since man took his first tentative steps. To this day San (Bushmen) make beads of ostrich eggshell. The African mother in certain tribes wears a necklace of large cylindrical wooden beads, both as carriers of magical medicine and for the eminently practical reason that they make very good gnawing for teething babies.

What could be more intriguing than a colourful glass bead from some far-off, almost mythical land? Today traditionalists, notably the Lobedu and Venda, still wear glass beads, which they claim their families have owned for generations and even brought with them in migrations from ancestral lands to the north. Notable in this respect are the small, blue 'beads of the water' found among these two tribes which, like all ancient beads, are associated with the lineage ancestors and are beyond price. Glass beads are also found in archaeological sites in Southern Africa, sometimes associated with locally manufactured clay and copper copies. Indeed, my parents, simply grubbing through the refuse heaps of the Valley Tonga in their former home, now beneath Lake Kariba, found many lovely old Venetian beads.

Attempting to trace the origin of old beads is often a hopeless task, even where modern methods of spectrochemical analysis are used. Nevertheless, it leads one to long-dead names and places that seemingly belong to the realm of myth and dreams.

THE EARLY BEAD TRADE

We do not know when the first bronze-smith pondered the significance of the fused sand which he found at the bottom of his kiln at the end of each firing, or when it was found that this glass 'frit', heated with seaweed or wood-ash (supplying sodium or potassium oxide, respectively), yields glass. However, the earliest glass beads, excavated in Egypt, the home of glass, are 4 500 years old, and by 1 500 B.C., the industry flourished at Alexandria and continued to do so, reaching a peak at the time of the birth of modern mathematics around 300 B.C., when this town was the glass centre of antiquity.

When the Jews fled Egypt, it is believed that they took with them the art of glass-making, and from them it spread all along the eastern Mediterranean seaboard — notably to the Phoenicians — and through the Middle East. With the conquest of Egypt by Alexander in the late fourth century B.C., and the later annexation of Egypt by Rome, trade boomed. The glass — and bead — industry expanded rapidly. Caravans struck southwards across the sand wastes of the Sahara laden with trade beads. The Arab dhows sailing the monsoon winds across the Sea of Zanj to trade with the inhabitants of East Africa in the early part of the Christian era were burdened with glass beads from the Mediterranean. Very ancient beads are still found in the possession of Africans. Professor van Riet Lowe reports one worn by a priest-diviner, believed to date to the Ptolemaic Period. B.H. Dick has suggested the Etruscans as the glassmakers responsible for teaching the art of bead-making to the Phoenicians.[1] Furthermore, he unequivocally identified the Venda 'beads of the water', mentioned earlier, with beads excavated from the ruins of Carthage, destroyed in 146 B.C. Whether the beads owned by the Venda originated at such an early date in Carthage, or later at colonies on the West African coast is not certain, but their name, beads of the water, suggests their having been brought by seaborne traders, probably Phoenician, and therefore at an early date.

With the changing fortunes of commerce and war in the first millennium of our era, first the Egyptians, then Syria and Palestine, Rome and Byzantium gained and lost supremacy of the glass and bead trade, and most of them are represented by occasional beads still found in Southern Africa. The eclipse of the great glass industry of the Byzantium empire was the cue for Venice, whose master craftsmen had learned the art of glass-making from wandering Jews early in this era, and later from the Byzantine glass-workers. From A.D. 400 there flowed a stream of beads out of Venice which, toward the end of the Middle Ages, swelled to a river, to pour out in trade to primitive peoples the world over and unite them in a brotherhood of colour.

Among the earliest and most coveted Venetian trade beads are the Aggry beads, still found in Southern Africa. Although the mode of manufacture differed in some respects from that of other beads, I will describe it in order to give an idea of the skills involved in the manufacture of these early beads.

Like many early beads, the Aggry started out as a tube of glass, later to be cut into lengths and bored. In the case of the Aggry beads, however, before cutting, the rod was ribbed by rolling (marvering) it on a corrugated surface while still hot and soft. It was then overlaid with a sheet of coloured glass and again rolled on the surface. This process was repeated several times, creating a striped pattern. Then, when the rod had been cut into beads, each bead was tapered pyramidally at the ends, creating an attractive zigzag pattern.

The advent of the Portuguese changed the slow and romantic (if bloody) Arab trade on the East Coast into a full-scale commercial operation. Among the objects of this commerce were the Venetian beads. In the years 1508-9 alone nearly 80 million beads were landed on the East African coast. These were carried far south by migrants, even reaching the Khoikhoi (Hottentots) in the Cape. In addition, organised trading expeditions carried the glittering beads deep into the heart of the Dark Continent. Early explorers such as Speke, Livingstone and Burton, reported long lines of slaves burdened with beads — to be traded for yet more slaves.

BEADS AND SOCIETY

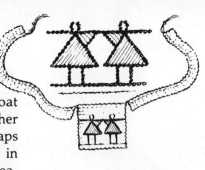

Beads featured in the first trade between European and African. A boat would land and the sailors walk up the beach to place their beads and other articles at the jungle's edge. They would then put to sea to return, perhaps the following day. There, on the beach, they would find ivory or gold in return for their wares — gold left by people who saw them as pale sea-beings, who lived in giant shells and ate ivory.

When, in the last century, these Europeans found Southern Africa opening up as a market, they discovered a people ravenous for beads, beads, and yet more beads. The two tribes to make the most use of beads were the Zulu and Southern Ndebele. Other Nguni, however, were not far behind in their love of beads as adornment. In societies with the central government wielding great power in the personal life of the individual, and with such clear social groupings and codes, the wearing of beads immediately became related to the wearer's status and relationship to society. When Mpande, as nineteenth-century king of the Zulu, adopted a pink bead as his emblem, it became a sign of royalty. Likewise among the Ndebele, where red became the bead of royalty. The Swazi royal family and those who serve them wear strings of beads made of red, white, blue and black in a special sequence. This shows their status and guarantees for them safe conduct anywhere (and, for any illegitimate wearer, a fine).

Every stage of an individual's life is marked by certain types of dress and beadwork. There are two reasons for this. First, the time of maximum emotional involvement with members of the opposite sex is bound to be marked by brightly coloured dress — and the dashing traditionalist, resplendent in a mass of coloured beads, is a fine sight. Second, as a result of high emotions, the codes of society must be more strictly enforced — a task made easier where the individual's status and certain aspects of his past and present commitments are manifest in his dress.

The period of peak adornment is at the time of courtship, when the pace of love and intrigue is especially heated. All or most of the beadwork worn by a young man has been given him by one or a number of girl friends — the more the merrier, and the higher his status. A youth's beadwork may weigh as much as fifteen kilograms.

All or most of the beadwork worn by a girl may be gifts from a young man, made by his sisters for his girlfriend. This beadwork has not only a deep emotional meaning, but very real social significance and is virtually beyond price — the sale of certain items is the equivalent of a European girl selling her engagement ring. More so in fact: in a culture without writing, these pieces of beadwork became valid legal documents produced as evidence in traditional courts.

Apart from the significance of the type of beadwork, the colours of the beads used and the patterns can have a meaning. While bead colours (or some of them) appear to have some meaning in most tribes, this use of colour meanings has seen the creation of singularly lovely bead poetry among the Zulu and some related tribes.

BEAD LANGUAGE

By the beginning of this century, a full colour lore had evolved among the

Bead love message recorded in the diary of O.J. Horrax, in the course of an expedition to Zululand arranged by Dr Hugh Tracey in July 1930. The meaning of the linked figures is obvious. The message is conveyed in the triangles: the small ones are green while the large (skirt) are royal blue. Together the triangles mean, 'We stand on the same platform of love, with nothing to separate us'. The blues ask, 'Have you the power to maintain me?' The greens state, 'My heart is as green as the grass,' meaning, 'My love for you will never die'.

The wearer stated emphatically: 'I understood the message without the girl saying a word. It would have been very unmannerly for the girl to have explained it to me and I would have been very angry with her had she done so.'
[Jill Tracey]

Zulu-speaking people of modern Natal and kwaZulu and among the Swazi. This involved the assignation of meanings to colours as well as the defining of certain acceptable colour combinations. Though the meaning of bead colours may vary from district to district, it is remarkably constant. The accepted colour combinations vary substantially from place to place, however, a fact which enables a person with a knowledge of beads to know from where a wearer of beads or a piece of beadwork comes.

While Mrs Estelle Hamilton-Welsh reported[2] that all questioning of Transkeian people about bead messages resulted in comments to the effect that such ideas were only the white man's nonsense or something indulged in by the Zulu, there are today many examples of 'talking beads' from this area. These have been described by Mrs Joan Broster in her most informative book, *The Thembu*.[3] These examples indicate that 'talking beads' are worn mainly by married women.

The traditionalist is a very discerning buyer, supersensitive to the size and precise colour of the beads and whether or not they are fashionable. This desire to be 'with it' and to manifest good taste, as well as the need for the correct colour to express a feeling in a bead message, has kept suppliers on their toes.

The vagaries of supply have made their mark, however. In the past, when the discerning buyer had several different shades of most colours to choose from, each had its own meaning, but today she must often be content with only one shade. The correct meaning is inferred from the context in which the colour is presented. Recently, plastic beads have begun to replace the original glass article. While they are not much cheaper, they are often chosen for their availability and lightness. One realises the importance of this latter characteristic when examining the bead adornment of the traditional individual: many a Western woman would be hard put to it even to lift the beaded blanket worn with apparent nonchalance by her Ndebele counter-part.

In Natal, prohibitive prices have driven many people away from the use of beadwork. Often when the beaux and belles parade through the local village on Saturday morning, they are resplendent not in beads but in a wonderful selection of gaudy cloths and studded belts. In many areas of Natal where the existence of the bead language is known, its use is a thing of the past and the pieces worn carry none of this poetry of the veld. It is hard even to find someone who properly understands the 'language'. If you ask for 'beads that talk', you might be shown some trite phrase in Zulu or English, worked on to a rectangular bead panel.

Western man is not in a position to appreciate the true poetry of

---

PAGE 239   Bead ornaments and bright cloths as worn by a Xhosa youth in Transkei announce that the boy has made the transition from childhood to manhood by circumcision. He has now been accepted by his chosen girl and is flattered with many bead ornaments. Horns and beaded bottles containing love potions are strung into necklaces. A beaded toy cutlery set suggests future plans.

The line drawing depicts the virtually extinct dancing dress of the circumcision period. The heavy skirt, mask and 'horns' are made of a palm from the Bashee River. The dance symbolised a virile young bull tossing his head and boastful of his strength.

Barbara Tyrrell

Styles of beadwork adapt and incorporate new features of the environment. This piece from the Natal Midlands states quite explicitly what its owner wishes to say: '*Ngizo shadá nawe*' — 'I shall marry you.' The following are representative of the Zulu beadwork of thirty years ago. [Arthur Smit coll.]

≡ RED
⦂⦂⦂ GREEN

'You think I don't see what you are up to — but I do.'

≡ RED
⦂⦂⦂ BLUE
⦀⦀ GREEN

'I am angry because you haven't brought the cows [bride-price].'

≡ RED
⦂⦂⦂ GREEN

'I don't want the child of the first wife to be the successor.'

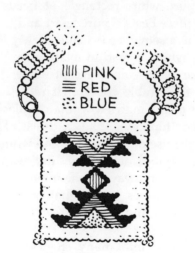

⦀⦀ PINK
≡ RED
⦂⦂⦂ BLUE

'You are poor and afraid.'

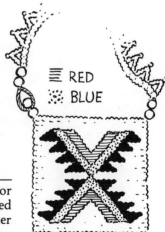

≡ RED
⦂⦂⦂ BLUE

'You are telling lies about all your possessions.'

PAGE 240   This Ndebele woman is seated in an attitude which shows her respect for her husband's family. She is newly married, as indicated by the single, beaded neckhoop worn at this stage. Her new ceremonial blanket is richly beaded, as is her married woman's apron and her ceremonial mat.

She has decorated her home in bright colours inside and out in the manner of her people, adapting, in her designs, impressions of life around her — more especially of the excitement of visits to the city, motorcars, trains, street lights and the novel architecture.

beadwork. Both the language and the way of thinking are foreign to him. The love letter from a girl to her lover will be made while she sits with a peer group, and its final form will depend on their combined advice — a true expression of the communal spirit of her society. It will be read with the help of the young man's sisters and her friends — who likewise make beaded love poetry for their young men — and such is the understanding that not only the same basic message, but the same subtle intonations of feeling are picked up. The true art and meaning of bead poetry — and this is a true poetry of colour and feeling — operate at a level of thought and perception beyond that of the word. Even a single odd bead, for instance, in a panel of another colour, is not a mistake but, if it is not locally accepted as a 'tasteful' colour combination, will tell the reader that the whole message is subtly but certainly altered.

Colour Meanings

In many of the remoter areas bead language is still used and even common. In describing the meanings of the colours below, I have tried to find the most common meaning, agreed on by people who have worked in different areas. Some colour meanings are best illustrated by placing the colour in context as it may appear in a string of beads.

White is the basic colour of much beadwork. As seems to be the case in most societies, it is symbolic of purity, truth, virtue. See a young man wearing a pure white rectangle of beads about his neck and know that somewhere there beats a pure heart and true. In almost all bead poetry, the first colour in a sequence is white — 'My heart . . .', followed by the rest of the message which is read in relation to 'My heart . . .'.

Black, like every colour except white, has both good and bad connotations. In a favourable context, it represents marriage — the *isidwabe* or leather skirt of the married woman is black. In an unfavourable context, it can mean anything evil, bad; a threat. The figure on page 244 is a good example of the use of both black and white.

Pink, the symbol of royalty, indicates poverty when it is worn by a commoner. A man away on the mines who receives a necklace of alternate white and pink beads knows that his beloved is gently chiding him: 'My heart is ever true and pure, but you are too poor to pay my bride-price (*lobola*).'

Blue is divided into many shades. A pale, greyish-blue, close to the Westerner's 'dove grey', is called 'pigeon' and, as such, is a messenger or agent to carry desires. A sequence composed of a white, a blue-grey, a pink and a black bead may be interpreted as follows: 'My heart is pure with love, my dear, and I would that I were a dove who could fly to your door; but, alas, you are too poor to pay my *lobola* and I am very unhappy that I cannot wear the leather skirt of marriage.' A deeper, royal blue can mean a loyal and true heart. A man away on the mines who receives a necklace of alternate white and blue beads knows that he has nothing to worry about at home. A different shade of deep blue can also mean a request, especially if placed at the centre of a mirrored sequence. For instance, the sequence white, black, blue, black, white, could be interpreted as, 'My heart is full of love and I want to wear the leather skirt of marriage: when will we be married?' A

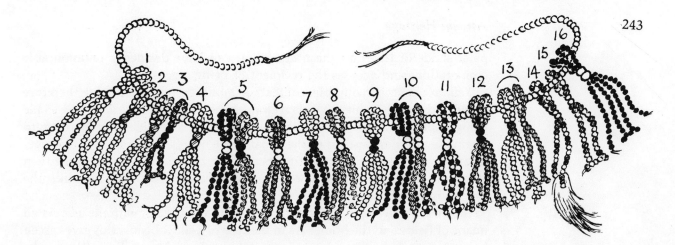

Bead love letter, dated 1978, from the Qudeni district of Zululand. It is one of the oldest types of letters, a style still in use, comprising bead tassels looped onto a single string of white beads. It is 'read' tassel by tassel, or in pairs, some tassels having four strand ends, or two, according to the value of the meaning involved. It is read from the end containing the pale yellow and black beads (i.e. starting at 1):

1 Pale yellow: Hear ye, boys of this home, for there is no dwelling, be it large or small, that has not something to tell. (Calling attention; introduction.)
2 White: My heart is white and pure like the sands of the sea. (Assurance of fidelity and innocence.)
3 One tassel pale blue, one red: Leave your home and let us go to the Maputo coast and return home when the corn is red. (A longing to elope.)
4 Pink: Your lack of wealth is an obstacle. (Frustration: he is too poor to afford her bride-price.)
5 One tassel deep blue, one smoky-green: I heard the warning cry of the ibis birds and I came out and looked, hoping it

was you, my lover. I searched until my eyes became smoky [hazy] but saw, after all, that it was the lovers of my sisters who came. (Her initial optimism in the relationship has been replaced by disappointment and despondency.)
6 Cornelian red: However, my lover, be confident, even as I am confident. (Reassurance and strength.)
7 White loops and black ends: I saw the great turkey buzzards taking wing and I thought it was you, child of man, but it was the Ignorer who stands aloof, like the maid who shuns the people of the kraal of her betrothed. (Hope and fear mingle over suspected coolness.)
8 Clear green: I am young and childlike, bright green as the grass that is not even eaten by cattle but only by the mambas [snakes]. (Too naive to comprehend or handle this situation.)
9 Pink: I suggest, my lover, that you leave the road that you are on, lest you be swallowed in its dust. (A warning against present behaviour.)
10 One tassel black, one green: I thought that I would marry at your homestead where there are little black cows, but when I arrived I found only that the inside of the cattle byre was green

with weeds. (His family has no cattle, nothing to offer — shattered hopes.)
11 Alternating deep blue and white: Happy is the guineafowl that calls wherever it runs, but like the hornbill I cry only when I return to my home, sorrowing. (A turning away in sorrow.)
12 One string red, one cornelian: I suffer and my nose bleeds clots as did the cattle that died of rinderpest and lay facing downhill. (Utter despair.)
13 One tassel white, one pale blue: The cattle egrets [white] will reveal to me in what manner the waves [pale blue] have eroded holes in our relationship and how deep the holes are. (Hoping to discover what is wrong.)
14 Alternating two pink, two green, with a tuft of goatskin on the end: My lover, do not treat me cheaply [pink] as you would your shabby leather buttock garment, the one you wear only at home. In return I [green] do not make of you my shabby fringe skirt. (A lament over being badly treated and a promise of respect.)
15 Alternating two red, two bright yellow: I command that, like the chameleon, you change your colours, your ways. (A threat and challenge to improve.)

16 Black: For I wander sadly around the hills, wearing the little black cloaks of widowhood. (She is lost, lonely and disconsolate.)

This deeply moving letter was given by a loving and faithful girl to a lover whose affections appeared to be on the wane. The frustrations of waiting, watching, and 'not knowing' are poignantly told in beads. Modesty and respect forbid that such sentiments be openly expressed.
   The young man for whom the letter is created must ask to be told the meaning. The girl will then read it back to him, losing neither 'face' nor modesty. She reads it in a fast flow of metaphor, tassel by tassel. Her 'reading' appears to be thoroughly memorised and she moves each tassel aside as its meaning is revealed.
   When a girl wishes to end a relationship, she may make an all-black letter of this type and throw it at the feet of her lover. He is then obliged to wear it for a day to announce the severance of their relationship.

paler shade of blue, on the other hand, can have decidedly unfavourable connotations and accuses the recipient of being a gossip.

Yellow, in its favourable context, symbolises pumpkins and therefore home and wealth, while its unfavourable meanings are very firm, one shade being called 'calf excreta' by the Ngwane people of Natal, according to Regina G. Twala.[4] Instead of the usual white bead as the start of a message, meaning 'My heart ...', the first bead may be yellow. The message then starts off with the rather uncompromising statement, 'You are like the excreta of a calf'.

Green, in its favourable connotation, symbolises grass, with the associated image of fields and the home. As in the case of yellow beads, this gives green beads the twin favourable meanings of domestic joy and wealth. In the alternative, less favourable meaning, a green bead tells the recipient of the message that its maker is pining away through sadness or sickness. A sequence of white, pink, black, green would say something like, 'My heart is pure and filled with longing for you, my beloved, but your poverty prevents your buying the *lobola* cattle for our marriage. I pine away like the wilting river reed when the summer rains do not come.'

Red, also has two meanings, which were once shared between the opaque and clear beads when the two types were both freely available. In its favourable meaning it refers to longing and passion of the heart. A sequence of white, red, black, translates as, 'My heart is white with devotion and purity and burns with a great passion for you. Oh! That I could wear the black skirt of marriage.' The fire symbolism may be changed slightly, however. A girl who is given a piece of beadwork with many red beads dotted about is being told, 'You light fires in many hearths' — you are too free with your affections. In its worst context, red symbolises blood, the negative passions of anger and pain: 'You have hurt me, and now the blood of pain and anger pours from the wound in my heart.'

Rectangular Love Letters

The meanings of sequences of beads on a string are easy to read and the interpretation will not change significantly from area to area. Local idiom in bead language becomes more important in reading the rectangular love letters. As already mentioned, their meaning is closely tied to the district where they were created and interpretation depends on the tacit sharing of meanings. Every district has certain acceptable basic colour combinations (e.g. white, black, green) which form a background against which the message is presented by means of elaboration and modification. In such rectangular work, the message is read from the centre outwards. Rectangular messages and strings of beads may be combined to create a document of considerable complexity.[5] Twala gives an example of one such piece which tells not only the complete life story of a widowed woman but also her present feelings and attitudes.[4]

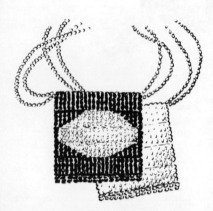

Two short necklets purchased from a young Zulu male in 1978 and given him by his betrothed. The first was all white, indicating absolute purity of heart and complete fidelity. The second, white surrounded by black, is a less happy message. It is an ultimatum, meaning that the giver is still faithful but anxious to wear the 'black leather skirt of marriage'. Unless positive steps are taken towards arranging a wedding, the betrothal will be terminated. Such 'letters' are precious personal and social documents and cost their present owner a considerable sum of money — which contributed towards the imminent wedding!

CRAFTS

POTTERY

THROUGH man's history as uncovered by archaeologists, there runs a consistent theme — the art of pottery. In South Africa the Khoikhoi peoples and later the Bantu-speaking people made and fired pottery. Our knowledge of the spread of the Iron Age into Southern Africa and of the history of the Bantu-speaking people is largely the result of the archaeological study of ancient potsherds.

Contemporary traditional pottery rests on these ancient traditions. The potters of traditional society are, and have always been, the women. In many tribes such as the Xhosa and Mfengu, the potter's art is today almost completely extinct. In many others, the potters are few and far between. But pottery continues to flourish in other areas, such as Swaziland. It has probably survived the onslaught of enamel and plastic ware largely because of its cheapness and traditional role, and the large beer-brewing pots and smaller pots for drinking beer are still to be found throughout Southern Africa. Porous pottery water containers are also popular, as they keep their contents cool through evaporation.

A Tswana clay drinking cup with typical stippled pattern. [S.A. Museum, Cape Town.]

Each potter has her own 'special hole' from which she obtains her clay. This is prepared by kneading and, depending on the individual, is left to mature for different lengths of time. Then a sand 'filler' is added before the clay is used to fashion a pot.

Different techniques are used by different groups of people. These have recently been comprehensively documented by A.C. Lawton.[1] The Swazi and Mpondo potters, for instance, build the base of their vessels first, by making a spiral of clay which they smooth over. The walls are then built up from this by means of a spiral 'rope' of clay which is smoothed over, leaving no trace of the method of manufacture.

The South Sotho and Natal clans, from whom they probably learned this method, build up the sides of their pots using sausage-like rolls of clay, which are smoothed onto the walls as they are applied. The western, Tswana, peoples build their pots from the widest diameter, either towards the rim or the base, turning the pot over to add the remaining half when it has hardened slightly. These people build up their pots by adding clay in large, flat chunks. When building small pots, the potters of all tribes follow the primitive method of simply moulding them from a lump of clay.

Potters always take care to work under cool, draught-free conditions to prevent over-rapid drying, and consequent cracking of the pots. The potter's art is also surrounded by taboos for the protection of their wares: many a craftswoman will not tolerate men or 'impure' people near her place of work for fear of cracked pots.

Pots are fired after a period ranging from several days to several weeks of careful air-drying. The fuel for firing may be wood, twigs or dung. Usually the pots are placed in a group and the fuel is packed in and around them before firing.

Decoration is peculiar to each group. Various designs may be grooved into the surface with a thorn or any sharp object such as a safety-pin, or stamped impressions are made using a variety of objects. Pots may be highly polished with graphite, a practice common with fine ware in Natal, or ochre may be applied in colourful patterns. The use of ochre, formerly common among the Sotho tribes, has to some extent been replaced by painting with gloss enamel.

Today bowls and shallow vessels are seldom made. The most popular traditional clay vessels are large pots, from 90-litre beer-brewing vessels to 5-to 10-litre cooking-pots and the smaller drinking vessels. Cooking-pots are not as popular as drinking and beer-brewing vessels, however, as they have mostly been replaced by the three-legged iron pot of European manufacture.

The high standard of African pottery was first brought home to me in Malawi. I was aboard a small steamer which plies Lake Malawi, when we stopped to send a boat ashore with supplies for a small village crouched beneath the looming green mountains which plunge into the northern parts of the lake. A huge beer pot, well over half a metre in diameter, was one of the articles loaded on to the boat. Unfortunately it was dropped, shattering into a thousand pieces — none of which was more than a centimetre thick!

A good proportion of beer brewed in the homeland areas comes from clay pots. Even in urban areas clay pots are often used for brewing. They are much in evidence in the black townships round my home village of Richmond in Natal. The illicit and potent brews encountered in urban areas are, however, unlikely to be brewed in pots because the brewers find it useful to have easily movable vessels to forestall the police. The almost universal vessel of choice in this case is the 20-litre paraffin tin! These tins are often buried and covered with sheet metal or hardboard, on which is spread a camouflage of earth and leaves.

An intriguing variation on a theme: pipe carvers in traditional society are apparently blessed with unlimited imagination. Note the owner's detachable mouthpiece tied by a thread: anybody else using the pipe must supply his own to avoid magical contamination. [After Shaw.]

CARVING

One of the requirements of man the world over is a strong, durable, easily shaped substance with which to make a large variety of objects and containers, and through which he can express his artistic urges. Such a substance is wood: wood to make milk pails, meat trays, spoons, assegai-stocks, drums, doors, smoking pipes — and the abstract grimace of the African mask, which has become symbolic of the dark continent.

Using only primitive tools — axe, gouge, knife — the carver of wood (always a man) can create functional articles as if they had always been there awaiting manifestation. Attractive patterns are often produced on these articles by charring them and then cutting through the burned, black outer surface to reveal the white wood underneath. Many carved articles are oiled to prevent cracking.

A feature as essential to African thought as it is incidental to that of the West is the *meaning* of all things — their psychological connections and significance. This meaning is carved into most objects, with the exception of some of those mass-produced for the tourist trade. Not all tourist-oriented objects are without meaning, however. I remember stopping beside the national road to the Cape, where it dives and winds through the deep Umkomaas valley in Natal, to chat to an old man carving knobkerries for sale to passing tourists. The knob topping most of the sticks was shaped into two bulbous halves. They were well-made sticks, clearly showing the care and craftsmanship of the old man and, at R1.50 each, he was doing a fairly brisk trade. Knowing the common symbolism of the stick (in Natal at least) I questioned the old man — and indeed his customers were going off with artistic phallic symbols! I wondered how many realised this.

Care and meaning are carved into even the most mundane of Zulu articles. The long-handled scoop decants beer from larger to smaller pots, while that above it is for dipping water from the stream. [Arthur Smit coll.]

GRASSWORK

For a people living close to the earth, the essentials for existence come from nature. Grasswork plays a fundamental role in a society which evolved on the hot African plains. Baskets used for carrying grain, and storing it; mats; neck, leg and arm rings; beer-strainers — all are made of grass. The most finely woven baskets can even be (and are) used for storing beer, and the large storage baskets of the South Sotho can hold up to 2 000 kilograms of grain.

Of all the traditional crafts, basket-making — because of the cheapness, lightness and utility of grass-woven materials — has been least affected by the advent of Western technology. In recent years, however, plastic containers have begun to take their toll.

Though traditional society can boast fine basketwork, the art of weaving was never developed. When Mohlomi, the famous mystic and wandering Sotho chief of the late eighteenth century, returned from his travels in the north, one of the most remarkable (to his subjects) of his achievements was his acquisition of a magical garment which, while it covered the entire body, could be crumpled up to fit in one hand. The closest these people came to cloth was the primitive bark-cloth produced by some tribes.

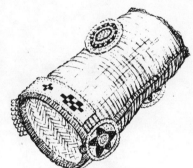

A modern Zulu head-dress for a married woman, constructed of plaited palm-leaf, covered with black muslin and red ochre. The top is covered with tufts of the wearer's own hair as a concession to the past when such headdresses were a fixture, built up from the wearer's hair. The beaded band worn at the front is a token of respect for her husband's family. [Arthur Smit coll.]

Although the art of basket-making is fairly universal among the tribes and each housewife makes most of her own wares, there are specialists in the manufacture of baskets who may be either male or female. Two basic methods are used in basketry. In one, grass-stalks (or other fibres) are woven, as is cotton; in the other, very common method, thick (0.5-1 cm) grass coils (wound on grass cores) are wound spirally upwards from a base, securely bound all the way to form firm, strong articles. Attractive patterns may be woven into baskets by colouring selected fibres with vegetable dyes.

MUSICAL INSTRUMENTS

The first 'homemade' musical instruments i recall came from a bamboo patch. Kehla was a good few years older than my six when he made the first flute I saw. It was constructed from a piece of bamboo about fifteen centimetres long, closed at either end by the nodes. In the side of this he bored a series of holes, four or five in number. By blowing into the last hole on the left and using his fingers to close the others, he produced a full-bodied series of notes, if not a melody. My efforts consistently rewarded me with no more than a windy chirping.

Imported Instruments

Since that time, however, I have seen few traditional instruments. Some are still found in rural areas where time passes as slowly as it always used to. But elsewhere the instruments are petrol-tin 'guitars' or 'violins' as well as their commercially obtainable counterparts (though violins are quite rare) and — much in evidence — harmonicas. I have always loved the cool, dim interiors of trading stores, and an essential amid the bric-à-brac has always been at least one hardy steel-string guitar suspended on the wall behind the rack of bright cotton frocks or blouses in the corner where the ox-plows are kept. And, in posh stores, a glass counter to reveal the pile of cheap harmonicas.

I referred to the guitars as being hardy. They have to be, as their owners take them out in all weathers, rain or shine, with no apparent concern for the instrument and, so it would appear, no ill effect either. Though the sight is becoming less and less common, I remember young men striding, guitar in hand, along the paths and winding dust roads I have walked and driven. Some of these people were true musicians, plucking out the sparkling, peculiarly African melodies that seem to speak the wistful-yet-jaunty language of Africa's great plains. Others, not so skilful, would walk for kilometres in step with a repetitive three-chord sequence.

Like the guitar, the harmonica is an integral part of the young person's courting image and, as such, a popular instrument. This is to be expected, as these Western instruments resemble the various traditional reed and bone flutes of Southern Africa.

Indigenous Instruments

We owe much of what we know of African musical instruments to a few dedicated men, notably Dr Hugh Tracey[2] and Professor P.R. Kirby who, when it was not fashionable as it is today, spent their time travelling and studying the music and musical instruments of Africa. Kirby wrote a definitive and authoritative book on the subject entitled *The Musical Instruments of the Native Races of Southern Africa* in 1934.[3] Writing today, any account of traditional musical instruments is at best a very brief précis of this work.

Wind Instruments

Briefly, the Bantu-speaking people played, and still play, a wide variety of wind, string, and percussion instruments. The horn bugle made from antelope (especially sable and kudu) or cow horn is a popular wind instrument which is still commonly used, blown in trumpet style.

Of pipes, the most impressive were the reed-pipe ensembles of certain tribes. Those of the Venda were passed on to the Pedi or North Sotho, while a subgroup of the Tswana in Botswana borrowed their reed pipes from the Khoikhoi. Each reed pipe played gave just one note, so that the melody could have as many notes as there were players. Venda pipes were tuned to a seven-note scale, while the Sotho tuned theirs to a five-note scale.

The one reed instrument still in use today is the pipe that is played by *Nonyana*, a creature cloaked in blackened bark fibre, with a scarlet-bean

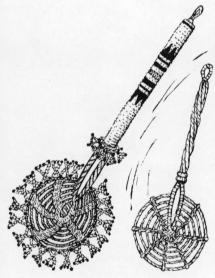

Two plaited grass beer skimmers, one for practical use and the other (beaded) as an ornament, symbolising a woman's pride in her domestic duties and home. [Arthur Smit coll.]

head topped with ostrich feathers, which is the central mystery of the highly secret dancing ceremony of the Venda circumcision school for girls. *Nonyana* uses this reed pipe as a voice-modifier to amplify the sound of the voice.

Stringed Instruments

Stringed instruments probably all derive from the bow. Even those peoples who apparently never used the bow as a weapon, adopted this type of instrument. In playing these, either the player's mouth or a calabash — more recently, a tin as well — is used as a resonator. Individual notes are selected by the fingers gripping, touching or pressing nodal points of the string. The harmonics are selected in one of two ways: either by movement of the calabash resonator to and from the chest, or by opening and closing the mouth as one does in playing the Jewish harp. The methods of playing and the traditional players (i.e. male or female, old or young) vary from tribe to tribe, for these instruments are widely distributed. Traditional stringed instruments, unlike drums, produce a soft, wistful sound and the melodic tinkle of a South Sotho maiden playing her personal tune as she wanders along a rocky path seems to harmonise with the remote grandeur and deep silence of the mountains of central Lesotho.

The lesiba is one of the world's few wind-string instruments. Originally Khoikhoi, it is now played by the Sotho, and is a stringed instrument operated by wind. It is played by placing the flattened quill between the lips and breathing in and out vigorously so that the quill vibrates. The strength of the suck and blow determines which harmonic is to be elicited.

Multi-stringed instruments, such as the guitar, violin and the autoharp, were introduced by the European. However, a rock painting copied by Stow and reproduced by Kirby, illustrates a traditional multi-stringed instrument, which was made by burying a series of bows of different lengths in the soil and striking them.[3]

Hand Piano or Mbira

The Iron Age brought hand pianos to the northern Transvaal. These hand-held instruments consist of beaten metal strips of varying lengths affixed securely to a wooden frame, and sounded by striking with the thumbs. They may be played inside a calabash, which acts as a resonator.

Xylophone

It is probable that the xylophone was introduced, together with its musical scale, some two thousand years ago from Malaysia via Madagascar, and today it is widely distributed in Mozambique and in West and Central Africa, especially in the forest areas. While the Chopi of southern Mozambique are the most famous xylophone players of Southern Africa, of those peoples dealt with in this book the Venda are the only xylophone players. The keys of the African xylophone are carved from wood; under each is a suitably sized calabash with a hole, which is covered by the egg-covering membrane of a number of household-spider varieties. The keys are struck with rubber-headed sticks to produce fast-moving music, made up of many complex rhythmic patterns, which is attractive though on the whole unintelligible to the Western listener.

A Zulu priest-diviner's drum, derived from the bass drum of European military bands, is beaten by a trainee priest-diviner.

Drums

Some of the traditional musical instruments have been displaced by those of the West. The exception to this rule is the ubiquitous standby for dancing and jollification: the drum. From the earliest days of man's emergence in Africa, the nights have been alive with the pounding of the big drums — drums made from pots, from buckets, even from pieces of oxhide rolled up on the floor.

In this continent of drums, the Nguni are notable in that they have no tradition of drumming. The closest they have come to the traditional drum is the rolled-up oxhide mentioned above, which is played for the dancing of priest-diviners. Closer to the drum, perhaps, is their method of beating a pot: one man holds a skin over the top, while another strikes it with his hands. Buried together with many customs of the past is the friction drum of girls' puberty ceremonies. Today most priest-diviners have their own style of drum, copied from the bass drum of European military bands, and this is also used almost universally among the Zulu and the Swazi for most types of dancing.

In contrast to the Nguni, the Venda are able to produce an impressive drum ensemble, the *domba* drummers. Here, four drummers, male and female, beat as many instruments, with a skill, flexibility and precision of timing that match the agility and grace of the dancers.

The Venda drums are of two broad types: the long *murumbu* and the large, squat *ngoma*. The former, shaped like a milk pail and often with a handle, is probably derived from these utensils. The large *ngoma* drums, with their heavy handles, have been compared with the bronze 'frog' drums of Tonkin China, and it has been suggested that this is no mere fortuitous resemblance.

Drums are traditional instruments in the Sotho/Tswana areas. Though the instrument is traditionally made of wood, the absence of this material has forced the people of Lesotho to use clay bodies for their drums.

METALWORK

A brief glance at traditional metalwork is necessary in a book on the Bantu-speaking people, whose single most definitive characteristic after their languages is the fact that they were the local carriers of Iron Age culture. Where they learned the art of smelting and forging iron is the subject of speculation, but wherever ore was available in Southern Africa, there is evidence of iron-working. The same applies to other metals such as gold, copper and tin, and the alloy bronze. Today, however, the traditional iron industry is a thing of the past: Africans have become another adeptly exploited market for Western technology and among the patient robots who tend its machines.

Mining

Mining was fairly primitive and mostly on the surface in the case of iron-ore, though tin and copper mines went down as far as 25 metres or even, in one case, to 40 metres. Ore was mined either by chipping with stone hammers and iron chisels or by alternate fire-heating and dousing with water to split the rock, which was then prised loose.

Smelting

Both open and closed furnaces were used for smelting the ore. The vast majority were used for smelting iron. The open-hearth furnaces consisted of a hole in the ground or sandstone almost half a metre deep and protected on either side by a mound of earth. The enclosed hearth was an earthen dome about a metre high, with an entrance in front for packing. Charcoal was used for firing. After an initial charcoal fire had been started, alternate layers of iron-ore and charcoal were packed on. Heat was maintained by the use of bellows, which were operated in pairs by an assistant. Air entered the furnace via a pair of longish conical clay pipes or a tuyère. The bellows were a pair of animal skins, each with all the limbs, etc. sewn closed, but for one, which was the air outlet and inserted into the tuyère. Air entered the bellows via a long slit, reinforced by thin planks, in the belly of the skin. The assistant placed his fingers through loops beside the inlet slits and, by opening and closing the slits as he raised and lowered his hands, pumped both the bellows.

Usually, the iron-ore was not heated sufficiently to reduce it to the liquid state and the spongy metal/slag mass was reheated and worked several times to produce the pure iron. The metal produced by this repeated reheating and forging was well tempered, and Africans looked down on drop-forged European imports. If temperatures were high enough properly to liquefy the iron, or if the metal had a lower melting point (copper, tin, gold), the molten metal was led by small furrows into moulds in the shape of implements, weapons or ingots, which were formed in the damp sand.

The Smith

Whatever its products, the traditional technology of Southern Africa was not a technology in the Western sense of the word, rooted in a scientific conception of the world, but was rather, based on a magical conception of nature. The life and work of the smith were wrapped in mystery and surrounded by taboos. The smith was a feared and respected man, who had inherited his calling from his father and was probably in much the same category as the priest-diviner — but with rather sinister overtones — in the minds of the general population. He usually lived on his own in the hills and his oven would glow in some dreaded, hidden valley. The ritual impurity of women, or that clinging to the smith's clothing, would be enough to block the magic smelting operation. The smith and his assistant, usually a small boy (free from ritual impurity), therefore worked naked. It was rumoured that an essential ingredient in the magical medicines to make the iron flow was human fat, so that people naturally steered clear of the smith's abode.

EPILOGUE

THIS book has been largely about the traditions of the Bantu-speaking peoples of Southern Africa. Tradition may be said to refer to the way a society does things: how it structures itself in its dealings with its environment.

This environment is, as far as the society is concerned, largely defined by its manner of coping, by its traditions. There is thus a complementary relationship and a slow co-evolution of tradition and its effective environment. This is exemplified in the case of beadwork. While the colourful beaded dress and bead poetry are justifiably regarded as a part of traditional dress in many areas, the fact remains that, only in the last century or so have beads been available in sufficient abundance for their incorporation into the body of tradition in this way. Beadwork is, then, an example of the adaptation of the traditions of society in response to an environmental change. The change in the patterns of agricultural work-sharing in response to the introduction of the plough is another such change.

However, hard on the heels of both examples used here, the plough and abundant beads, came the colonial era. And it is in this that one is confronted by a phenomenon very different from this gradual co-evolution of the tradition and environment of a society, even where this environment was substantially modified by another society. A whole new environment was effectively opened up to the African individual exemplified by the city.

There he made three very significant discoveries: the first, awesome and good; the second, threatening and demoralising; the third, challenging. First, he discovered that the world was amenable to styles of living previously denied by both his society's morals and its commonsense. Second, he discovered, to his detriment, that the lords of this new world were, justifiably perhaps but just as certainly, jealous guardians of their own realm and therefore unmotivated to help him to adapt, or to give him the tools to exploit their world. He experienced the fearful impact of their power within this alluring world. Third, while his desires might relate to this new reality, he discovered himself, for all practical purposes, to be constituted by the old reality and both incapable of fulfilling a role in and being fulfilled by this new world as he saw its lords were.

In order to relate to — survive in — this new environment, he had to create for himself a new society, complete with traditions adapted or taken direct, as dictated by the new circumstances, from the old society. This achieved, two distinct things happened. With the consolidation of this African culture or set of traditions geared to survival in the Western economic domain, many individuals became capable of living according to both the old and the new sets of tradition: later generations emerged, moulded by and belonging to the derivative African traditions, existing in symbiotic relationship with the Western industrial economy, yet able to relate to, to varying degrees, the old traditions as those of their own people.

Before introducing the second event, it must be noted that the notion of a single derivative corpus of tradition regulating the new society is simplistic: a continuum of options has become available, ranging from those more closely related to the old traditions (or, to put it more succinctly, less adaptive to the new socio-economic reality) to those which are very well adapted. What is pertinent here, is that this adaptation can largely be characterised by the emergence of an understanding of the new world and the administrators of its riches, the white men. This is the second event.

More specifically, the most significant aspect of the African's understanding of the white man is his ability to see his own image in the latter's eyes. In so far as he remains true to his traditions, the tension between the role expected in terms of this image and the necessity to survive and fulfil his psychological needs, demands a social awareness vouchsafed few other South Africans. Furthermore, in speaking of this understanding one is aware not only of a strength to change society but, in so far as bitterness and cynicism have not been engendered, of a responsibility to South Africa.

At present the black man's reaction to the image that the white man has of him is to do something the individual white has had little need to achieve so far: to manipulate another culture's perception of him.

On the individual level this image manipulation has often been an attempt to keep the white man as ignorant as possible of his true self in order to leave him free to get on with self-fulfilment on his own terms. At the societal or political level the situation is more complex. On the one hand the black has demanded the right to share in the economy as the fully competent creator of a system of traditions unique to him and adapted to his reality. On the other, whites have persisted in the recognition of the black in terms of the old culture and largely ignored the contemporary, extremely mobile traditions the better to justify their political economic hegemony and the relegation of the black to a limited role as a source of labour. Predictably, in his rejection of this caricature of himself, the black man is reacting by shifting and unifying his new, derivative traditions further and further away from the old life-style, and even going to the extent of adopting exotic ideologies.

Today, any description of the old traditions is thus incomplete without mention of the contemporary cultural options. Without this, it can be used as a millstone to hang on the neck of the black man. On the other hand, the old culture, still to a large extent embodied in rural life, feeds the new, dynamic life-styles and increasingly acts as their point of reference in the global context.

As we find it today Southern Africa, especially South Africa, is exceptionally well blessed with natural and industrial potential. I believe that, as soon as black society is allowed its right to participation and progress, the heirs to the culture described in this book will use that culture's vigour not only to participate economically, but will bring as a gift for all, their unique perspective as the inheritors of a set of traditions which makes them the self-conscious inhabitants of two worlds. This injection of a new concept of reality should reinforce the humanitarian values of caring and sharing in a world dominated by utilitarian exploitation of man as an object.

I believe that Southern Africa, however divided up (preferably united) politically in the future, is destined to become one of the great places on earth, but that this can happen only when the unique contribution of the majority of its inhabitants is actualised and built into the economy and society as a whole. I believe furthermore that as the black man comes to participate economically and politically, so he will become a real person to the white man, and as such accessible and able to share with him the perspective of a quite different culture.

This subcontinent is sufficiently wealthy for us to share in its rewards and growth. Instead of sinking into a slough of encrusted non-adaptive values, tailor-made for mutual exploitation, the contenders for Southern Africa can create together not just an economic giant but a source of ideas and inspiration for both present and future generations.

APPENDIX 1

A 'SMELLING OUT' OR DIVINATION

THE following is an example of a typical divination, which took place in the Natal Midlands in 1976. The patient, or client, in this case was a man whom I shall call Nkomo. The reason he and his wife sought professional help was twofold: not only had the man's hat been lost, but a bird, seldom present in the area, had been seen running across the yard in front of their hut. This alone portended evil, but the loss of the hat made it certain, as the sweat within the brim could be used in witchcraft against Nkomo. The loss was viewed in a very serious light. The couple came immediately to our home in Richmond, earnestly requesting that we take them to a certain priest-diviner of repute who lived some 50 kilometres away. Their concern was patently obvious, and we (my mother and I) at once agreed to take them.

Mbege, as I shall call the *isangoma* (Natal Nguni priest-diviner), was rather well known and had eight novices (*amathwasa*) she was training in her homestead. Of these, five participated in the proceedings, as a part of their training and to assist their teacher.

As in all *isangoma* homesteads, Mbege's had the all-important hut of the spirits, used solely for professional divinatory purposes. The troubled couple and ourselves were taken to this hut by five novices, four of whom entered. The fifth took Nkomo and his wife aside where they could not be overheard and, in whispers, questioned them concerning their problem. The *isangoma*, as yet, as not to be seen.

Having obtained the requisite information, this novice led the husband and wife inside and settled them and herself on mats on the right-hand side of the hut near the door; all three remained there throughout the divination. This made it obvious to all in the hut that no information could be passed from the novice to the *isangoma*, who would eventually conduct the enquiry. On the left-hand side of the hut sat three novices, while the fifth rested on hands and knees in the centre of the hut, facing the *umsamo*, or place of the ancestors. She was in charge of proceedings and is therefore referred to as the 'leading novice'. The novice who sat with the clients is referred to as the 'informant novice' for, by the tone of her responses, she revealed the information she had received.

The leading novice had carried in with her a *dengezi* (large potsherd used for preparing medicine) on which glowed a few coals. Onto these she placed the *imphepho* herb, blowing the small fire to life and filling the hut with sweet, pungent fumes.

Small talk dwindled. All knew that the ancestors, in the 'clearness of head' created by this characteristic scent, would be gathering around. The leading novice, holding a short staff upright in her hand and pounding its end on the hut floor to give weight to her words, began to speak: 'You must respond to my questions if you know, for you have been ill [because of the presence of the ancestral spirits] for a long time.'

To this the informant novice replied, 'I would agree, but I fear this person I walk with.' (This was said mainly to create fear in the minds of Nkomo and his wife.)

Following this exchange, the leading novice said softly: *'Shaya s'bona'* [Strike, let's see].

To which the informant novice replied, equally softly: *'Ezwe'* [Hear].

This call and response were repeated several times, the two voices gradually becoming louder, faster, and more excited, until the gloom of the hut was electric and tense with the wildness of the exchange. Now the divination commenced in earnest:

LEADING NOVICE (LN): 'I thought the home was strong' [well protected].
INFORMANT NOVICE (IN) [with Nkomo and wife]: *'Ezwe!'*
LN: 'Was it this home, really?'
IN[with Nkomo and wife]: *'Ezwe!'*

This dialogue continued at length in the same atmosphere of electric excitement, the leading novice groping towards the nature of the problem by the enthusiasm or otherwise in the response of the informant novice to the possibilities ventured. One had to remind onself that the leading novice was, in fact, ostensibly addressing the ancestral spirits. As the whole process was very detailed and laborious, the full transcript is drastically cut. The response of the informant novice is bracketed after the guesses of the leading novice.

'Was it a human's home, really?' (Response)

This was repeated 4 times, followed by the exhortation, 'Strike well!' meaning 'respond well', in order that she — the leading novice — could know whether or not she was on the right track in her guessing.

'Was it an old man, really?' (Mild response)
'Was it a person's home, really?' (Mild response)
'Was it Nkomo's home?' (Enthusiastic response)
'Was it a person's home, really?' (Mild response)
'Was this mischief *in* the home?' (Enthusiastic response)

This questioning continued with the leading novice ascertaining from the response that it was 'mischief' that took place 'in the home' rather than 'in the yard', and that the perpetrator of the mischief was a 'thing that breathed' and that the problem revolved around the loss of something 'from the top of the body' which was 'suddenly not there', which statement was followed by the deduction, 'It is a hat'. This was greeted with a jubilant response. The leading novice then proceeded to discover that there were many people present at the time and to say (still ostensibly addressing the ancestors):

'Does he really want the water of help?' (Response)

'He's come for help because his hat has completely baffled him.' (Response)

'You saw during the day that the hat was gone.' (Response)
'It was put down while there were a lot of people present.' (Response)
'All agree that there were plenty of people present.' (Response)
'There were really a lot of people present at the home?' (Response)
'He was shocked to find that it wasn't present.' (Response)
'There were outside people — non-family — present.' (Mild response)
'Only the family were present.' (Enthusiastic response)

At this point the proceedings were interrupted by a wild-sounding yawn from the doorway of the hut. The *isangoma*, her yawns proclaiming the presence of the ancestors within her, swaggered into the hut, emitting strange exclamations and hysterical sighs.

Quietly, the leading novice passed on to her the information that had been obtained and quickly gave place to her on the mat near the *umsamo*. She settled herself with much ado, blowing the burning herbs into new life, placing her special snuffbox open beside her, taking the snuff with a long spoon, and yawning gustily. Taking up her wildebeest tail switch, she whipped it through the air, now towards the *umsamo*, now over each shoulder where her spirits stay, in order to alert and summon them. The assembled company, with eyes downcast, stirred by their teacher's ritual and aware of the assembly of shades, gave greeting: '*Makhosi!*' — 'Chiefs!' — a respect term for the ancestral spirits.

One of the novices commented that their 'mother' — the *isangoma* — was acting in a somewhat odd manner as there was evil abroad, a statement likely to instil awe in Nkomo and his wife. The ancestral spirits of this particular *isangoma* communicated by means of whistling and the novice's remark was cut short by the first whistling of the ancestors.

There followed a smelling-out similar to that which had been conducted by the leading novice, with the *isangoma* posing questions to which the whistling spirits provided answers, translated in turn by the *isangoma*. Only the content of her words betrayed whether she was speaking for herself or translating for her spirits. This conversation was interspersed at regular intervals by the cries of the company — Great Chiefs! — and dragged on and on in a guessing game of hot and cold. The transcript below is again considerably abbreviated.

(Whistling) 'We've come on a big matter.'
'Chiefs!'
'What is it, Chiefs?' (Hearty sighs and whistling.) 'We've come on this matter which has completely baffled us.'
(Whistling)
'Chiefs!'
'What is it, Chiefs?' (Hearty sighs and whistling.)
'We've come on this matter which has completely baffled us.' (Whistling)
'Chiefs!'
(Sighs) 'What is it Chiefs?' (Whistling) 'What, Chiefs? . . . What has happened, Chiefs?!' (Whistling) 'What?! . . . Hat?!'
'*Chief! Great Chiefs!!*' (Extremely excited) 'How did it get lost, Chiefs?' (Whistling) 'It simply got lost.' (Whistling) 'These is confusion in my mind as the people are not responding properly.'
(Whistling) 'Because he does know well that he had placed it somewhere.'

(Whistling) 'This thing is very hard.' (Whistling) 'We look but we cannot see.'

(Whistling) 'Where did it go, Chiefs?' (Whistling) 'Where then did it go?'

(Whistling) 'What then can we say about this thing?'

Leading Novice: 'What, Chiefs?'

(Whistling) 'Because the hat really did get lost.' (Whistling) 'Then how is it they don't agree?' [i.e., why is their response so unenthusiastic and not pointing out the direction to take?] (Whistling) 'When that hat was lost, who was present?'

(Whistling) 'Nkomo doesn't know who was present at the time. The last he knew of it was that he had placed it in a certain spot.'

'Chiefs!'

'When he put down the hat, who was present?' (Whistling) 'They were present.' ['They' being the person(s) who stole the hat for evil purposes.] 'And what did they end by doing?'

After a good deal of elaborate beating about the bush, the *isangoma* (or the ancestors) felt ready to make the revelation:

'What kind of creature was it that took the hat while everyone was inside the hut?!' (Whistling) 'What?!' (Whistling) 'I don't hear.' (Whistling) '*Great Chiefs*!' [loud exclamation by the *isangoma*] 'The thing is taking sweat from the hat to make medicine for killing Nkomo.' (Whistling) 'He came in while the others were present. We ask for enlightenment.' (Whistling) 'Tokoloshe is a *very* clever creature!

'*Great Chiefs*!'

(Whistling) 'He did this in order to confuse all present and for each to point to the other as being the person who took the hat.' (Whistling) '*Great Chiefs*!'

'What does he want with it [the hat]? (Whistling)

'He wants the sweat?!'

'*Great Chiefs*!!' (*Extremely* excited.)

(Whistling)

'Great Chiefs!'

'A person sent him [*Thikoloshe*].'

The invocation of this evil symbol, *Thikoloshe*, was followed by a vivid affirmation by the ancestors of the mal-intent of the man (witch) who had sent the creature. Furthermore, it emerged from the (translated) whistling of the ancestors, that the witch, with the help of *thikoloshe*, was intending to send lightning to the home; a grave situation commented on by the spirits: (Whistling followed by a loud sigh) 'A bad matter, this.'

'*Great Chiefs*!'

The ancestors went on to recommend that Nkomo consult a herbalist to obtain medicine for the protection of his home. This medicine was preferably to include the ashes of the missing hat which he was exhorted to retrieve. Now the *isangoma* changed her tack:

'We have a further request, Great Chiefs.' (Whistling, loud sigh, whistling.) 'The child is asleep. We ask the big spirit to open his ears very carefully for what we are about to ask now.' (Breathless pause and then, dramatically) 'Great Chiefs, Great Chiefs! Great, great Chiefs!' (Whistling, huge sigh, whistling) 'What further matter do you cry after?' (Whistling) 'We've come on a different matter now.'

'Great Chiefs.'

(Whistling) 'What is this matter?' (Whistling) 'What is it' (Whistling) 'There is one other thing they [the ancestral spirits who were present at the losing of the hat] saw.'
'Chiefs.'
'What is it, Chiefs, Great Chiefs?' (Whistling) 'What is it like?' (Whistling) 'A bird?!!'
'*Chiefs*! Great, *great* Chiefs!!
(Whistling) 'What was the bird doing?' (Whistling) 'It came and settled in the yard.'
'Chiefs! Chiefs!'

The unease that Nkomo felt about the bird he had seen in the yard and passed on to the novice, had been in turn given to the *isangoma* when the two consulted the informant novice. This bird became the dreaded magical *mamtsotsi* or lightning bird and it became apparent that not only was the witch sending *thikoloshe* to the home, but had plans to destroy it with lightning as well. It was almost predictable that here too another magical bird, *impundulu*, would be invoked, and it was. Both her spirits and the *isangoma* herself rebuked Nkomo severely for not (magically) protecting his home better than he had been doing.

The investigation now went on to deal with the depths of wickedness to which the witch had stooped, or at least planned to, and eventually came to his motives:
(Whistling) 'He [Nkomo] works well and and everyone is jealous of him.'
'Chiefs.'
(Whistling) 'And when you walk abroad, don't forget, for one moment, this matter.'
'Chiefs.'
(Whistling) 'Why do you think you're always feeling unfit?'
'Chiefs.'
(Whistling) 'Look out for your blood [health]!'
'Chiefs.'
(Whistling) 'Yes, he hears Great Chiefs.' (Whistling)
'This witch who kills does not come from Zululand.'
(Whistling) 'Yes, he hears, Great Chiefs.' (Whistling)
'This matter of death; it stems from a person who lives right here, in this vicinity.'
'Great Chiefs!'
(Whistling) 'Do you hear well?'
'We do hear well, Great Chiefs.'
(Whistling) 'Everybody is satisfied now, Great Chiefs.'
'Great Chiefs.'
(Whistling) 'We are going now.'
'Great Chiefs!'
(Whistling) 'We salute you all.'
'Great Chiefs. Chiefs. Great, great Chiefs!'

This concluded the proceedings, and an atmosphere of indulgent and good-humoured relaxation prevailed in the hut. Everyone chatted amicably for a while before Nkomo and his wife left. They received medicines and instructions on how to use these and were quite satisfied and apparently pleased, rather than disturbed with the somewhat drastic findings of the *isangoma* and her spirits. Today, although the hat remains unfound and the matter is not forgotten, appropriate medicines have been used and it is no longer a cause for concern. Although the individual responsible for the bewitching was not identified, the suggestions made by the *isangoma* were enough to lock suspicion firmly onto a local person. In the past, this could have had fatal consequences for this individual, but now it was Nkomo who was threatened: a person may even decide to move house to escape a suspected witch.

A switch, well-stocked snuff-box, and *imphepho*, burning in a broken piece of pot, all of which are important to a priest-diviner as a means of attracting the ancestors.

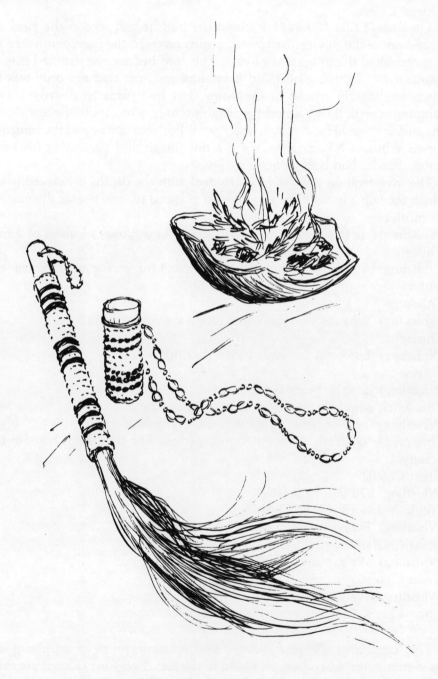

APPENDIX 2

PRIEST-DIVINER'S GRADUATION

THE final 'coming out' or graduation ceremony of a Natal priest-diviner — *isangoma* (plural *izangoma*) — is held at home in order to bring him or her home. I have witnessed several such ceremonies and will describe one that I attended in Zululand, which is a good example: in this case the *isangoma* being 'born' to the world was a strapping young man whom I shall call Timothy Khumalo. For nine months he had trained, along with ten other novices, in the Natal Midlands some 65 kilometres from Pietermaritzburg, and now he was ready to become a fully fledged *isangoma*.

Because his home was in Zululand, we were asked to transport him and some of his colleagues there for the ceremony. In exchange for this, we were welcome to watch the rituals.

His departure from the home, where he had spent the nine long months of his training period, was touching. To the accompaniment of the singing of all the inhabitants of the homestead, he walked slowly off down the road, never looking back. (The tone changed somewhat, however, when, a kilometre down the road, we picked him up in a van pungent and noisy with twelve joyous *izangoma* and novices!)

The initiation or coming-out of an *isangoma* is referred to above as a 'birth'. This is an important part of the symbolism, for the initiate is regarded as 'born from the earth' at his or her coming out. In fact, she should spend the night prior to initiation outside 'with the earth' to stress this symbolism. This respect was omitted by Timothy, however, as we set off for his home in Zululand late in the afternoon and arrived only at nine o'clock at night.

Timothy's home was some 65 kilometres from Eshowe, near the end of a long stretch of winding, swooping, bumping side road. The headlights of the van sliced up and down, back and forth, through the thick darkness, sometimes shining out into nothing for long moments before swinging back to reveal the road twisted to this side or that and descending yet another sinuous ridge in its journey into the Tugela valley.

The end of the road left us with a 3-kilometre walk to the homestead. Under a full moon, the path wound through a wonderland of dusty silver thorn trees, sturdy aloes, and the deepest of inky shadows.

The homestead, when it finally appeared before us, was cosy with the orange glow of the fires in the huts. We were cordially greeted by the occupants, who showed no surprise at our arrival. Soon we were in a new hut and were presented with a great deal of beer. We commented on the fact that no-one had been surprised to see us. 'Oh,' said Timothy's mother, 'we dreamed that you would be here tonight.'

Before long the *izangoma* were dancing with wild abandon clockwise around the hut, while the spectators, who sat on the left-hand side of the hut, clapped in time. In the midst of this we were provided with orange squash in clean, patterned glasses on a tray covered with a delicate gauze cloth. We had been provided with chairs, too, and these apparently were the only ones available, for when the headman appeared, resplendent in a lounge suit, he sat on the floor, refusing my offer of a chair. According to tradition, we had brought him a gift — a folding suitcase — and he was well pleased, which eased relations considerably.

After half an hour of intense dancing to bring the looming shades nearer, the headman made a handsome speech to them, thanking them for the return of Timothy. It was only then that we learned that he and the headman were brothers! They made a striking contrast: the headman dapper in a well-pressed, blue suit, and his wild-eyed, vigorous brother, clad in tatty T-shirt and khaki trousers, and wearing on his head the bladder and beaded black wool wig of office.

After the speech, the sacrificial goats appeared at the door, led by a teenage boy. One was black and white, the other pure black with a magnificent 'beard'. Each in turn was made to face the *umsamo* while the headman delivered a short address to the ancestors. Then Timothy burned the medicinal herb *imphepho*, holding the pungent, smoking coals under the nose of each goat in turn.

The smaller, black and white animal was the first to be sacrificed. It was manhandled into an upside-down position by two burly men who grasped its front and back legs. There was discussion concerning the suitability of the knife for the job and the correct positioning of the blackened storm lantern, which provided the sole, dim illumination. Timothy had to suck the blood of the sacrificial animals while they still lived, in order to partake of their life: he stabbed the goat on the right side of the thorax, making it cry pitifully, and then went down on his knees to suck the wound. The goat was then despatched by a deep stab in the heart.

The second goat was sacrificed in the same way. The wound bled fairly profusely, however, and some blood fell on the floor. This caused a great deal of consternation, and a child was despatched to fetch a basin in which to collect the blood. Not only was this spillage repugnant to the ancestors, but the blood could serve as the basis for a very destructive medicine in the hands of an ill-disposed witch.

I have encountered blacks in their traditional setting who are nauseated or pained by the sight of a sacrifice, and on this night one woman fled in the midst of the proceedings. 'Gracious!' somebody exclaimed, laughing disparagingly. 'She is scared.'

While the goats were being dismembered in the middle of the hut, the company shared the beer. The various parts of the goat which had ritual significance were preserved and the two *izincekwa* or third stomach(s) were hung with sticks from the thatch above the *umsamo*, to be licked by the ancestral spirits.

During these proceedings we were presented with a half-cooked portion of goat liver to eat. At every ritual sacrifice I have attended, I have been presented with some portion of the animal, usually the liver (although occasionally only the beer of the ancestors). This is an essential gesture of friendship: by partaking of the meat, we the visitors, are included in the communion with the ancestors.

The goat sacrifices were followed by a session of vigorous dancing. Then came the time for the more important beast sacrifice. The *izangoma* and novices began chanting and, swaying with the rhythm, they left the hut. Led by the head *isangoma* (who had trained Timothy) with Timothy in second place and the rest following in a long swaying, chanting line, they made a strange and very ancient spectacle in the dispassionate light of the moon.

The procession entered the cattle byre. Inside, the cattle, dark shadows, were sleeping. The intent humans gathered about the animals and they began to stir. Timothy indicated the sacrificial beast. In accordance with his sex, and like the goats, it was a male, a black bullock. The other cattle were driven out and the bullock was caught and its head tied to the fence. The *izangoma* and novices approached it in turn and switched it with their wildebeest tail whisks, thus blessing it and consecrating it to the ancestors. Then a young boy, under the direction of Timothy, stabbed the animal in its right side. It jumped and bellowed frantically. When it was still, Timothy leant forward to suck the wound. This done the beast was neatly dispatched by severing of the spinal column. The entire procedure and the final reflex twitchings of the animal were accompanied by a quiet, haunting chant with all the lingering wistfulness of a dirge: '*Inkomo ai vuga*' (The beast won't awaken).

The bullock was skinned and disembowelled then and there, and the same sacrificial knife was used as for the goats. On the throax, under the front legs, is flesh which twitches for a long time after death, called *isipiko*. It is said to be strongly associated with the ancestors and, in most sacrifices, a portion must be presented to those beings immediately, before any mortal may eat of the animal. The portion, as usual, was cooked to cinders on a potsherd. These cinders were then mixed with certain medicines and set aside for a later part of the ceremony.

Meanwhile, the *izangoma* and novices returned to the hut where, all in high spirits, they continued dancing. When we left them at midnight, they were still dancing energetically. As we drove silently back, we could picture the scene within the hut, lit by the red glow of a storm lantern, and it made perfect sense in the context of the brooding, moonlit mountains of the Tugela valley.

The Second Day
We returned to the homestead the following day at 10 o'clock, to find several *izangoma* in Timothy's hut. They sat before a basin full of blood and body juices, fishing therefrom various bladders from the sacrificial animals, which they inflated like balloons to be later worn by Timothy.

Outside, Timothy donned the two crossed circles of skin on his chest. It was surprising that this activity was accompanied by neither interest nor ritual. According to Reverend Berglund, the cross formed on the chest has some symbolic significance: in olden times, when one man accused another before a tribal court, he was required to lay a stick on the ground to represent each charge. Should the judge find the accused innocent, he would instruct him to place another stick on the first to form a cross. This signified that the matter was cleared up and that wholeness prevailed. The symbolism of the cross worn by the new *isangoma* is similar — his training is 'closed' or complete.

The day was primarily for dancing and celebration and three local *izangoma* had come to join in. One was a memorable lady: she appeared on the horizon dancing and wailing excitedly, following a tiny girl who beat a small drum suspended from her neck. During the dancing that followed, this lady stole the show with her abandoned, wild-eyed performance, which convinced all present of the power of her personal spirits.

Initially the dancing was in Timothy's hut, but then all the *izangoma* emerged in procession to dance into the cattle byre as they had the night before. There, stuck in the stomach contents of the bullock, was the sacrificial knife. This is commonly practised in sacrifices as a safeguard against the depredations of witches: should such a person take some of the stomach contents with the intention of bewitching Timothy, he or she would feel stabbing pains in the stomach, caused by the knife.

After Timothy had retrieved this knife (holding it in his left hand) the whole company danced out of the cattle byre to a flat area, where they danced all afternoon before an awed gathering of local people. Towards evening, more and more people gathered, attracted by the beer, meat, and festive atmosphere. By nightfall, the entire neighbourhood was participating in a grand party.

The Third Day

The next day I discovered that Timothy was married, and that his wife had been present in the vicinity all the while. Yet, despite his absence of nine months, he has not been able to see her or his infant son (born in his absence) until their two sets of ancestors had been introduced and joined. The rites on the third and last day of his graduation were directed to this end.

The first rite was performed before sunrise. Timothy stood with his arms outstretched before the *umsamo* of the hut, while his wife poured the gall of one sacrificial goat along his arms and on his right big toe. As all things are reversed in the ancestral realm, gall is very sweet to the ancestral spirits and attracts them. By pouring gall on her husband, Timothy's wife induced her personal ancestors to lick it and thus become acquainted with his shades. He did the same to her, ensuring that the two groups were well introduced and would not quarrel.

When this rite was completed, Timothy, his wife, and the company made their way to the cattle byre, the reunited couple singing and the head *isangoma* carrying a pot of *ubulawu* (white medicine). In the cattle byre, the mixture was heated over a fire and husband and wife repeatedly dipped their fingers in the boiling liquid and sucked them (a common way of taking medicine). They then took handfuls of hot preparation and rubbed it onto their arms, faces and legs. This was followed by both husband and wife jumping back and forth over the fire through the smoke — another form of medication. All these rites were to create in the ancestors a beneficent and benign attitude.

Suddenly Timothy and his wife jumped up and raced each other to the hut, where her victory was the source of much hilarity. In the hut, laid in two rows, were alternate pieces of the lung and the liver of the bullock, which had been treated with the remaining 'twitching meat' medicine in order to involve the ancestors in the ritual. Without further ado Timothy and wife began an eating race, which Timothy won hands down, thereby eliciting much ribald comment concerning the size of his mouth! (Similar rites are performed to reunite man and wife or reconcile enemies: the two parties involved eat from either end of a strip of meat.)

Timothy then sat down on the hut floor, legs extended and crossed before him. In this position, he was switched by each of the *izangoma* and novices in turn to 'bless' him in final farewell.

Having done this, the entire group of people from Natal — the *izangoma* and novices alike — quickly left the hut. Outside, they hastily removed skins, wigs, bladders — all the trappings of their calling — before rushing off into the bush, out of sight of the huts.

The purpose of this was to leave without luring away the ancestral spirits of the new *isangoma* who, meanwhile, sat happily in the hut chatting with his wife and, for the first time, seeing his son — who burst into tears at the sight of his garishly attired father!

This concluded the graduation ceremonies. Those of us not involved with the ancestors, said our goodbyes along more conventional lines before setting off on the long journey home.

REFERENCES

ORIGINS AND HISTORY

1. D. Dalby, 'The prehistorical implications of Guthrie's comparative Bantu. Part I: Problems of internal relationships', in *J. Afr. History* XVI (1975) pp. 481-501.
   M. Guthrie, 'Some recent developments in the prehistory of the Bantu languages', in *J. Afr. History* III (1962) pp. 273-82.
2. N. van de Merwe, 'The Iron Age: a prehistory of Bantu-speaking South Africans' in '*Occasional Paper No. 2.*' Cape Town: University of Cape Town, Centre for African Studies. 1979. p. 96.
3. T. Maggs, 'The Iron Age sequence south of the Vaal and Pongola rivers: some historical implications', in *J. Afr. History* XVI (1980) pp. 1-15.
4. Van de Merwe, in *Occasional Paper*, p. 101.
5. J. Campbell, *Travels in South Africa*, London 1822 (reprinted by Johnson Reprint Corporation, U.S.A., 1967) Vol. I, p. 221.
6. R.J. Mason, 'Transvaal and Natal Iron Age settlements revealed by aerial photography and excavation', in *African Studies* XXVII (1968) 167-80. See also, T. Maggs, 'Iron Age patterns and Sotho history on the Southern Highveld, South Africa' in *World Archaeology* VII (1976) pp. 318-32.
7. P.B. Borcherds, *An Autobiographical Memoir*, Cape Town: Africana Connoisseurs Press. 1963 (Facsimile reproduction) p. 83; see also p. 124.
8. V. Ellenberger and J. MacGregor, *History of the Basuto, ancient and modern*. London: Caxton. 1912.
9. J.D. Krige, 'The traditional origins and tribal relationships of the Sotho of the Northern Transvaal' in *Bantu Studies* XI (1931) pp. 321-356.
10. D.W. Phillipson, 'The chronology of the Iron Age in Bantu Africa', in *J. Afr. History* XVI (1975) pp. 321-42.
11. A.T. Bryant, *Olden Times in Zululand and Natal*.
12. M. Wilson, 'The early history of the Transkei and Ciskei' in *African Studies* XXVIII (1959) pp. 167-78.
13. J.H. Soga, *The South-Eastern Bantu*.
14. J.D. Omer-Cooper, *The Zulu Aftermath*.

THE KING AND HIS COUNTRY

1. A.T. Bryant, *The Zulu People as they were before the White Man came.* pp. 474-5.
2. H. Kuper, *An African Aristocracy*.
   B.A. Marwick, *The Swazi*.
3. Bryant, *Zulu People*, pp. 485-6.

4. B. Sansom, 'Traditional economic systems' in Hammond-Tooke (ed.) *The Bantu-speaking Peoples of Southern Africa.*
5. A. Vilakazi, *Zulu Transformations.* p. 106.
6. J.H. Soga, *The Ama-Xosa: Life and Customs.* p. 43.

BELIEFS AND RELIGION

1. W.D. Hammond-Tooke, 'World-view I: a system of beliefs' in Hammond-Tooke (ed.) *The Bantu-speaking Peoples of Southern Africa.*
2. A. Vilakazi, *Zulu Transformations.* p. 89.
3. B.J.F. Laubscher, *Sex, Custom and Psychopathology.* p. 108.
4. H. Ashton, *The Basuto.*
5. H.O. Mönnig, *The Pedi.* p. 51.
6. B.J.F. Laubscher, *Where Mystery Dwells.* Cape Town: Timmins 1963.
7. This does not refer to the 'heaven herds' or 'lightning doctors' found in Zululand. (For an excellent account of the activities of these people, see Berglund, *Zulu Thought Patterns and Symbolism*).
8. H. Stayt, *The BaVenda.* pp. 269-70.
9. A. Mafeje, 'Religion, class and ideology in South Africa' in M. Whisson and M. West (eds.) *Religion and Social Change in South Africa.*
10. *Drum* magazine (March, 1977) pp. 14-15.
11. The *Cape Times.* (April 30, 1977) p. 1.
12. H.J. Moller, *Stedelike Bantoe en die Kerk. Deel II: God en die voorouergeeste in die lewevan die stedelike Bantoe.* Pretoria: Report submitted to the Human Sciences Research Council. 1972.
13. W.D. Hammond-Tooke, 'Urbanization and the interpretation of misfortune' in *Africa* XV (1970) pp. 25-39.
14. B.A. Pauw, 'Ancestor belief and rituals among urban Africans' in *African Studies* XXXIII (1974) pp. 99-112.
15. A.G. Schutte, 'Dual religious orientation in an urban African church' in *African Studies,* XXXIII (1974) pp. 113-120.
16. Mafeje, in Whisson and West, *Religion and Social Change.* p. 167.
17. S.G. Lee, 'Social influences on Zulu dreaming' in D.R. Price-Williams (ed.) *Cross Cultural Studies: selected readings.* Harmondsworth: Penguin 1969 pp. 307-28.
18. A. Kiev, *Transcultural Psychiatry.* Harmondsworth: Penguin 1972 p. 42.

THE HEALERS

1. A. Boshier, 'E.S.P. among African priest-diviners' in J.C. Poynton (ed.) *Parapsychology in South Africa.* Johannesburg: South African Society for Psychical Research 1975 p. 18.
2. F. Laydevant, 'The praises of the divining bones among the Basotho' in *Bantu Studies,* VII (1933) p. 349.

BIRTH AND INFANCY

1. I. Schapera, *Married Life in an African Tribe.* p. 193.
2. H.O. Mönning, *The Pedi.* p. 101.

GROWING UP

1. D.H. Reader, *Zulu Tribe in Transition,* p. 200.
2. H.A. Stayt, *The BaVenda.* p. 96.

INITIATION

1. E.J. Krige, *The Social System of the Zulu*. p. 87.
2. H. Ashton, *The Basuto*. p. 55.
3. B.A. Marwick, *The Swazi*. pp. 155-6.
4. H.O. Mönning, *The Pedi*. pp. 125-6.

COURTSHIP AND MARRIAGE

1. I. Schapera, *Married Life in an African Tribe*. p. 49.
2. A. Vilakazi, *Zulu Transformations*. p. 63.
3. H.A. Stayt, *The BaVenda*. p. 149.

MARRIED LIFE AND THE HOME

1. H.O. Mönning, *The Pedi*. p. 211.
2. H.A. Stayt, *The BaVenda*. p. 153.
3. J. Bird, *The Annals of Natal 1495-1845 I* Cape Town: Maskew Miller (facsimile reprint by Struik, Cape Town, 1965) p. 42.
4. H.S. Alverson, *Africans in South African Industry: the human dimension*. Manuscript in the University of Cape Town Africana Collection. 1971 p. 20.

OLD AGE AND DEATH

1. I.A. Berglund, *Zulu Thought Patterns and Symbolism*. p. 79.
2. *ibid*. p. 369, Fig. 27.

LIVESTOCK

1. H. Epstein, *The Origins of the Domestic Animals of Africa*. (2 Volumes) New York: Africana Publishing Corporation 1971.
2. J.H. Soga, *The amaXosa: Life and Customs*. pp. 374-5.
3. L. Alberti, *Ludwig Alberti's Account of the Tribal Life and Customs of the Xhosa in 1807*. (translated by W. Fehr) Cape Town: Balkema 1968. p. 54.
4. B.A. Marwick, *The Swazi*. p. 81.
5. H.A. Stayt, *The BaVenda*. p. 95.
6. H.O. Mönning, *The Pedi*. p. 86.

AGRICULTURE

1. J.D. Clark, 'The spread of food production in sub-Saharan Africa.' in *J. Afr. History*. III (1962) p. 211.
2. M. Wilson and L. Thompson, *The Oxford History of South Africa*. p. 109.
3. A.T. Bryant, 'The Zulu People as they were before the White Man came. pp. 254-5.
4. I. Schapera, *Rainmaking Rites of Tswana Tribes*. Cambridge: African Studies Centre 1971 p. 90.

HUTS

1. E.J. and J.D. Krige, *The Realm of a Rain Queen*. pp. 18-19.

BEADWORK

1. B.H. Dick, *The Bush Speaks*. Pietermaritzburg: Shuter and Shooter 1936 pp. 405-9.
2. E. Hamilton-Welsh, in *Catalogue of the Estelle Hamilton-Welsh Collection as Compiled by Mrs. Juliet Louw for the Collection* Fort Hare: Fort Hare University Press 1938 p. 19.
3. J.A. Broster, *The Thembu*.
4. R. Twala, 'Beads as regulating the social life of the Zulu and Swazi' in *African Studies* X (1951) pp. 113-123.
5. H.S. Schoeman, 'A preliminary report on the traditional beadwork in the Mkhwanazi area of the Mtunzini district, Zululand. Part 1' in *African Studies* XXVII (1968) pp. 57-81.
   H.S. Schoeman, 'A preliminary report on the traditional beadwork in the Mkhwanazi area of the Mtunzini district, Zululand. Part 2.' in *African Studies* XXVII (1968) pp. 107-133.

CRAFTS

1. A.C. Lawton, 'Bantu pottery in Southern Africa' in *Ann. S. Afr. Mus.* IL (1967) p. 1.
2. H. Tracey, *Ngoma: an introduction to music for Southern Africans*. London: Longmans 1948.
3. P.R. Kirby, *The Musical Instruments of the Native Races of South Africa*. London: Oxford University Press 1934 frontis.

SELECT BIBLIOGRAPHY

J. Argyle and E. Preston-Whyte, *Social System and Tradition in Southern Africa: essays in honour of Eileen Krige*. Cape Town: Oxford University Press. 1978.

H. Ashton, *The Basuto*. 2nd ed. London: Oxford University Press. 1937.

I.A. Berglund, *Zulu Thought Patterns and Symbolism*. London: C. Hurst & Co. 1976.

J. Broster, *Red Blanket Valley*. Johannesburg: Hugh Keartland. 1967.

J.A. Broster, *The Thembu: their beadwork, songs and dances*. Cape Town: Purnell. 1976.

A.T. Bryant, *Olden Times in Zululand and Natal*. London: Longmans. 1929.

A.T. Bryant, *The Zulu People as they were before the White Man came*. Pietermaritzburg: Shuter and Shooter. 1949.

H. Callaway, *The Religious System of the Amazulu*. Springvale, Natal: Blair. 1870.

P.A.W. Cook, *The Social Organisation and Ceremonial Institution of the Bomvana*. Cape Town: Juta. 1931.

V. Ellenberger and J. MacGregor, *History of the Basuto, Ancient and Modern*. London: Caxton. 1912.

W.D. Hammond-Tooke, *Bhaca Society*. Cape Town: Oxford University Press. 1962.

W.D. Hammond-Tooke (ed.), *The Bantu-speaking Peoples of Southern Africa*. 2nd ed. London: Routledge and Kegan Paul. 1974.

R. Inskeep, *The Peopling of South Africa*. Cape Town: David Philip. 1978.

E.J. Krige, *The Social System of the Zulus*. London: Longmans. 1936.

E.J. Krige and J.D. Krige, *The Realm of a Rain Queen*. London: Oxford University Press (Reprinted in paperback with new preface by Juta, Cape Town, 1980)

H. Kuper, *An African Aristocracy*. Johannesburg: Witwatersrand University Press. 1947.

L. Kuper, *An African Bourgeoisie*. New Haven: Yale University Press. 1965.

B.J.F. Laubscher, *Sex, Custom and Psychopathology*. London: George Routledge and Sons. 1937.

A.C. Lawton, 'Bantu pottery of Southern Africa', in *Ann. S. Afr. Mus.* 99 (1967) 1.

S. Marks and A. Atmore (eds.), *Economy and Society in pre-Industrial South Africa*. London: Longmans. 1980.

B.A. Marwick, *The Swazi*, London: Cambridge University Press. 1940; London: F. Cass & Co. Ltd. 1966 (reprint).

H.O. Mönnig, *The Pedi*. Pretoria: Van Schaik, 1967.

H. Ngubane, *Body and Mind in Zulu Medicine*. London: Academic Press. 1977.

J.D. Omer-Cooper, *The Zulu Aftermath*. London: Longmans. 1966.

B.A. Pauw, *The Second Generation*. Cape Town: Oxford University Press. 1973.

D.H. Reader, *The Black Man's*

272

Portion: history and demography and living conditions in the native locations of East London, Cape Province. Cape Town: Oxford University Press. 1961.

D.H. Reader, *Zulu Tribe in Transition.* Manchester: Manchester University Press. 1966.

W. Sachs, *Black Hamlet: the mind of an African Negro revealed by psychoanalysis.* London. 1937.

I. Schapera, *Married Life in an African Tribe.* Harmondsworth: Penguin. 1940.

I. Schapera, *Migrant Labour and Tribal Life: a study of conditions in the Bechuanaland Protectorate.* London: Oxford University Press. 1947.

M. Shaw, 'Native pipes and smoking in South Africa.' *Annals S. Afr. Mus.*, 24, pp. 277-302.

J.B. Shephard, *Land of the Tikoloshe.* London: Longman Green and Co. 1955.

J.H. Soga, *The South-eastern Bantu.* Johannesburg: Witwatersrand University Press. 1930.

J.H. Soga, *The amaXosa: Life and Customs.* Lovedale: Mission Press. 1932.

H.A. Stayt, *The BaVenda.* London: Oxford University Press. 1931.

B.G.M. Sundkler, *Bantu Prophets in South Africa.* London: Oxford University Press. 1961.

L.M. Thompson (ed.), *African Societies in Southern Africa: historical studies.* London: Heinemann. 1969.

B. Tyrrell, *Tribal Peoples of Southern Africa.* Cape Town: Books of Africa. 1968.

B. Tyrrell, *Suspicion is My Name.* Cape Town: T.V. Bulpin. 1971.

N.J. van Warmelo, *Contributions Towards Venda History, Religion and Tribal Ritual.* Ethnological Publications Vol. III. Pretoria: Government Printer. 1932.

N.J. van Warmelo, *A Preliminary Survey of the Bantu Tribes of South Africa.* Ethnological Publications Vol. IV. Pretoria: Government Printer, 1935.

A. Vilakazi, *Zulu Transformations.* Pietermaritzburg: University of Natal Press. 1962.

M.G. Whisson and M. West, (eds.), *Religion and Social Change in Southern Africa: anthropological essays in honour of Monica Wilson.* Cape Town: David Philip. 1975.

M. Wilson, *Reaction to Conquest.* 2nd ed. London: Oxford University Press. 1961.

M. Wilson and L. Thompson, *The Oxford History of South Africa.* Vol. 1. London: Oxford University Press. 1969.

D. Ziervogel, *The Eastern Sotho.* Pretoria: Van Schaik, 1954.

INDEX

Page numbers in *italic* denote main entries, while those in **bold** type indicate the pages on which illustrations occur.

Barbara Tyrrell

ENDPAPER Lesotho is a land of mountains, all impressive and characteristically flat-topped or conical like the famous hat of its people. Villages nestle among the peaks, some accessible by often incredible roads but many — mostly in the east — only by winding bridal paths. Horses are the main form of transport, but when workers go home on holiday the walk from the bus stop can take very much longer